MAGIC HOUR

Jack Cardiff, portrait by Annigoni

MAGIC HOUR

Jack Cardiff

Foreword by Martin Scorsese

faber and faber
LONDON · BOSTON

First published in 1996
by Faber and Faber Limited
3 Queen Square London WC1N 3AU

Photoset by Avon Dataset, Warwickshire
Printed in England by Clays Ltd, St Ives plc

Plates 9 and 13 courtesy of BFI Stills, Posters and Designs

A CIP record for this book
is available from the British Library

ISBN 0–571–17640–2

2 4 6 8 10 9 7 5 3 1

To my Nicki
who has helped and supported me over the years and made me finish this book before rigor mortis set in.

Author's Note

'Magic Hour' is a film term denoting that time in early evening – that late twilight – just before the sky goes completely black.

If one chooses the right moment, the under-exposure from the last light in the sky appears as a stunning deep blue. That's the magic part.

The hour part is nonsense. The swift evanescence of the dying day is more like a magic minute.

Where did the phrase come from? I have no idea. But if I might speculate: perhaps one day a cameraman had chosen this time for a shot, but the camera crew took so long that the sky had faded to black by the time they were ready. So the next time, the cameraman covered himself by allowing a 'magic hour' for the crew to prepare.

Contents

Illustrations

Foreword

When I was a child there was a promise of wonder in the movie theater experience. The nicest theaters were spectacles themselves and the screens were huge. This is something that has been lost to younger audiences, who see films either on television or on tiny screens in small cinderblock rooms. But when I was growing up, the great movie palaces were still intact, and they intensified the expectations that a child brings to any experience. And there were some movies that fulfilled those expectations, that possessed a fullness of imagination and a richness of experience that left me satisfied – and to have childhood dreams met is something you don't forget. *The Black Rose*, *The Red Shoes*, *The Magic Box*, *Pandora and the Flying Dutchman* and *Scott of the Antarctic* – each of these films was unique, and felt very different from other films. Now, looking back at them, I realize that it was the pungency with which they were visualized, particularly the richness of the color. The color in those five films is so vivid and richly imagined that you can virtually *taste* it. Now, I didn't really understand what cinematography was when I was ten or eleven, but I remember noticing the name 'Cardiff' in the credits of all these films and being struck by the Englishness of it. Very soon I would understand Jack Cardiff's special contribution to these films, and to the cinema in general. I've never met Cardiff, but I feel a deeply personal connection with him through all that he's given me in the films that he's photographed and directed, and that's why I considered it an honor to be asked to write this foreword.

Magic Hour is a wonderful opportunity to survey the career and artistic evolution of this man whose name had become synonymous with Technicolor, from his itinerant beginnings on the vaudeville circuit with his parents to his apprenticeship in silent cinema, from his work as an operator on films like Hitchcock's *The Skin Game* and *The Man Who Could Work Miracles* (a childhood favorite) to his acing of a Technicolor exam with his knowledge of painting, from his adventurous days shooting travelogues and war footage with the mighty Technicolor camera – 'in steel foundries (inches away from molten ingots), in battleships in wartime seas, on top of erupting volcanoes, in burning deserts and steaming jungles', as Cardiff puts it so beautifully – to his magnificent work as a cinematographer and his experiences as a director.

Here is a way of seeing not just the historical context in which Cardiff worked but also how some of the most precious images ever created for the movies made their way to the screen. And into the bargain, Cardiff gives us a raucous history of the British cinema from the inside looking out.

The wealth of experience covered in *Magic Hour* makes it compelling reading, and some of Cardiff's adventures, especially during his early years touring with his parents, have an almost Dickensian flavor. There is also a marvelous, eye-opening description of the atmosphere of his beloved Paris in the thirties, given an added poignancy by the fact that it would soon fall away. His memory for visual detail (the image of himself as a boy backstage watching a 'ranting Devil spring through a burst of orange smoke'), his vivid evocations of Henry Fonda, Marlene Dietrich, Noël Coward and especially Sophia Loren, and the black comedy (the story of the aerial photographer who nearly had his legs severed by a helicopter but happened to be flying over a surgeons' convention at the time) give his book some of the vivid three-dimensionality of his film work. An entire book could be devoted to the year-long ordeal of filming *Western Approaches*, a semi-documentary war movie shot with the cumbersome Technicolor camera in the worst conditions imaginable. But the spiritual center of *Magic Hour*, and its most wondrous aspect for me as a film-maker, is the revelation of painting as Cardiff's greatest source of inspiration and light as its shaping force. In the mid-thirties, he was called to Denham Studios to take the Technicolor exam (the winner would go to Hollywood to learn the process). Much to his surprise, he passed the test by spurning all references to the technical and concentrating on the value of light and color in painting. Aside from the obvious appeal of this story as a lesson in sticking to your guns, there's something so moving about the image of a group of business people coming to discuss technology and being won over by a young man's passion for light in the work of his masters: 'Rembrandt, Vermeer, Pieter de Hooch and the mighty Turner', and the Impressionists, who taught him about pure color and reflections. There is so much joy and care in Cardiff's descriptions of painting. A wonderful moment comes later in the book when he is shooting a Technicolor travelogue in Italy. In the process of working out how to properly shoot Bernini's fountain in the Piazza Navona, his colonnade in St Peter's or Michelangelo's Pietà, Cardiff achieves a fuller understanding of the artists; it's as though he is paying tribute to his beloved painting *through* film. It is only fitting at this point to say that his achievement as a cinematographer was to make cinema into an art of moving painting. In this sense Cardiff was a true pioneer of color.

For me, the most indelible moments of this book are his memories of film shoots: he worked in one capacity or another on many of the greatest pictures ever made, films that have captivated me from childhood to middle age. *The Four Feathers*, on which Cardiff worked as an operator, was one of my favorite films as a boy; the locations seemed so beautifully remote that they appeared to have been shot on the dark side of the moon. It all looked so real, so tough – and in *Magic Hour* we learn that it didn't just *look* that way. The stories about the shoot – a blistering, arduous three-month affair in 115-degree heat, during which director Zoltán Korda suffered from a skin disease and Cardiff's tempestuous marriage all but disintegrated – make it clear why that film's images more than live up to the world of the imagination. Cardiff got his first big break as a cinematographer on Powell and Pressburger's *A Matter of Life and Death*, because Michael Powell had been impressed by the way Cardiff shot inserts of the animal trophy heads on the wall for a passage of time montage in *The Life and Death of Colonel Blimp*. (I was astonished to read that Cardiff shot those particular inserts: a co-incidence, since I first saw *Colonel Blimp* as a child on television, in black and white, and while I was too young to really appreciate it, that montage stayed in my mind for years.) But this film, which I missed during its original release as *Stairway to Heaven* and which I recently helped distribute in its original version, was the beginning of a truly great collaboration between director and cinematographer: both Powell and Cardiff were bold experimenters who flew in the face of convention, and both were passionate about their art.

It's fascinating to read the details of studio and artistic wizardry behind *Black Narcissus*, for which Cardiff won an Oscar for Best Cinematography. *The Red Shoes*, Cardiff's next movie with The Archers, is simply one of the greatest films ever made and it's a film that lives in my heart. So, to read Cardiff's descriptions of his preparations – his initial resistance to ballet and his slow conversion over many evenings at Covent Garden – as well as the shoot itself, is an experience to be cherished. But beyond that, the technical details of how he filmed the ballets – he actually invented a device that allowed him to change camera speed in the middle of the shot – brought me back to his love for painting in the earlier chapters. Because, in effect, what Cardiff did was to *paint* with the camera. He was the one who taught the movie camera how to become as supple as a paintbrush, and in moments such as the one where a dancer seems to hover in the air and fly down to the stage, we're seeing the cinematic equivalent of the brushstroke. This aspect of film as painting in Cardiff's work was something that I recognized as a child but could not put into words. As opposed to the wildly expressionist palette of an American Technicolor film from the same period such as *Duel in the Sun*, Cardiff worked with a subtler, warmer and more sumptuous field of color, very much in the spirit of late nineteenth-century painting. And, as opposed to many films that have *copied* paintings, Cardiff made cinema *through* painting. It seems incredible now to realize that *The Red Shoes* was something of a disaster when it was originally released in England, but it shares the now august company of *L'Atalante*, *Rules of the Game*, *Citizen Kane*, *The Magnificent Ambersons* and Powell's later *Peeping Tom*.

Cardiff's descriptions of technical misadventures during the shooting of Hitchcock's *Under Capricorn* offer a hilarious look at the kind of on-the-spot ingenuity required on a film set, carried in this case to an outrageous level. *The Black Rose* is another difficult shoot in which the reality lives up to the movie and vice-versa. It was because of this film that I'd always wanted to shoot in Morocco and when I finally did, on *The Last Temptation of Christ*, I was delighted to have a crew member who had worked on *The Black Rose*. *Pandora and the Flying Dutchman*, with its sumptuous color, exotic real locations, and strange, mystical love story, is a precious film, unlike any other. (Because of all these elements, in addition to that name 'Cardiff', I originally mistook it for a Powell/Pressburger film.) One of the small gifts of *Magic Hour* is that it allows a rare glimpse of that film's director, Albert Lewin. Lewin was a very special film-maker with a refined, literary sensibility.

The African Queen offers yet another series of mishaps and near-death experiences; a boiler that almost toppled over on to Katharine Hepburn and John Huston, the sinking of the *African Queen* itself. As a child I remember watching the film and knowing from the images that they actually *went* there. This is an ongoing theme in this book, which reflects a moment in film history that may sadly be over now. You had the sense of the people behind the film caring for and *respecting* the audience enough to go to real locations, to make the film *feel* real as opposed to merely *look* real (that you can do with digital technology). *The Magic Box* is the other side of the coin – a film made entirely in the studio with a rare sense of care and craftsmanship. The story of the film pioneer William Friese-Greene, this movie taught me about the 'persistence of vision' phenomenon, the very essence of 'moving pictures'. It's well directed by John Boulting, but what makes it extraordinary is the world created by Cardiff's light. The mysterious dream which is cinema, in all its womb-like warmth, is captured in this film. In my mind, this light is the light in which the cinema was invented. In the scene where Robert Donat's Friese-Greene summons Laurence Olivier's bobby from the street to behold his invention with bewildered amazement before he looks behind the screen (as kids we all wanted to look behind the screen and see if anything was there), we *all* saw the cinema for the first time.

So many memorable films, so many memories. Mankiewicz's *The Barefoot Contessa*, a film in which passion equals color and Ava Gardner; Hathaway's *Legend of the Lost*, an extraordinarily sensual film with exotic locations that I find myself watching at least once a year; King Vidor's *War and Peace*, which I saw for the first time at the New York Capitol projected in VistaVision and which had a scale that is no longer possible (the magnificent battle scenes in that film would probably be digitally enhanced now, but although you save money with digital you lose the senses of both distance and texture); Richard Fleischer's *The Vikings*, an old-fashioned adventure film with a real edge which holds up remarkably well (I still remember the huge Viking ship billboard with moving oars over the Astor and Victoria theaters in Broadway, and I also remember that my friends and I couldn't be admitted to see it before three o'clock because we were in school.)

The sad story of Cardiff's first job as a director – the abortive *William Tell* with Errol Flynn – is the kind of heartache that only a fellow film-maker can understand. Cardiff had a happier experience with *Sons and Lovers*, one of the most honest and straightforward adaptations of D. H. Lawrence we have. I'm fond of both *The Lion* and *My Geisha*, again films with wonderfully authentic locations. I remember seeing *The Long Ships* on its first release and feeling that we in the audience were privy to something special – here was an unusual film for this genre, a film of style and self-deprecating humor. It's a surprise to learn that there was acrimony on the set because there's not a trace of it in the finished film, a tribute to the professionalism and artistry of everyone involved. *Young Cassidy* had a true sense of empathy for Sean O'Casey and offers us a view of one of the great Irish artists, as well as a vivid depiction of the world in which he lived. Another startling film is the little known and little seen *Dark of the Sun*, which surprised me with its unexpected ferocity the first time I saw it back in 1968 in London's Leicester Square.

An entire history of cinema seems to be contained in this wonderful book. But *Magic Hour* is not merely a history but a piece of it as well, a graceful act of remembrance during a time when the memory of the past is not valued very highly. Its author has more than completed his apprenticeship with the old masters of painting he admires so much. I hope he knows what an inspiration he's been to me and to so many others. *Magic Hour* will give young film-makers and cinematographers a precious gateway to a vital body of work. And it will also serve as an announcement to new students of cinema that there's now another old master to study. His name is Jack Cardiff.

Martin Scorsese, 1996

Fade In . . .

The music soared into the usual persuasive volume over the end title. *Sons and Lovers*, my first important film as a director, was up for judgement at the Cannes Festival and I sat in the front row of the circle, my mouth completely dry.

The lights came up. The applause exploded with delicious vehemence. A spotlight swung to me as I bowed and smiled mechanically at the blurred images of faces, black ties, and glittering gowns. The applause went past conventional politeness, and there was no longer any doubt. I had made it.

It was a 'like a dream' cliché. All the battles and heartaches I'd had making the film were forgotten in this blissful hosannah. Standing next to me was my boss, Buddy Adler, the sovereign lord of 20th Century Fox. Tall, white haired, with pearly sad El Greco eyes, but he was smiling now, and had to lean close to my ear to make himself heard: 'Jack, you must enjoy every second of this. Who knows, it may never happen to you again.'

My father was playing billiards in a pub at Yarmouth on the night I was born. He was a good player – he made breaks of over a hundred sometimes – but this time, on 18 September 1914, he dashed off to welcome me with a bottle of champagne.

My parents were old-time music hall 'pros' (they liked to call themselves) who travelled every week to theatres all over England. At the time I was born they were appearing on the sands at Yarmouth in an alfresco minstrel show. Dad, his face burnt-corked black, with a white silk suit and a jaunty boater, was singing and twanging his banjo to a deckchair audience sluggish with sun and beer, while my mother watched in her usual sunny world, awaiting my arrival. They used to do the traditional seaside concert party most summers, as a long vacation 'lark' – one of the last echoes of Edwardian pleasures. Some miles away across the English Channel the 'War to end all Wars' had started a month before.

What had also been termed a 'lark' by so many was already becoming a horrendous charnel-house.

Across the Atlantic my own future world – the cinema – was bawling lustily like an infant Gargantua. De Mille was in his first year as a director, D. W. Griffith had just made *Birth of a Nation* and Charlie Chaplin, who had worked with my father before he went to America, was already a star.

In the realm of painting, which was to become so important to me, Renoir was still working away, his brush strapped to his withered hand. Degas, nearly blind, was reduced to fumbling his hands over his models, making his famous wax ballet dancers, which he hid in dusty cupboards until they were discovered after his death and bronzed to glory. (I was later to own one after I had photographed *The Red Shoes*.) But I don't remember my parents – simple, uncomplicated people without much education – ever talking about painting, or any of the Arts; the entire landscape of their minds was show business.

My parents had lost their first-born, also Jack, two years before when he was seven. He had been a child prodigy, singing and dancing in his own act, and was obviously something special in the stage world. Paul Singavelli, a well-known magician and illusionist, had been so enraptured by his talent that he begged my father to allow him to adopt Jackie, and offered Dad ten pounds a week for life. My father was more amused than outraged, and told Singavelli he must be out of his mind – that his son was his very life.

Two weeks after that preposterous offer my young brother caught pneumonia, and died. A long and lifeless two years went by before my parents recovered from this tragedy. When I grew up, my mother, with her ever-delightful ingenuousness, told me that they had tried desperately to have another child, but nothing happened until a friend suggested that Dad should go away for a couple of weeks to recharge his procreative abilities. Sure enough, it worked.

My childhood was spent travelling to towns all over England; every week was another home, another world. We stayed in digs, usually a bedsitter, and I always called the landladies 'Auntie'.

As a baby, my nursery was the theatre dressing-room until the show was over, when I was carried back to the digs. When I could just walk, I used to be seated on a stool in the wings watching the show. One night, I squirmed down off my stool and toddled on to the stage, up to the footlights, blew a kiss to the audience, and toddled back to my stool – to thunderous applause. After that, I was strapped to the stool.

(Strange how tiny slivers of memory can pierce the years. I can still see a man in evening-dress saying to a chorus girl: 'Not even if I gave you this gold watch?')

My nursery continued to be backstage; sometimes, if the stagehands were indulgent, I would climb the dizzy heights above the proscenium – the 'flies' – where the scenic backdrops were raised and lowered by incredibly complex systems of ropes and pulleys; or I would sit perched up in the gantry, where the spluttering arc lamps followed the actors below. Laurence Olivier told me that, in the early days of the primitive lime lamps, the electricians used to pee in the earthenware pots that served as accumulators for the limes – the chemical that made the term 'limelight' a mark of fame. Certainly, the magic everlasting fragrance of backstage will stay with me always: greasepaint, powder, cheap perfumes, glue and urine.

I spent many evenings in the chorus girls' dressing-room, and took it as a natural part of life that the girls would pee in the washbasin as they gossiped and swore whilst making-up and dressing. They taught me their dance routines, and I could do the splits almost well enough for the can-can.

When I was older, I would sometimes be the call boy: calling the actors when their time approached to be 'on'. Occasionally I was allowed to appear on stage myself, in some child's part, and that was heaven.

I used to go to a different school every week – about three hundred schools in all – and learned virtually nothing. As I was always a 'new boy' I was never punished or driven to study anything. Not much could be done with me in a week. I was a curiosity passing through, a scholarly eunuch. The friendships I made at school were sadly ephemeral. I enjoyed a brief popularity each week, as I was allowed to take my transitory friends to see Dad's show, free; this also applied to the local cinema shows, where tradition allowed stage people and cinema people free access to each other's domains.

There is no doubt I missed many things in my fragmented schooldays. Apart from the shocking absence of education, I missed the character-forming crucible of adversity, having neither friends nor enemies. I never came home with a black eye from a fight. I never failed an exam; I never passed one, either. However, what I lacked in schoolday slings and arrows was compensated for by a childhood spent in the protean fantasies of the theatre; I certainly never felt deprived.

My mother and father adored each other, and were sweethearts all their lives. They used to sing old vaudeville songs together: 'Lily of Laguna', 'Swanee', 'Moonlight Bay', 'Danny Boy', and so on. It seems incredible in today's grim world, but whether they were in digs, or out shopping, or in the theatre dressing-room, they sang together. Both had good voices. Dad used to sing in melodious and accurate counterpoint, and music was as natural a part of my childhood as eating and sleeping.

My father was always a hero to me. Short – about five feet eight inches – he had a well-built, muscular body; he'd done a bit of boxing, and played football as a professional for Watford. He had finely cast features with a strong chin, and proud serious eyes that often lit up unexpectedly with mischievous humour.

As a lad of fifteen he had seen a Scottish regiment march by his home in the East End of London, and was so taken by their jaunty marching, their bright kilts swinging in unison, the grimy air filled with the wheezy arrogance of their bagpipes, that he ran away from home to endure the rigours of army life in the Seaforth Highlanders up in Scotland – until his age was discovered, and he was sent home.

His first job was as a door-to-door salesman, and on his very first day he met with disaster. He rang a doorbell and waited in the rain until the door was opened at last by a woman who, the moment Dad started his sales talk with a beaming 'Good morning, Madam', slammed the door in his face. Dad lifted up the letter-box flap and yelled 'Bollocks!' at the top of his voice – and that was the end of his brief career as a salesman.

I don't know how he got started on the stage. He had sung in the local clubs during the time he played football for Watford, and this must have given him the spur to go 'on the green', as the stage was called.

There were stage connections in our family; the singer Marie Kendal was his aunt, and probably helped him on his way. In fact, she allowed him to sing one of her own songs, 'Did Your First Wife Ever Do That?' (I suppose he changed 'wife' for 'husband'). But dancing was his first success. He had a natural grace and sense of rhythm which probably came from his footballing skills. His tap-dancing was softly dexterous, and quite dazzling to me. I wanted to become a 'hoofer' too but, perhaps because of the tragedy of my young brother's early death, my father never encouraged me to be a dancer. I picked up a few routine steps and was even able to 'wing' – a pretty difficult manoeuvre – but Dad didn't want me to go any further. He was a very superstitious person, and felt it would tempt providence to set me up as another child wonder.

My father was in a double act billed as 'Morrin and Cardiff'. They danced in white tie and tails, top hats and twirling canes, with twinlike precision, every movement a double image. The act was so effective that Dad and his partner were honoured by a Royal Command Performance in front of King Edward, who said: 'Their dancing was capital. I have never seen dancing like it in my life.' He gave my father a huge cigar and, from that triumphant evening, the Morrin and Cardiff act was booked solid for a long time.

But there were problems. Morrin took heavily to drink, and this made their close-knit dancing less than perfect as he would sway drunkenly in all directions, obliging Dad to sway with him to maintain their dual precision. It became intolerable. Dad broke up the partnership and became a comedian. However hazardous the transition, it was successful. He was able to use his dancing talents and physical fitness to good effect as a knockabout comic, and eventually topped the bill all over England.

In the early days, however, there were much more illustrious names above him; Charlie Chaplin, for instance. Dad was in a revue with Chaplin – Fred Karno's 'Mumming Birds'. Half a century later I was having dinner with Chaplin (we were neighbours in Switzerland) and mentioned my father having worked with him. To my surprise and pleasure, he remembered working with Dad at the Palace Theatre, Maidstone, and said they had often played billiards together.

Chaplin described his act to me: how he played an Eton schoolboy, sitting in a theatre box which was on the stage. Every time a dancing girl kicked her legs high in the air, he would lean forward and drop his hat on the floor so he could get a good look up the girl's skirts. The girl – a 'soubrette' – sang in the quaint innocence of those days: 'You naughty, naughty man!' Dad told me that, although Chaplin was very young at the time, it was obvious that he had great talent. He would go close to the footlights, just looking at the audience, and they would soon be in stitches.

On the bill every week there were many who became famous: Gracie Fields, Sir Harry Lauder, George Robey, and many others including Dad's aunt, Marie Kendal. One act I watched from the stalls with my mother is still fresh in my mind today. A woman was dancing in a manner I had never seen before. My mother told me it was ballet. In this act there was just a single figure, not several chorus girls, and the music was not the brazen gaiety of music hall; it was hauntingly sad as the lone dancer glided on tiptoe, seeming to drift through the air, with her long fragile arms waving in delicately expressive gestures, depicting a swan in its fluttering death-throes. It was the legendary Pavlova, dancing her 'Dying Swan' late in her career; although so many years have passed, I shall never forget the overwhelming sensation of a beauty never before encountered. I remember that I cried seeing Pavlova die as a swan and, as my mother hugged me, she was crying too.

My mother radiated purity like a Raphael Madonna. I have never stopped wondering how she survived the smutty sophistication of show business. She had a serenely beautiful face, a busy smile, and huge brown eyes that always seemed to shine with simple happiness. Her whole life was focused on my father. She lived to please him, and there was extra-ordinary love, trust and understanding between them, without jealousy or rancour. During shows Dad would often receive bouquets of flowers, and sometimes expensive gifts from women admirers, which he would at once hand over to Mother, who would happily receive them without the slightest resentment.

In spite of her delightful innocence, there were times when she used a shrewd ploy to avoid a tricky situation. My father had a fiery temper and when a row with another actor was accelerating to punch-up propor-tions, with Dad about to take a murderous swing, Mother would faint. I saw her do it once, and later she confessed that it was all put on. It was brilliantly performed, and I don't think Dad ever caught on. At any rate, it always worked.

Once, though, my mother was unable to do her fainting routine to avoid fisticuffs. Dad was playing a dying man and had a line before the curtain came down for the interval when he uttered his last request. On this particular night a drunk in one of the boxes was shouting loudly and ruining the show. His companion, quite sober, was trying to keep his friend quiet – but without success. When my father was asked what would he desire before he died, Dad changed his curtain line, and instead said: 'I'd like one minute with that idiot in the box.' There was tremen-dous applause. The drunk in the box bawled his acceptance of the challenge and tried to climb out of the box on to the stage, being re-strained with great difficulty by his sober friend as the interval curtain came down. My father leapt up from his death-bed and, still in his make-up and wig, ran full-pelt to the theatre lobby and up the stairs to the box. As he burst the box door open, he hit the occupant's jaw so hard that the man had to be taken to hospital. Unfortunately the man he hit was the sober one, who happened to be the town's Lord Mayor! The next day, Dad had to go to the hospital to apologize.

Although we lived so happily together, the family bliss would sometimes be shattered – mostly because of something I had done. I would get hell from Dad if I offended my mother in any way, and hell from Mother if I upset Dad; but it would all be over within a few seconds, with hugs and kisses all round. I was never punished, as long as I told the truth. This was a strict rule. Once, playing in the back yard of our digs, I relieved myself in a handy bucket. It turned out that the bucket was full of oysters, and the landlady was understandably hopping mad. But I wasn't punished as I owned up at once when my father questioned me. He pacified the irate landlady, and later we all had a good laugh.

Dad's sense of mischief was spontaneous – sometimes alarmingly so. During a lively family tea in the digs before the show, he threw the remains of his kipper at me. I ducked, and it stuck on the wall like a Picasso collage. The landlady entered at this point, and furiously berated me as the culprit. Dad acted in horrified anger, as though he hadn't seen it before, and gave me a stern lecture on the gravity of my offence. He gave such a good performance as an outraged parent that the lady, seeing me on the point of tears (of laughter, had she but known!) forgave me, and left. We laughed ourselves silly.

Somewhere on tour, Dad took me to meet Jimmy Wilde – perhaps the greatest flyweight boxer Britain ever produced. He was a world champion, tiny and thin (only 98 pounds) with arms like matchsticks; but such was his skill and the incredible power in those frail arms that he could beat the daylights out of any opponent. He had learned to box the hard way – in a boxing booth: fighting to eat, and for pitiful amounts of money, he knocked out dozens of much heavier men every day. When I met him, he showed me the famous coveted Lonsdale Belt, and put it on me for fun. He also gave me a lesson in self-defence. 'When you hit someone on the nose,' he said, 'and he touches his nose gingerly, seeing a little blood on his fingers . . . hit him again – as hard as you can. But if he just stares at you as he draws the blood back fiercely up his nostril' – he gave a graphic illustration – 'run for your life!'

Like most stage people we used to speak 'stage slang', a rapid and seemingly meaningless gibberish to outsiders, which could be very useful at times. Even today, I can rattle it off at a good rate. Once, in a bus, I was commentating rudely on a woman's hat to my parents. The woman turned to us as she was getting off the bus and said, cuttingly in fluent slang, that we weren't the only stage pros in the world. Oops!

A good example of this esoteric jargon was 'You're starring', meaning your flies were undone. Dad would sometimes use this to cruel effect when an actor was emoting passionately at the footlights; Dad would only have to whisper 'You're starring' to cause the actor to become glassy-eyed with panic and forget his lines.

My father was extremely funny on stage, but quiet and serious off it, never speaking much. Whenever we arrived in a new town, those who were used to the gusty ebullience of extrovert comics were dismayed at the sight of the silent figure in the corner but, after the first night's performance when they had seen his sparkling comedic talent, he was always highly popular for the rest of the week.

I used to sit in the audience, knowing all the gags that were coming up – indeed, I usually knew all the actors' lines by heart – and would glow with pride when people all around me were convulsed at my Dad's antics. I actually saw a woman carried out, in pain from laughing too much.

Sometimes I was a 'gee' – someone planted in the audience to make a gag work. Dad would expound on how people in the street are always inquisitive and, if someone looks up at nothing, the crowd would do likewise. Dad would then bet that he could make the entire audience turn round. The bet was taken – and that was where I came in. Sitting right at the back of the theatre I would start a loud argument. In seconds, the entire audience would turn round to stare at me. I would then leave the theatre in a huff and, as the audience turned round again, they would see that my father had won his bet.

Mother was usually in the chorus, always looking radiant; sometimes she would have lines to speak – 'a bit of patter', as she called it – which pleased her very much.

Sundays were travelling days. My mother, not always so innocent, used to carry me in her arms (even when I was far too big) to avoid paying my train fare. Babes in arms travelled free up to the age of four, but I was carried – with increasing difficulty – long after that tender age. The inevitable end to this cumbersome fraud came when, for some reason, we were travelling on a weekday. When my mother staggered up to the ticket barrier, the inspector (seeing the enormous bundle in my mother's arms) enquired what age I was. My mother gave the usual age of four. 'No, Mummy,' I piped from the depths of my swaddling, 'I'm seven today – I'm only four on Sundays!' Perhaps the conductor had a sense of humour – or a child of his own – for there was no immediate arrest, but that marked my début as a fare-paying rail passenger.

Dad had a special strategy to keep our railway compartment to ourselves. He would feign madness, contorting horribly, and mouthing insane gibberish at the carriage window to frighten away passengers about to enter. This worked with dramatic success until one Sunday; in spite of his lunatic frenzies, a woman, taking not the slightest notice, entered the carriage, and calmly seated herself next to my mother saying, 'Shame, isn't it? I have a son like that . . . but they're quite harmless, aren't they?' And Dad had to act out his noisy lunacy for the rest of the journey.

One Sunday, as we were speeding north, there was sudden, screaming terror as the train went off the rails at speed and careered over the sleepers in a series of gigantic kangaroo vaults, soaring up, and crashing down to nightmare sounds. We were thrown all over the place, bouncing in the air as though on a devil's trampoline. My mother, convinced it was the end, was trying to reach me to hold me in her arms – but it was hopeless. Fortunately the driver kept his head and gradually slowed down the train over the distance of a mile, to prevent the coaches becoming concertinaed. It saved our lives, but by the time the train had stopped every window was shattered and many carriages smashed.

At Christmas there was pantomime. If I was deprived of the convivial family reunion in a proper home, I never missed it. I think I loved pantomime more than Father Christmas. *Ali Baba and the Forty Thieves*, *Aladdin*, *Mother Goose*, *Puss-in-Boots*, *Dick Whittington*, *Jack and the Beanstalk*, *Cinderella* – that was my Christmas. What child could desire more?

Even more enchanting was to be backstage; to see at close quarters the ranting Devil spring through a burst of orange smoke or the benign fairy, refulgent in flashing sequins, spring up from the stage waving her tinselled wand to banish the nasties. The entire stage troupe seemed to cast off their cares at panto-time. Just like any normal family unwinds at Christmas, so did the pros enter into the Christmas spirit, and the usual stage tensions and temperamental flare-ups were absent.

I was thoroughly spoilt, playing with the giant cat, chased by the two-man donkey, playing hide-and-seek in Ali Baba's jars, being made-up and costumed to appear on stage when the whole cast came on for the finale.

Dad was often in drag in these Christmas shows, and was a riot as Widow Twankey, with an enormous floppy hat, great balloon breasts and a monstrous wobbling bottom that would slide down from time to time. It was all for the kids and, for me, a non-stop Christmas party. How sad that this has all but disappeared forever from the English scene.

No matter how successful a show had been, there were periods when Dad was 'resting' before another one came along. My father earned good money as a provincial comedian, but he certainly wasn't the thrifty type; in the periods between shows, there was little money left to live on. We 'rested' in London in a state of near-poverty, usually in the cheapest rooms in Kennington Road, Lambeth. It was the same street that Charlie Chaplin had lived in, but that didn't make things any easier. Our squalid digs were usually overrun with bugs, which Dad used to hunt and burn with a candle. How we never started a fire remains a mystery. However, this grim existence didn't stop Mum and Dad singing the next morning; we would catch the bus 'up West' where we would tour the theatrical agencies, hoping another show would turn up before we became completely broke.

During these periods, we were able to fill-in with film work. The British film industry was nothing like as busy as Hollywood, but I remember it fondly. If my stage childhood was a fairytale existence, the film world in those days was pure enchantment. There would be a train journey out to the studios – St Margaret's at Twickenham, or Wharton Hall at Isleworth – where the sets were lit with huge banks of violet klieg lights. The make-up was a heavy yellow (Leichner No. 5) with the eyes shaded in a dark red, and lips brilliant crimson to accommodate the orthochromatic film then used which had little sensitivity to the red end of the spectrum. The cameras made a merry whirring noise with the handle – not on the side as many picture it, but at the back, so the cameraman cranked away at right angles, and the noise on the set as we worked could be deafening in those 'silent' days.

Each studio had (and still has) a back lot: a surreal graveyard of dismantled sets and props left outdoors for possible further use. After the ravages of the English climate, everything became eroded and overgrown.

For me as a child, this wasteland of cast-off dreams was a wonderland. In the times I wasn't required on the set, I would wander about entranced. Of course, I was used to stage sets – this, however, was not just flats of painted canvas on a small stage, but outside in the open air, an infinity of mysteries to be explored. There, cuddled in vines and wild flowers, was an old horse-drawn bus. Through tall grass I would jump as a face reared up, revealing a huge ship's figurehead, the flowing hair and haughty eyes staring blankly; I would climb on to the massive shoulders and be a sailor, peering at Arabia, where the distant gas-holder was. Here was my own dream warehouse, which shaped my future world of make-believe.

During these film interludes we worked as humble extras. Sometimes one of us would have the odd line of dialogue, but that was rare. My father's quiet, serious exterior could never have intimated to a film producer his talent as a comedian. He wasn't a polished actor of the 'legit' stage, as he called it, and I don't think he had any ambition to exchange his happy vaudeville life for a new film career. It was only a lark to us, to get a few days' film work at the considerable sum of a guinea a day.

On one film, *Mary Queen of Scots*, the large crowd was paid off from a tiny booth set up in a field. The cashier could only see one person at a time through a narrow window. As the crowd filed past, they would be handed a guinea, and move on. What the cashier didn't see was that the extras were rejoining the line, having disguised themselves – changing hats or spectacles – and receiving another guinea!

I was sometimes given a little part to play, the first being at the age of four in 1918 in a film called *My Son*, starring Violet Hopson and Stewart Rome. What acting I had to do was simplified by the director shouting instructions through a long megaphone: 'Look over to Miss Hopson . . . You LOVE her . . . SMILE a little . . . Take his hand, Violet . . . Jackie, look up at her and SMILE . . . More, son – that's good . . . .'

I loved it. With my stage background I was never nervous or shy and it all came naturally. I even played the lead in a film when I was eight years old. *Billy's Rose* was a typical weepy of that time. I played an Oliver Twist-type beggar boy with drunken parents – acted with brio by Mum and Dad – who forced me to beg in the streets for money. I had an ailing bedridden sister who told me wistfully how she would so love to have a real rose. I trudged through the mushy streets and, as a posh car went by, saw a lady throw some discarded roses from her window. As I darted eagerly forward to pick them up, I was knocked down by a following car and fatally injured.

I lay stretched out in a garret bed for a whole day, and died many times before the director was satisfied. It was a weirdly painful experience for Mum and Dad. They had to watch me 'die' as they had watched my brother die – at the same age – and there is little doubt that their tears were real. Dad said afterwards that it had been a nightmare for them both. Just as my last moments came, I looked up to heaven and saw angels gliding around, Isadora Duncan style. I had to imagine that bit, as the angels were to be filmed next day to be superimposed above my death-bed.

The next morning, now healthily resurrected, I watched the 'angels' dancing outside on the lawn, and remember vividly the sharp voice of the dancing mistress as the girls, dressed in flowing white robes, danced in dreamy, gentle movements to the stern metronome commands of the dancing mistress: 'And ONE, and TWO, and ONE, and TWO – Mabel, catch up!'

*

During out-of-work periods we nearly always 'rested' at grimy Kennington. My mother did her best to put me in some school – a kindergarten on a temporary basis – and it was at a kindergarten that I had my first love affair. The object of my pangs of passion was a little girl the same age as I was – about six – who had flaming red hair which her mother had ironed into clusters of tight curls, Mary Pickford style. She might have been pretty – I don't remember – but what made such a chaotic upheaval in my soul was that she simply reeked of eucalyptus. Her mother took no chances of her darling catching a cold and soaked her in the stuff every day. Ever since then, whenever I smell eucalyptus, I still have starkly erotic feelings.

During another of these resting times which my family was filling in with film work, and soon after my olfactory lust for the little eucalyptus girl, I worked on my first commercial. It was for Sharps Creamy Toffee. Not for television, of course, but for the cinema, and I had to play the challenging role of a duck.

In an establishment in a cobbled street near St Pancras station, a cane basket in the shape of a duck was made to fit me, and this was covered in goose feathers. I had to waddle about in a low stooping position around the bucolic farm set with other members of the toffee cast, showing the pleasures of Sharps Creamy Toffee. Everyone had a happy time except me: I had to keep my head down, with increasing cramp, straining to keep my knees from bending, while the unseen cast was pleasurably chewing toffee. I had to concentrate on not crashing into the other actors as I couldn't see anything except the ground. At the end of the day, I was a very lame duck.

More shows and another spin of the carousel and I was back in digs again in the familiar streets of Kennington. One evening I went for a walk. I had just had my ninth birthday, but I hadn't received any expensive presents because my parents had been out of work for months and things were tough.

As I passed a large building which looked like a concert hall I heard music and applause, so I nosily edged inside. It was a talent show. Children were singing to a piano accompaniment and the packed hall was showing their verdict by applause. At that time I had not the slightest shyness or inhibitions that most children have and went right up to the stage asking if I could enter. I sang one of my father's songs, 'Beaver, You're Barmy', the piano picking up the tune without any trouble. I sang a verse and a chorus then started to dance, but after a few moments the master of ceremonies stopped me saying, 'That will do son – you've won.' When I saw the prize I nearly fell over. It was a Tan-Sad scooter, a magnificent machine with a pedal on a spring which, as you bounced up and down on it, propelled the bike along at some speed. I drove it home in delight to show it proudly to my astonished parents. My mother said that God had arranged it, giving me the sort of birthday present they would have liked to have given me themselves.

When I was ten I made my first appearance in a play – the legitimate theatre no less – which my father (bless his heart) looked upon as a snobbish world. The play was called *The Octoroon* and featured Frank Livesy, the father of Roger Livesy with whom I worked years later on *A Matter of Life and Death*. The theatre was The Little Theatre, which is just off Soho. I had a very small part as a negro boy, and the play had a very short run, but I loved it.

My character opened the show. As the curtain came up, I entered on stage to say one of my few lines, and exit. Big deal! But even though I was used to being on stage, I had that indescribable thrill – part rapture, part terror – feeling the sea of blurred eyes reflected in the faint light from the proscenium. I wore a curly wig and had black greasepaint all over my naked loinclothed body which took ages to get off. At the end of the first night, I couldn't wait to get back to our digs (my parents were rehearsing and weren't able to see the show). I caught a tram back, and as I sat there I became conscious of people staring at me with considerable distaste. In my rush to get dressed, I had forgotten to take the black greasepaint off my knees.

*

Most kids aren't too impressed by a famous name, and I was no exception. Here I was, working on a film with Dorothy Gish and the great Will Rogers, and I wasn't aware of their fame until years later. Will Rogers was, in the twenties, the folk hero of all America. A tall, lanky cowboy, with a Southern drawl, he used to stand on stage making trenchant political wisecracks, at the same time tossing a piece of rope about eighteen inches in length into the air and making a knot, then switching the rope in the air again and untying the knot. It looked easy, but anyone trying it would soon realize it was maddeningly near-impossible.

The film was *Tip Toes* and it was made at the charming rural St Margaret's studio at Twickenham. The director was Herbert Wilcox, who years later was to be my big boss at Elstree Studios. I don't remember exactly what I did on *Tip Toes* (probably very little), but during waits between shooting, Will Rogers generously taught me how to 'throw the knot'. Eventually I had some kind of success, but my piece of rope had to be tied at the end, so that its weight would help the forming of a knot. Rogers did it without such assistance, but I had a tiny suspicion that his rope had a hidden weight in the end. Anyway, I used to show off on studio sets for years afterwards and have fun watching people trying to do it.

At this time my family moved to the new studios at Borehamwood, called 'Elstree' by the press even though the village of that name was several miles away. My father was getting less and less stage work and, since his health was deteriorating, he found film work less of a strain. We rented a small bungalow next door to the studios, and I went to a permanent school for the first time: Medburn, which was a Church of England council school and a three-mile bike ride away.

My acting career was over. I was too big for children's parts and too small for grown-up roles. My last bit of acting – if you can call it that – was for a competition for Nurses for the St John Ambulance Brigade. First, in a studio kitchen set, I played a boy getting on my screen mother's nerves by bouncing a ball. She was perched on a high stool getting something out of a cupboard. As my mother turned to tell me to stop bouncing the ball, she fell off the stool and lay inert on the floor. I ran out to get help. Then the kitchen set was taken to a theatre in London where, sitting in the audience, were the Duke and Duchess of York – our future King and Queen. The film was shown, then the screen disappeared as the curtains rose, to show the mother in person lying on the floor. I enter with a nurse who decides what has to be done.

This was repeated a dozen times, and according to which methods and procedure each nurse showed, a winner would be chosen. I had to make myself useful – heating some water, getting blankets, etc. It was fun, if somewhat repetitious. I was awed by the presence of royalty in the audience. Hardly a command performance like my father had achieved, but something to tell my school chums about.

I had to leave school two weeks before my fourteenth birthday. Dad was too ill to work and I was able to get my first job, at Elstree studio. The film was *The Informer*, the 1928 silent version, several years before John Ford's film with Victor McLaglen. Lars Hansen and Lia de Putti were the stars. My most important function was to supply the German director, Dr Arthur Robison, with Vichy water as he had a flatulence problem. I had to be ready to hand him a full tumbler throughout the long day.

*

A complete Dublin street had been built on the old silent stage. It was packed with four hundred extras, and looked splendidly authentic. There were several shops, including a pawnbroker's with its three brass balls hanging outside, and for this haven for the hard-ups, the property department had really gone to town. The shop was crammed with clocks, watches, rings, riding boots, silver cups, hats, golf clubs, cameras – you name it.

When we returned from lunch there wasn't a single solitary article left in the pawnshop. Everything had been stolen. All that was left to mock us were the three brass balls.

At that time there were no studio gates or security men. On one film, the leading man's suit was taken from his dressing-room. The director appealed in vain on a loudspeaker for the thief to return the suit as the film couldn't be completed without it. In the end a new one had to be copied from a photograph.

There was a most extraordinary and chilling incident on our Dublin street. The actors had been given Colt 45 revolvers and somehow one real bullet got mixed in with the blanks. The gun was fired in a crowd scene and the real bullet, miraculously, missed four hundred extras before embedding itself in the far studio wall.

We worked extremely long hours, and most Sundays as well. (This was before the existence of unions.) One Sunday Lia de Putti arrived very late, coming on the set just after lunch, carrying an armful of flowers. The director screamed out in fury: 'Where the hell have you been?' and Lia, beaming with seraphic innocence said, 'I've been to church.'

In the final sequence Gippo, the informer (Lars Hansen), leaves his girl (Lia) and walks down the stairs from their apartment, to certain death. He had locked the door to stop Lia following him. Lia screams, entreating him not to go, and sinks to her knees, beating on the door in a frenzy. The door had six panels of glass, and Lia had to break most of these panels with her bare fists. Nowadays we use sugar glass but in those long ago silent days, sugar glass was unknown and real glass was used.

Lia was persuaded to drink most of a bottle of whisky. Very soon, she was in a mood to do anything. We cranked the camera and Lia beat the door with hysterical desperation, smashing several panes of glass, before collapsing on the floor. Yes, her fists were bleeding badly. And yes, it was cruel and stupid. All that can be said is that times have changed. There are still accidents, but there is much more consideration for safety. Still, it *was* a great scene . . .

*

A very young Alfred Hitchcock was making what is said to be the first sound movie in England – *Blackmail* – in the same studios. Probably because of this, it was decided that *The Informer* should have one sequence with sound. Our stage had no soundproofing, and because we could hear the traffic and other daytime noises, it was decided to shoot the sequence at night. At night, however, we had birds singing away in the gantry, so we had to fire revolvers (with blanks this time) which kept them quiet for a couple of minutes while we hurriedly shot the scene.

The actor, Johnny Butt, was very nervous about this first speaking scene and kept forgetting his lines. 'Don't worry,' said the director, and gave him a whisky to settle his nerves. This went on for take after take until his voice became so slurred that nobody could understand what he was saying anyway. Our brave, new sound scene ended with poor Johnny Butt collapsing in a drunken stupor across the table, and we all packed it in and went home.

At one point during the shoot, the assistant cameraman called me over and showed me two pencil marks on the lens. 'Now, when I tell you, during the shot, I want you to rotate the lens from this pencil mark, to the other one.' We shot the scene and I asked the assistant what I had done. 'Well, sonny,' he said, 'you followed focus.'

And that was the beginning of it all.

2

Crossing the Rubicon

The Informer was the last big silent film to be made in England. When it was finished, my career as a Vichy waterboy ended too. I now stepped on to the lowest rung of the camera department ladder as a number boy. I knew nothing about cameras, optics, or laboratory work, but I wanted to work in the camera department because camera people went on location abroad: Egypt, France, Italy, perhaps India – how I yearned to visit these magical places! In my new world I soon came down to earth. I found out how heavy the camera equipment was to carry, and at night I had to unload and reload all the magazines with fresh film. On location this was usually in a hotel cellar. On *The American Prisoner* (Carl Brisson and Madeline Carrol) we worked excruciatingly hard on the savage terrain of Dartmoor, shooting an average of fifty setups a day while at night I would be loading film in the cellar with rats shuffling about me. I would listen to the convivial merriment above my head, hoping that I would finish in time to get something to eat.

Over the dying days of silent films I did actually crank the camera occasionally. You had to keep a precise rhythm. In fight scenes, the cranking had to be slower, which made the action faster.

The cameraman who trusted me to do this was the delightfully named Theodore Sparkle. When cameras had to be silenced for the new sound movies he built a blimp (a box to muffle the camera noise) out of horse-hide, which was fairly successful. But it wasn't long before the first pro-fessional blimp arrived, heavy and as unwieldy as a suit of armour on a bridegroom.

The first sound films were treated with almost religious reverence. At first, we were told to hold our breath during the scene but this drastic piety soon died out as those with wheezy chests would burst out in paroxysms of coughing. We were also ordered not to rattle coins in our pockets and to stand perfectly still during a scene – in our frozen attitudes, we must have looked like wax figures at Madame Tussaud's.

The way of effecting synchronization between the picture image and the soundtrack (a separate film then, now tape) was by clapping two pieces of wood together. This ritual was considered so important that the director had to do it. He would order the camera to roll then, with the solemnity of a sacred rite, intone the scene number and clap the two pieces of wood together. After scrambling back behind the camera he would then call 'action'. Very soon after, the clapper ceremony was relegated to the humble number boy. Sometimes, it was complicated. One director, Thomas Bentley, had a complex system of numbers and I had to learn my lines like an actor: '*Harmony Heaven* sequence 115F, scene 312B7, section 4H, take 12.' Sometimes there would be jokers. Having got my announcing right, I would discover that someone had nailed my clappers together. There were variants: rubber bands over the clappers, so that they snapped back prematurely, or glue spread inside so that as the clappers came apart, a horrible gooey mess would be revealed. Sometimes children's pistol caps were stuck inside creating a loud bang and sending the sound engineer crazy. One day, while performing my clappers act, I observed a group of visitors laughing themselves silly as they watched me. When the scene finished I was invited over to speak to them. This was difficult as they only spoke German, but an interpreter told me that the chief cameraman Heinrich Gartner and his assistant Bruno Mondi wanted me to do the clappers on their next film (which was going to be shot at the same studios) which had the recondite title *The Flame of Love* starring Anna May Wong.

I soon found out there was more to it than clapper work. Every morning at 7.30 I had to assemble two Debrie cameras on tripods while Bruno Mondi gave me instructions for oiling the mechanism with a hypodermic syringe. There were over twenty oil positions on each camera. After this I had to load the film in the magazines and carry all the equipment on to the stage, including the cameraman's special case filled with arcane aids for artistic effects: special diffusion filters; trick glass for all kinds of magic; a plain glass on which Vaseline could be smeared to make various diffusion effects; extremely fine gauzes with different shapes burnt into them by cigarettes. I learned a lot from that case.

Hardly anyone spoke English, but within a few days I was speaking a few words of German and desperately trying to understand the instructions bellowed at me. The Debrie cameras were too delicate to be switched straight to full speed (24 pictures per second) so a preliminary switch was introduced which started the camera slowly. It was my job to do this and at first it was frantically embarrassing. The German word for 'on' is *auf* which sounded very much like 'off', so when they rapped out *auf* I would say 'Yes, sir, it is off'. Eventually, after much bellowing and clips around the ear, the pfennig dropped.

It was long and weary work. The only rest I remember having was when Anna May Wong had to cry in a scene and couldn't. A pianist was brought on the set to play stiflingly dull Russian music. Still no tears. I thought of suggesting a little menthol up the nose – my goodness, what a whack I would have received – so I kept silent, enjoying the rest. Towards the end of the day, a violinist came on the stage and played so badly that all of us had tears in our eyes except Anna. Then – perhaps because she was bored out of her mind – she made a slight movement of her hand and the camera turned. Finally the suspicion of a tear brimmed in her eyes. A low cathartic sigh was heard from the company and we resumed work.

Soon after this I was working with Hitchcock on *The Skin Game* (Edmond Gwenn, John Longden and Jill Esmond, the first wife of Laurence Olivier), unaware that this enormously rotund man, with his lugubrious demeanour and his plummy, posh-cockney voice, was to become the most famous film director in the world.

I was still a clapper boy, far too ignorant at sixteen to be aware of his directorial skills. All I knew then was that he had a revolting sense of humour. There were many stories of his macabre jokes. On a previous picture, when the camera assistant had married and moved into a tiny apartment, Hitchcock sent a wedding present of several tons of coal with instructions to deliver it outside the fourth-floor doorway so that the newlyweds could not get within yards of their apartment for days.

Film workmen are usually called by their first name, then their jobs: Charlie Wardrobe, Jack Stagehand, Jimmy Sound, etc. Our property man was Harry Props and he became the butt of Hitchcock's terrifying sense of fun. Jack Cox the cameraman was often a close ally in these monstrous games as on one occasion, when Harry was used as a stand-in (proper stand-ins were unknown then). Harry stood, while Jack Cox was supposed to be lighting him; in reality, he had signalled all the lamps on the spot-rail to be focused at full intensity on poor Harry's head. I think he must have sweated off half a stone. Once Hitchcock offered Harry five pounds if he would have his head shaved, which he promptly did, and Jack Cox promised a further three if he would wear handcuffs for the next twelve hours. That was the start of the cruellest joke of all. At the end of the day's shooting Hitchcock gave a shaven, manacled Harry a lift as usual, but beforehand he had phoned the pub at Elstree and told them to put a strong laxative in Harry's beer. On the way to London after their usual drink, Hitchcock suddenly exclaimed that he had to go back to the studio as he had forgotten some important documents and pushed a bewildered Harry out of the car in the middle of nowhere. Not only was Harry arrested on suspicion of being an escaped convict, but he also spent the night sleepless from acute diarrhoea.

I have described my rootless, nomadic schooling at hundreds of weekly schools, where I learned little, but I ended up being educated at one of England's most famous schools – Greyfriars, a former ancient monastery near the coast of Kent, founded in 1551 by Edward VI. Sounds a grand *alma mater*, doesn't it? Unfortunately, of course, Greyfriars School never existed. It was a fictitious establishment in a weekly boys' magazine called the *Magnet*, which was so popular and widely read that it became a British institution, as immortal as Sherlock Holmes, and *Alice in Wonderland*. (It's not that absurd: Homer's heroes of Troy, Switzerland's William Tell and England's Robin Hood probably never existed, either.) George Orwell said that Greyfriars was known wherever the Union Jack was flying.

Its creator was a phenomenon; there's no other word for him. His real name was Charles Hamilton, but he wrote for the *Magnet* under the pen-name of Frank Richards. At the same time he wrote about another school, St Jim's, under the pen-name of Martin Clifford; and yet another school – Rookwood – under the name of Owen Conquest. As well as all this, he wrote weekly adventure stories and crime fiction under other *noms de plume*, churning out over seventy thousand words a week on a battered old typewriter. His output was almost unnerving. At his peak he was writing a staggering three million words a year – without doubt, the most prolific magazine writer that ever lived. But it was the *Magnet*, with the stories of Greyfriars School, that was so fondly cherished, by barrow boys and barony alike. The first issue came out in 1908 and the last in 1940 at the start of the war. I still have over a thousand originals, starting with the 1908 issue.

I entered Greyfriars in 1926 when I was twelve years of age. My family had moved to Borehamwood in Hertfordshire. My father, now a semi-invalid, was doing occasional work at the new film studios. We had very little money, but I was able to spend tuppence a week on my *Magnet*, and attend my dream school. I knew all the boys' names in every form – I still do; all the form masters, prefects, down to old Gosling, the school porter. Since the first issue in 1908 until the last, thirty-two years later, the Greyfriars' boys – like Peter Pan – never grew a day older, and I rejoiced in their never-never-land.

During my time at Greyfriars I did, in fact, spend two years at a real local school. It was vastly different from Greyfriars, but I made it appear the same. The village school headmaster, Mr Cooper, I looked upon as Dr Locke, the headmaster of Greyfriars. My form master became Mr Quelch and I assigned Greyfriars' pupils' names to the unwitting local boys. It was a happy game of make-believe.

From reading Richards' stories I experienced all the ups and downs of a public-school environment. All the fun and adversities that are said to build character. So much was subtly inculcated in the reading: the schoolboys' code of honour and self-discipline; never to sneak, even under threat of punishment; to have courage to face anything, however unpleasant, for one's convictions of right and wrong; to be loyal; not to bear malice; to insist on fair play. I may never have achieved anything like these high ideals of character, but at least I became aware of how I should strive to act as I grew up.

Apart from inculcating codes of honour, Frank Richards planted crafty seeds of learning in his schoolboy tales. He treated his young readers with respect, and never talked down to them. There was a wealth of literary and classical terms that made one curious to find out more: who was Sisyphus? What was the Pass at Thermopylae? What were the Labours of Heracles? You had to look it up, and something new was learned every week. I wonder how many thousands of boys profited as I did from these subtle lessons at tuppence a week?

No doubt my extra cramming from Greyfriars helped me at my little local school. I became captain of the school, and won several prizes for writing, including a coveted county prize: 'The Best Essay of the Year [1928] on the subject of The League of Nations'. There were prizes for my paintings and for an essay on the mythological figure, Endymion – not perhaps realizing that the schoolboys of Greyfriars were under the same trance of immortality. Thus was my threshold of learning acquired from a school which never existed.

But there was an even more bizarre development in my education. Towards the end of my surrogate schooldays at Greyfriars, I read the notorious pornographic book by Frank Harris: *My Life and Loves*. Aside from the strident and detailed sex life of the author, there were constant references to great minds – writers, poets, musicians and painters – and I became aware of something wonderfully exciting happening to me. It was a realization that my little world had a much more powerful meaning. There were qualities of thought, ideals of perfection, of art and philosophy, of which I had had no inkling until now. I had the sensation of opening a treasure chest crammed with the most bounteous riches, knowledge and learning, and I had an instant lust to learn all I could from then on. All this, from a pornographic book!

The literary Titans quoted throughout the volumes of Frank Harris were awesome: Plato, Socrates, Goethe, Carlyle, Emerson, Dickens, Voltaire, Chaucer, Shaw, Wilde, Keats – *et* marvelling *al*. I scraped together enough money to buy as many from this noble list as I was able, and so began the stimulating process of educating myself. I found that reading about one illustrious name would lead me on to the study of the whole subject: Carlyle's *French Revolution* led me to Rousseau, Mirabeau, Danton, Robespierre and Burke; Walter Pater's *Plato and Platonism*, which influenced the young Oscar Wilde, took me on to Wilde's works – and this branch led to Bernard Shaw, and my first awareness of social problems.

I became a chain reader . . . a golden chain of enthralling links that hooked me securely on subject after subject. I read most of Maupassant and Dickens; all of Pierre Louÿs (it was he who opened my mind to the Greeks: Socrates, Plato, the *Iliad* and the *Odyssey* – a feast on which I am still gorging). With some innate caution, I kept a distance from Shakespeare. It wasn't difficult to see that he was something sublime, but I knew it would be wiser to enjoy him when I was more mature.

In my riot of reading, I didn't at first realize that what I was studying was only a thin outer layer of a wondrous whole. Shelley said: 'The more we study, the more we discover our ignorance' – and he hit it right on the nose, so far as I was concerned. I knew I would never be capable of more than scratching the surface of a complete education. But nothing could stop me scratching.

When I started to work in the film business I soon realized that, if I couldn't go to a university, working in films could be the next best thing. I know it sounds frivolous to equate academic erudition with the uncultured fantasy world of movies – yet, in some ways, a film-worker can learn more than a university undergraduate. The film industry often delves into subjects rarely found in any textbook study.

For example, an undergraduate in English Literature studying D. H. Lawrence could not (as I did when directing *Sons and Lovers*) work at the actual Nottingham coal mine where Lawrence's father toiled, use Lawrence's terraced house, and meet the actual people upon which he based his story – including the daughter of Alice Dax, from whom

Lawrence had drawn the character of Clara, and the brother of Jessie Chambers – 'Miriam' in the book. How many university students could have had that Lawrence experience?

A director making a film concerning crime may visit prisons, talk to criminals and work closely with the police. A man came to my house one evening when I was preparing work on a murder story. He had heard that I was making a film about the condemned murderer Oscar Slater. 'I've just come out of prison for murder – maybe you'd like me to talk about it,' he wondered. I doubt if my murderer would have dropped in for a chat at any university campus.

Whilst working on *The Diary of Anne Frank* in Amsterdam, I filmed in the actual house of this tragic girl, and talked often with Otto Frank (her father) who told me one day that he knew the identity of the man who betrayed Anne to the Gestapo. No, I didn't ask who it was. It would have been in questionable taste and, anyway, if he told me a name I would have been none the wiser.

Once, filming at night, I stood alone in Anne Frank's small, secret room at the top of the house, lit only by moonlight, where she had been forced to hide for two years. Easy to say, my imagination was nudged by the circumstances; but as I stood there in silence, with the faint aroma of old spices still coming up from the now-empty store below, staring at the large tree in the garden which she had seen only under threat of danger, I felt a chilling sense of the paranormal.

When working in the South of France I was able to visit the asylum at Saint-Rémy de Provence, where Van Gogh had spent a year, suffering from mental illness and epilepsy. The asylum had originally been a twelfth-century monastery, but when I saw it the building was a deserted ruin.

Wherever I looked in the long-overgrown garden there were semblances of the paintings I had seen in books and museums. A man came up to me, the old caretaker, perhaps. I asked him if I could go inside. He shrugged an assent but warned me that the floors had rotted away.

Inside the hall, I instantly recognised the mute echoes of more of Van Gogh's paintings. I made my way upstairs, stepping gingerly across the gaps, and there, along a dark passage, I was motioned inside the actual cell where Van Gogh had spent the penultimate year of his life. I can't express how moved I was to look through the small, barred window from which he had watched, and painted, the changing seasons – the outside scene transforming into the paintings.

I also visited Renoir's house, les Collettes at Cagnes, and Cézanne's studio at Aix and undertook excursions to the actual places that shaped the Impressionists' creations: Argenteuil, Chatou, and so on along the Seine to Etretat and Honfleur – sheer resuscitating joy.

I have worked on films where I had to learn about bull fighting, Viking history, ballet, crime, Irish history, horse racing, plastic surgery, Egyptology, and geisha girls – to name a few. The variety is boundless. There will always be something different to study and learn.

My education in the film world has surely been the equal of that available in any university. True, there were no amiable dons to converse with, no seminar discussions on subjects in which I was interested – but instead of dry discourse, I had the real thing in front of me. And, wonder of wonders, I was also getting paid for it!

Sometimes, not being content to travel at a film company's expense, I visit the hard-to-reach places I've read about in the Classics. Like fathers who buy their sons a train set so they can play with it themselves, I confess to the same stratagem: I take my sons to remote places because I want to see them myself.

Over the years, with various sons (I have four) I have seen truly wonderful things. In the early seventies I took my youngest, Mason, then aged thirteen, on a fabulous journey through Greece, Turkey and Troy, which was not only an education for Mason, but for me as well.

It is one thing to read a book about King Agamemnon and Mycenae, but to actually be there, before the still-extant walls of the great palace; to stand on the hilltop and see dust from the columns of Agamemnon's soldiers coming towards us (I swear I saw them!) or at the famous Lion's Gate through which Agamemnon's chariot would have swept, was awesome. His wife, Clytemnestra, would have seen him enter, accompanied by Cassandra, his trophy of war and now his mistress, before killing them both with an axe.

And the pass at Thermopylae! I couldn't believe I was actually at the place of that great drama in Greek history when Leonidas and his few Spartan soldiers held the narrow pass against Xerxes' enormous Persian army, bent on conquering Greece.

Then Mason and I hired a boat to Salamis and circled round the spot at the base of Mount Aegaleus where Xerxes had sat on a golden throne ready to watch the complete annihilation of the Greek fleet, which was greatly outnumbered by his navy.

But the Greeks had a saviour in the wily Themistocles, a statesman who had persuaded the Atheneans to build a navy in the first place and was now in command of it.

I always felt Themistocles was a man like Churchill. Both had an uphill struggle in politics and each helped to save his country from disaster. Themistocles sent his devoted family slave in a rowing boat at night to the Persians with a letter purporting to be from a Greek commander who had changed sides, saying that the entire Greek navy were panic-stricken and were withdrawing from Salamis under cover of darkness. Xerxes fell for the ruse and sent his navy in the pre-dawn light to annihilate the Greek ships.

Soon, the Persians saw what they had been waiting for: Greek ships heading away in flight to the north. The Persian fleet gave instant chase to the fleeing Greeks, whose billowing sails suggested they were escaping at speed.

Suddenly the Greeks lowered their sails and turned completely around to face the oncoming Persians who saw, too late, that they couldn't manoeuvre in the narrow channel and, so, were rammed by the Greeks.

The wily Themistocles, who was hiding in another channel, now pulled out into the strait and attacked from the rear. The Persians were thrown into complete disarray, crashing into each other, oars smashing like matchwood, the ships' hulls torn to pieces by the deadly bronze rams of the Greek vessels; a floundering, chaotic mass. Most of Xerxes' navy was destroyed and his dream of conquering Greece was practically over, right before his eyes as he watched on his golden throne.

All this I had read about and now my son and I were there on the spot, reliving that mighty page of Greek history.

The last stop on our enthralling odyssey was the one place, above all, I had dreamed of seeing for years – Troy. Perhaps, after the Bible, the greatest story ever told: the ten-year siege by the Greeks; the wooden horse; the final defeat and sacking of Troy, then the ten further years of the wanderings of Odysseus, has haunted the imagination for well over 2,000 years.

Its close proximity to myth made scholars doubt that Troy ever existed until Heinrich Schliemann's sensational uncovering of a large mound at Hisarlik in Turkey disclosing what must surely be the remains of the great city. And here I was, at the place where it all happened. An English-speaking guide was sent from a nearby village and we spent the whole day wandering around in wonder over the complex levels (there are nine, and Priam's Troy is now reckoned to be the seventh). Seeing this fabled place which Xerxes visited after crossing the 'swift flowing Hellespont', as did Alexander the Great and many others over the centuries until it was covered over for thousands of years, was worth a thousand school books.

Before I started work on *Tai-Pan* in China during the 1980s, I took my eldest son, John, who was now my camera operator, on a trip to see the extraordinary terracotta warriors at Xi'an – a whole life-size army made to guard the Emperor when he died in 206 BC. An amazing absurdity, but over 6,000 warriors had been made to protect the Emperor from any problems in the afterworld. All this had been buried under the earth for thousands of years.

We flew from Canton in a small Russian prop plane, spent a day seeing Beijing and the Great Wall of China, then flew in an even smaller plane to Xi'an which had once been the capital of China. The figures had been unearthed only a few years before and excavation work was still going on. A hangar-type building had been constructed over the vast pits, which held the most realistic figures, each one possessed of a different facial expression. There were also several magnificent full-sized bronze chariots, each one drawn by four of the most superb bronze horses I have ever seen.

Housed nearby were crossbows which had been set up in the Emperor's burial chamber to automatically shoot any who entered the room. It was all simply astounding.

3

Elstree

Next, in my pursuit of fame and fortune, was the British and Dominion studios at Borehamwood – Elstree, hailed as the 'British Hollywood'.

I was taken on as more productions were starting, including the new 'British Quota' quickies: full feature films that were made on shoestring budgets and shot, incredibly, in three weeks. One could never make a mistake, there was no time to shoot anything again. You just mustn't get the mike in the picture, and the actors must be on camera and sharp-focused at all times. It was exciting, nerve-racking, and great training.

The head of the camera department was Freddie Young, the undisputed doyen of British cameramen, who collected Oscars for *Lawrence of Arabia*, *Doctor Zhivago* and *Ryan's Daughter*. His crew was the A team, working on much more prestigious films, all directed by Herbert Wilcox, a mild, undemonstrative little man, but a great showman, who was the grand vizier of the studios.

There was a touch of cosy nepotism about the A team. They were not so much a team as a family. Apart from Freddie's operator, Francis Carver, whose father was a lord, there was John Wilcox, nephew of Herbert Wilcox, as focus puller; Kenneth Wilcox, another nephew, as the clapper boy; Gwen Wilcox was make-up, her sister Sonia Wilcox was assistant make-up, and Gwen's husband, Derek Williamson, was the editor.

And, of course, Anna Neagle, who starred in all the Wilcox films, was Mrs Wilcox.

Everything about the A team exuded class. The camera equipment was impeccably efficient, all cleaned and polished daily – even the wooden stools on the set were painted a bright regal red. Freddie Young was called 'Chief', with the same obeisance paid to him as to a headmaster.

I was in the B team. The camera I was given was in very poor condition. Ted Moore was my assistant (he later won an Oscar for his photography on *A Man for All Seasons*) and together we set about making our camera work properly.

The camera viewfinder had an inverted prism. This meant not only that up was down but also that left was right. If you panned the camera to follow the action, you would usually pan the wrong way and lose the shot altogether – a devastating shock to the operator and hardly the equipment to use on a quota quickie. Fortunately, I managed to find a normally aligned prism fairly quickly.

In those days there were no camera-hire companies like Joe Duntons and Samuelsons. The studios owned the cameras and we had to keep them in perfect condition all the time. I worked on a film with the Samuelsons' father, who was a producer. There's a charming story about when he phoned the great actor Matheson Lang (the Laurence Olivier of those days) and asked him how much he charged for his services. 'Eighty guineas a day, sir,' replied Lang. 'Oh, I'm sorry Mr Lang,' said Sammy, 'we'd never finish you in a day.'

Ted Moore and I made a good team. I was the focus puller (first assistant) and Ted did the number board – clapper boy – and loaded the film. We took a pride in trying to be extra good, practising quick loading of the camera, sometimes in total darkness; I also became adept at estimating distance so I could keep the actors in focus as they moved about the set.

Before sweating on the quota quickies, I worked on some normal feature films: *Diamond Cut Diamond*, directed by Fred Niblo who was famed for silent classics including *Blood and Sand*, *Ben Hur* and *Camille*.

On another stage, Alexander Korda was making screen history for England with the hugely successful *Private Life of Henry VIII*. Apart from making stars of several of the cast – Robert Donat, Merle Oberon and Charles Laughton (who won an Oscar) – it put England firmly on the international market, and later got a knighthood for Korda. Everything was humming, but I still had had no luck in getting an assignment to go abroad. I worked on some comedies with Tom Walls and Ralph Lynn. The cameraman was Stanley Rodwell. One night the camera was perched high on a fifteen-foot tower in the centre of a circular stairway. The camera had to follow the actress, Anne Gray, running from the top of the winding steps to the bottom, and then through the hall doorway. I set up the camera for Roddie while he dealt with the setting of the many lamps for this very complicated shot.

Suddenly, Roddie told me he was too involved with the lighting and I had better operate the camera myself. This was my big break – and Ted Moore's too, for he was now upgraded to focus puller. I had just enough time to rehearse with the stand-in, who descended the circular stairway leisurely while I panned the camera, walking carefully round the tripod legs and tilting down at the end. I felt elated. Then we shot the scene. Anne Gray sped down the steps like a panicking gazelle. I desperately whizzed my camera round trying to keep her in the picture. But I lost her and tripped over a tripod leg with a crash and nearly fell off the tower. The director called 'Cut!' and 'What the hell happened?' Roddie had already taken the camera from me, saying gently, 'It's too much for you, Jack – I'll do it.' I was crushed.

Anne mounted the stairs again, and again she hurtled down. This time Roddie tripped over the tripod and fell on his knees. On take 3, Anne came down at half speed, but Roddie still tripped over the tripod. On the next take Anne trotted down sedately and Roddie kept both her in the picture and himself upright. The director was satisfied but Roddie called for one final take. He thrust the camera into my hands saying 'Have another go, Jack – you'll do it now.' This time I made no mistake. Now I was an operator.

Occasionally I worked on Freddie Young's unit when a second camera was used and one of my duties was developing test shots. After Freddie had shot a few feet of film as a test I had to dash to the camera room, develop a few frames in a Thermos flask, then print an enlargement to show Freddie how it was looking. In this era of high-tech photography a cameraman uses a photometer to give him the correct exposure; the luxury of developing tests is a thing of the past. It's remarkable how cameramen used to judge light levels by eye alone but, even more remarkable, Billy Bitzer, the great cameraman of silent films who worked with D. W. Griffith on classics like *Birth of a Nation*, used to take the exposed film home and develop it himself!

The B & D Studios were going strong. New camera boys came on the payroll: Gilbert Taylor, who became a top cameraman, and Skeets Kelly, who later was considered to be the best aerial photographer in the business. Only eighteen, he was well over six feet, very skinny, with a sly wit and great sense of fun. Years later he was tragically killed in a helicopter crash. This brought home the dangers of helicopter photography. We all take silly risks, like sitting with legs hanging outside. Johnny Jordan, another fine aerial photographer, was sitting in this crazy position when another helicopter rose up from below and almost severed his legs. By incredible luck, he happened to be flying over a surgeons' convention and he was taken immediately to the operating table where his legs were attended to with brilliant skill. Like Skeets, Johnny later died in a chopper accident.

Ted Moore, Skeets Kelly and I formed a strong friendship, and most evenings we went out together to a movie or party. I would ride from the studios on my 1924 Raleigh motorbike along narrow, serpentine roads with Skeets perched on the rear mudguard, his long legs angled high in the air like a grasshopper's. Ahead, we recognized the car of our studio manager, Hector Coward – a formidable housemaster type who was very strict with us. We had to pass him of course, for the honour of the camera department. I throttled to maximum speed (fifty miles an hour) and passed Coward. Unfortunately, I realized too late that I couldn't make a sharp bend and had to go straight on, through a hedge, over a bumpy field, and through another hedge to get back on the road again. How Skeets held on I shall never know, but we emerged triumphantly on the road again, scratched and bleeding and covered with hedgerow and wild flowers and in helpless laughter.

Then I exchanged two wheels for four, Skeets and I sharing the expense of a 1926 air-cooled Rover, bought for thirty shillings (one pound fifty today). It was dismantled and reassembled every week, but it never saw a road. Sometimes we drove it crazily around a field pretending we were racing drivers.

Then we became big spenders and bought an old Morris Oxford for the huge sum of three pounds. We often drove to London. In those days you could drive to any restaurant and park right outside the door.

There were trips to Wembley Stadium to watch tennis (Vines and Tilden), or ice skate, or to see all-in wrestling at Blackfriars ring, marvelling at the notorious Jack Pye. Even then the wrestling was all rehearsed, but it was great fun; in those days it was less well organized and sometimes the injuries were real.

One night we were watching Jack Pye getting a hell of a beating. He was thrown all over the place. Unfortunately, I simply had to relieve myself and hurried down to the lavatory which was underneath the ring. As I stood urinating there were great crashes from above me of bodies thrown to the floor and cheers for the end of the fight. Then came another crash close by as the door flew open and to my horror Jack Pye himself tore in like a tornado breathing out great gasps from his lost battle, cursing away in petulant fury as he stood right next to me peeing. He was streaming with sweat, and his mouth was bleeding and the awful thing was I couldn't stop peeing, I had to just stand there and pray that this steaming, cursing monster didn't turn on me and tear me to pieces.

Because of my father's bad health he wasn't able to work much, but with my salary raised to six pounds a week I was able to buy a bungalow at Borehamwood for a mortgaged £650. With upstart conceit, I called it Granville, after our original family name.

Cardiff was my father's stage name. Our real name was Gran, which has Hungarian origins. Dad thought that Gran was rather stodgy for music hall, and decided that Cardiff was to be his *nom de théâtre* after performing in that Welsh city. Our Magyar ancestors must have twitched in their graves.

I retained my name of Gran for some time until problems with passports and remittances abroad became too confusing and, rather reluctantly, I changed it legally to Cardiff. I thought that the name was unique, but I was wrong. Many years later I sent a dozen roses to my wife and, as a freakish term of endearment, frequently used in show business, I just wrote 'fuck you' on the card. When I arrived home there were no roses. I realized I had foolishly addressed them to the next block of apartments by mistake. I hurried over and asked the porter if he had some roses in the name of Cardiff. 'That's right, sir,' the porter said, 'they've gone to Lady Cardiff on the first floor.' I'm sure her ladyship must have been puzzled by the 'Fuck you' message I had written on the card and I decided to leave the roses where they were.

More good fortune followed my lucky break as camera operator with Stanley Rodwell. Cameraman Cyril Bristow, who was next in importance to Freddie Young, was to photograph some tests for MGM of Freddie Bartholomew for the part of the young David Copperfield. On the day of the tests Bristow sent a message that he was ill. Freddie Young was on location and there was no other cameraman available at the studio. The MGM officials asked me if I could photograph the tests. Next day, the results were seen. The MGM boys were delighted and I was on cloud nine. But my joy of achievement was short lived. Cyril Bristow was upset at what I had done, and Freddie Young was furious when he returned from location. How dare I presume to take that sort of responsibility? Suppose my work had been unusable? I was duly chastened, but in my nineteen-year-old heart triumph shone like a spotlight. I knew I could do it.

One weekend, whilst taking my mother and father for a drive, I saw the huge half-built Denham Studios. This was to be the new Korda empire, London Films. I was fascinated and felt a foretaste of an exciting new era of film-making and an urge to be part of it, despite the fact that I was still working at B & D. I was granted an interview with the general manager at Denham, David Cunningham; 'Yes,' he said, 'I think we could use you, how about a two-year contract at fifteen pounds a week?'

I gulped my agreement. I went back to B & D and gave them two weeks' notice.

My new studio at Denham wasn't ready yet so Korda was using Wharton Hall studios at Isleworth, where I had acted as a child of six. I started in the trick department – now called special effects – run by Ned Mann, a one-time professional roller-skater and actor. It was engrossing work, but the hours were painfully long. On a scene for *The Man Who Could Work Miracles* we had to film a close-up of a foot growing to immense size. We shot it in reverse, starting with the immense painted clay foot, exposing a single frame (the normal camera speed is twenty-four frames a second). The sculptor then scraped a millimetre of clay away and the foot was repainted before we exposed the next frame, and so on. The whole thing took a day and a night to complete.

I worked with Ned Mann for some time, including on H. G. Wells's *Things to Come* with William Cameron Menzies, a truly great art director (*Gone with the Wind*, *Thief of Bagdad*, *Around the World in Eighty Days*).

It was during this sojourn in the trick department that I was faced with a dilemma. René Clair had just started *The Ghost Goes West*, a delightful story that had originated in *Punch* magazine, reporting on a Scottish castle being dismantled and shipped to America with its ghost unintentionally included.

The cameraman was Hal Rosson from Hollywood who had been married briefly to Jean Harlow. Hal had established himself in the studio as an outrageous tyrant, firing one camera operator after another, dissatisfied with the standard of their work.

The studio manager, the nice David Cunningham, sent for me, and told me yet another operator had been fired and would I like to replace him. I quickly declined, saying I was quite happy working with Ned Mann. Why should I take on something which would result in me sharing the same fate as the other operators? Cunningham acknowledged my rejection and I was let off the hook, but not for long. Cunningham sent for me again soon after. The last of the operators had been fired by Rosson and Cunningham told me I simply had to take the job myself. With the perfunctory air with which an army officer sends a soldier over the top, he said, 'I wish you luck, Cardiff.'

And that was it. I made my way on to the set to start work with Rosson. If marching into machine-gun fire produces a certain bravery from sheer fury, I had that same fury, knowing that I was going to lose my job. Right from the beginning I treated Hal Rosson like a bad smell, which surprised him considerably. All the operators who had lost their heads to Robespierre Rosson had been so terrified that they had treated this ace cameraman with awed obsequiousness, but I was too furious to care.

Hal Rosson was a small man with splenetic brown eyes, red-rimmed and piercing. He wore a tiny moustache (presaging Hitler), and his thin lips pursed when he was about to make a sarcastic insult. He showed me a large-handled camera panning head he had brought from America, saying with clipped finality, 'This is the best way to pan the camera – with handles' (handles were not used in England at that time). 'Well, Hal,' I said (no one had called him Hal before), 'you may like handles, but I don't. Since I'm the one who has to operate the camera, I'll try it out for a while and if I don't like them I'll change to a normal grease head.' No one had spoken to him like that before, and he was somewhat taken aback. (Actually I fell in love with the handles right away and used them ever after.)

Somehow I survived Hal Rosson. Working with René Clair was a joy, Hal and I eventually became good friends. We worked together on *As You Like It*, directed by Paul Czinner and starring Laurence Olivier with the fascinating Elisabeth Bergner as Rosalind. The Forest of Arden was built in the studio. It was the largest set I had seen, with many hundreds of trees and bushes. Hal was doing an excellent lighting job, but one morning he phoned the studio to say he was too ill to come to work. Luckily Lee Garmes, who had just won an Oscar for photographing *Zoo in Budapest,* was in London and had agreed to come to the studios for that day. As he wouldn't arrive before midday I was asked to rough light the huge forest set – 'Just do what you can until Mr Garmes arrives, and he will finish the lighting himself.' I was still only an operator and I had to set over two hundred arc lamps. This wasn't like doing tests of Freddie Bartholomew against a small backdrop; this was the Forest of Arden and a group of actors which included, in the foreground, a young Laurence Olivier.

When Garmes arrived I was introduced to the great man and the producer explained that I had just done a rough lighting job to prepare for him to light the set properly. Garmes looked at the lights I had set and then said calmly, 'Well, this lighting is extremely good. Why don't we shoot it as it is?' How magnanimous. A less able man might have reset several lamps to justify his position, but his position (and his good nature) was unassailable.

Although I had left B & D Studios, I still had my bungalow at

Borehamwood. At about 2 a.m. one morning I was awakened by Ted Moore on the phone: 'Jack, the studios are on fire, meet you outside the camera room.' I looked out of the window. The sky was violent red – like a crazily painted backdrop. The whole studio was blazing.

Ted and Skeets were there when I arrived. The camera room was smoking, but not yet alight. We decided to save some of the cameras, so I squeezed through a small window and let in Ted and Skeets. We humped camera cases outside until a fireman ordered us out for our own safety. We ran to the main corridor, but halted, unbelieving, as enormous roof girders hurtled down. Our beloved studio, with so many memories, collapsed in flames all around us.

But the inferno wasn't over yet. The fire had begun to spread next door to the British International studios. The studio manager, the legendary Joe Grossman, had his own fire brigade which had been the butt of many a joke up to that moment, but which now proved its worth and managed to prevent the fire from destroying his studio. Even so, it was not until dawn that the fire was finally brought under control.

Joe Grossman was a pure Cockney and a most surprising person. Stories about him are as legendary as those about Sam Goldwyn. If Goldwynisms are rarely accurate, I can vouch for a few Grossmanisms. While escorting the King of Greece on a tour of the studio, he explained the various technical film terms as follows: 'That's the microphone, your Majesty, and that box on the camera, that's what we call a blimp; all the walls are soundproofed and this is a dolly – of course, this will all be Greek to you.' The night his fire brigade put out the fire he turned to those who had helped him – odd workmen and technicians like us – and gasped: 'Well, boys, we've saved 'arf the bleedin' studios, now only 'arf of you will get the bleedin' sack.'

During the excitement of that sad evening, I ran into Ronnie Neame, an old cameraman friend who was working at BIP. He and I somehow got a camera working and we took several shots of the tumultuous evening. Next day, a newspaper reported: 'Cameraman Ronald Neame and his tripod carrier Jack Cardiff faithfully recorded the tragic blaze on film.' Much as I resented being called a tripod carrier, it was a thrill to see my name in print for the first time. Better a tripod carrier than nothing. Next morning, amid the still-smoking ruins of the lost studio, we discovered that the management was not deliriously happy that we had saved so many cameras. They said that the cameras had been heavily insured, turning our heroic adventure as flat as the ground where the studio used to be.

But there was an unexpected twist to this disappointing reaction. One of the cameras we had saved was a brand new Debrie – and it had not been insured. The French makers were extremely grateful and bestowed rewards on us. Skeets and Ted received fifteen pounds each and I was invited to Paris for a three-day, expenses-paid trip. At last! I was leaving England for the first time.

It may be a cliché, but to me there is no doubt, Paris is the most beautiful city in the world. That visit, fifty years ago, was the first of dozens, and still each time I gaze around enchanted.

Someone said 'Paris is a woman'. I know exactly what they meant. Even the architecture is voluptuous. The sensuous curves of the baroque, the romantic eighteenth-century buildings, with delicate wrought-iron balconies, the windows, winged with shutters that seem to cloak the secrets within. Even the language is sexy! A French menu caresses you with lip-licking lust: *Sole farcie Pompadour, L'agneau de Sisteron aux aromes de Provence, Fricassée de langoustines à l'estragon.*

Paris is a city of the senses. Beauty pervades and spreads through all the arts. So many artists flocked to Paris; there is culture everywhere, vibrating so much energy one wants to purr. Who hasn't sat in a Parisian café, addicted to the sport of watching the world go by, as they sip their glasses of wine or, with friends, enjoying that true elixir of life, good conversation. I have sat at tables at the Dome or the Rotond talking, but mostly listening, to fertile minds – Lazar Meeson, the brilliant art director (*Sous les toits de Paris, La Kermesse Héroïque*), and the equally brilliant Vincent Korda, René Clair, Claude Renoir (not a painter like his grandad but an excellent cameraman). I felt like Boswell when he listened to Doctor Johnson's famous guests; 'I listened and hugged myself with my mind.' But all that was on later trips. Ah, that first overture in Paris – only three days, it was like waking up too soon from a lovely dream. I remembered my stage nights as a call boy (aged ten). I used to shout, 'Overture and beginners please'. Well I was now a Parisian beginner. The overture had been played, and it was 'curtain up' on a ravishing show. I didn't have time on that first trip to see it all, but I left Paris determined to return as soon as possible.

This happened quickly enough. My new studio at Denham was now finished but there was nothing for me to do yet, so I was given three weeks' holiday. Paris again, but this time I drove there in my new sports car, through Paris, on to the famous route seven for the Côte d'Azur where, at St Tropez, I spent a happy day with René Clair. His house on the beach was decorated entirely in white: walls, furniture, leather settees – the only relief were old coloured maps of St Tropez on the walls. René had a guest who had just flown over from London. 'Isn't it sad about Denham Studios?' she said at lunch. 'What happened?' I croaked, afraid to learn. 'It's burned to the ground,' she replied.

I finished lunch without tasting anything and hurried to the village to phone London. Only one stage of the studios had been destroyed. I could breathe again. It was surely more than a coincidence that two studios had been set ablaze within weeks, although arson was never proved. The main thing was that I could carry on working.

London Films, Alexander Korda's new empire at Denham, was magnificent. It didn't have the intimate charm of my old Borehamwood studio, but the vast stages, workshops – which could build anything from a battleship to the Colossus of Rhodes – the opulent theatres, cutting rooms, and the adjacent film laboratories (which are still going strong) were on a par with any Hollywood studio.

Korda's heroic vision brought about a glittering fluorescence of the Britain film industry. He had an awesome charisma and, very important, good taste. There was financial backing from United Artists and the Prudential Assurance Company, and he used the money with the sensibility of an artist.

The Denham dynasty produced so many fine films: *Rembrandt*, *The Four Feathers*, *Hamlet*, *Henry V*, *The Third Man*, *Brief Encounter*, *Knight without Armour*, *Fire over England*, *Elephant Boy*, *The Thief of Bagdad*, *The Drum*, *Richard III*, *Anna Karenina* and *Wings of the Morning*. At one time, every one of the seven stages hummed with film-making. If the stages hadn't been soundproofed, the whirr of all the cameras would have sounded like fields of cicadas. The studio restaurant was packed with glitterati: Charles Laughton, Marlene Dietrich, Henry Fonda, Miriam Hopkins, Laurence Olivier, Orson Welles, Noël Coward. When visitors like Bernard Shaw, H. G. Wells and the occasional member of the Royal Family were sitting at nearby tables, it was like Madame Tussaud's with sound.

Several ace cameramen came over from Hollywood; as well as my old friend who ate operators, Hal Rosson, there was Charles Rosher (who started many years before me, was Mary Pickford's cameraman and photographed classics like *Sunrise*); my good friend Lee Garmes; the legendary Jimmy Wong Howe who had started as a floor sweeper in the studios and became a truly great cameraman – I watched him doing magical things with lights; and Harry Stradling, another 'great' for whom I operated on *Dark Journey*, which had a young and so very beautiful Vivien Leigh playing opposite Conrad Veidt. I continued working with Harry on *Knight without Armour*. Before this film started, we had to do the usual artists' tests and on this occasion I was late for work. I ran full pelt to the door of the stage and crashed into a woman coming out, just catching her before she fell to the ground. Not a sensible thing to do, especially to Marlene Dietrich.

Amid desperate apologies I introduced myself and the star, shaken, but still magically beautiful, forgave me. Throughout the picture she was friendly. She seemed to like me, I don't know why. Perhaps, seeing how young and callow I was, she had a motherly affection. Anyway she was always kind and considerate – once when I had a bad cold she phoned Germany for a remedy.

She spoke a lot about her mentor Josef von Sternberg, who had, with his superb visual talent, spun her in a cocoon of sensual beauty that radiated throughout all the films he directed with her: *The Blue Angel*, *Shanghai Express*, *Blonde Venus* and more.

It was an extraordinary relationship. Sternberg had complete domination over her, yet relied on her instincts in many ways, particularly in the editing of his pictures. He idolized her as a screen goddess and gave his whole artistic existence to make her the star she eventually became. She had such reverence for him. It was always 'Mr von Sternberg told me . . .' and 'Mr von Sternberg always prefers this lighting . . .' As our work developed on the film I realized what an enormous amount she had learned about lighting from him. She showed me photographs he had made of her and would point out the technicalities of light and shade with convincing authority. On the set she had a full length mirror alongside the camera and would study her reflection and advise Harry Stradling as he was lighting her. Many cameramen would have resented this interference, but Harry was tolerant and wise: 'She's right – she knows so goddam much,' he would mutter to me, but there must have been times when he harboured dark thoughts about Mr von Sternberg.

I remembered a story told to me by George Pearson, a distinguished pioneer of early British films who had started in the industry before 1900. When he visited Hollywood in the late twenties he had seen someone on the set whom he recognized as a prop man he had worked with at the old Ideal Studios at Borehamwood. 'I walked up to him,' he told me, 'and exclaimed, "Well, if it isn't Joe Stern" ' – and the man retorted in a hissed whisper, 'Josef von Sternberg'.

Apparently he was born in Vienna as Josef Sternberg and worked under that name until he embellished it with 'von' on credits of his

37

films. Success cemented this title of a high-born German.

Marlene Dietrich was the epitome of a film goddess. She would arrive at the studios like royalty in a sleek limousine driven by her trusted American chauffeur/bodyguard, who was dressed in full uniform, carried a gun and looked like he would kill you if you touched his car. (In fact, someone did touch his car and received a hefty crack on the jaw.)

Marlene was also an expert on make-up. She used highlights and shadows to complement the single high key light she always insisted on – whether she was in a ballroom or in a dark cellar. As her nose was turned up, she painted a pale line down the middle which minimized the tilt. She never liked to be seen in profile, anyway. Then she performed what I would have thought was a most painful trick to her lower eyelids, painting a white line on the inside edges, emphasising the reflection of the key light. Finally, just before shooting, her maids would bring a tray of gold dust which she would sprinkle carefully on the contours of her hair. All this was done in front of that full-length mirror by the camera. She would study herself for a long time, trying a twist of a lock of hair, or moving a fold of her dress in various positions, until, finally, she was ready for the scene.

I felt that setting everything in such detail was all right for a still photograph, but for moving pictures it could inhibit her freedom of movement and give her a mannequin's stiffness. Her leading man in *Knight without Armour*, Robert Donat, got fed up with all this and insisted on having his own full-length mirror placed near the camera; he would take his time touching up his hair and costume, but he eschewed the gold dust. Donat then complained to Korda that he was always framed on the side of the picture as Cardiff always centred on Dietrich, and all he got from Stradling was leak light! Harry and I received a mild rebuke from Korda, but I could see by the twinkle in his eye that he hadn't taken the complaint seriously.

The director Jacques Feyder (of *La Kermesse Héroïque* fame) was stimulating to work with. He had grey, untrusting eyes in a pale stress-worn face, a voice hoarse from smoking. He carried a small flask of whisky which he would sip during the day. He wore a Parisienne trenchcoat that hung to a couple of inches from the ground, and a brown trilby from Locks of Piccadilly. He was a sensitive director and I learned much from him. He had a sure sense of composition, grouping actors in unusual ways, reminding me of Degas whose interest in the new photography had prompted a ruthless cropped-picture style which gained much power from asymmetric grouping.

Feyder's manner was typically French: rather sardonic, though sometimes acerbic with impatience. However, on one occasion he used a stratagem which was more subtle and effective. Korda came on the set, carrying a copy of the script, and talked earnestly to Feyder. It appeared he was so enamoured of a certain sequence that he wanted to direct it himself. Korda used all his persuasive charm and tact, but obviously Feyder wasn't overjoyed at the idea. He shrugged, with as much dignity as possible in the circumstances and said, 'All right, I'll go to Paris for the weekend.' We worked on the new sequence all day Sunday – Korda directing with great enthusiasm, but the crew with quite a lot less.

On Monday, Feyder carried on directing. Korda came on the set and enthused about his Sunday shooting. Feyder then told him, with quiet but devastating finality, that the sequence Korda had shot was from an old script, and couldn't possibly be used unless several long sequences were retaken at great expense.

On another weekend we had to shoot a bathroom sequence. The studio was almost empty (nobody likes working weekends). We were resigned to it, but the atmosphere was hardly vibrant with enthusiasm.

The set was a small Russian bathroom. There were few people about – an electrician was reading a newspaper on the spot-rail; two more were listlessly setting some lights below; and a few technicians were making desultory preparations for the bath scene. 'Just a few close-ups,' the assistant director had said. 'We'll be away by five.'

The prop man was pouring the last bucket of hot water into the bath, stirring the frothy foam until the jewelled flakes had swollen like iridescent spittle.

We had shot many bathroom scenes before. Standard procedure was that the actress wore a bathing costume, and the covering foam gave the illusion of nakedness.

Marlene strode regally through the cluttered stage, followed by her two maids, hugging bundles of warm towels. She was draped in a dazzling white bathrobe, her hair swept up in cunning disarray; an extra-long cigarette holder was clenched gently in her teeth so that her mouth was parted in just the hint of a smile, her Prussian-blue eyes gazing blankly ahead. Saturday or no Saturday, it was good to look at her.

The 'blonde Venus' nodded graciously to us mortals on the set as she walked to the bath and tested the water with her finger, then casually took off her bathrobe and immersed herself in the foam.

It was a simple action – but it had devastated the entire film crew, for in that brief moment Marlene had shown herself to be stark naked. We were completely unprepared for this. In those early days at Denham, the sight of Marlene Dietrich, gloriously starkers, was cataclysmic. We were stunned as we shot the first scene.

Jacques Feyder said 'Cut', and told Marlene she could rest while the next scene was being prepared. Her two maids came either side of the bath with their huge towels and flung them swiftly around her. Those who had looked forward to another vision of Aphrodite in the buff were disappointed. However, there were several more scenes to shoot, and I was aware of a new spirit in the air; there now seemed to be many more technicians around. The little bathroom set was filling up like a cocktail party getting underway.

We shot more scenes. After each one was over, Marlene would jump out of the bath, her maids throwing the towels around her with slick teamwork, and very little was seen in the swiftness of the cover-up. But each time she jumped out, the floor was getting wetter and soapier. The spot-rails were now packed with enthusiastic onlookers, and below the audience stretched deep into every corner of the stage. I heard later that pictures being shot on other stages were becoming bereft of technicians.

As the last bathroom scene finished, Feyder thanked Miss Dietrich with a certain frosty politeness. He wasn't happy with the conversion of his tiny Russian bathroom into Carnegie Hall. The maids advanced on Marlene with professional confidence and Marlene already had one foot over the bath when disaster struck. Her foot slipped on the soapy floor and she fell over with a wet crash, the towels passing east and west in the air. Ten seconds followed that seemed like ten minutes, while Marlene slipped, flopped and skidded helplessly in all directions, frantically trying to get up from the soapy floor and showing a transfixed audience her magnificent charms from every conceivable angle. Eventually the frantic maids retrieved the towels and flung them over the blonde Venus as she was helped to her feet.

A deep sigh was heard all over the crowded Russian bathroom – like a child sighs when the last present comes out of his or her Christmas stocking.

Next we had a large 'exterior' set of a forest with a lake which had been built for Dietrich and Donat to hide from the Bolsheviks. At one point Marlene had to undress and take a dip in the lake. This time there was no total nudity (perhaps Feyder had spoken up for a more secluded ambience than the crowded bathroom). In the scene Marlene had to undress, with her co-star discreetly retired. As the camera was about a hundred feet away with a wide angle lens, it was thought that Marlene could wear flesh-coloured underwear which would be invisible to the camera. We shot the scene. As I was the operator, looking through the lens, I was the only one able to judge if the panties and bra showed up. Even at that distance I could see the puckered wrinkles of the wet material. Marlene shrugged. 'OK, I take them off.'

Later she told me she really preferred nudity to showing her underwear, 'I feel more embarrassed at people seeing me in undies, which to me is a private thing. But everyone knows what a nude body is like – it's more natural.' They don't make Godesses like that anymore.

One evening I received a phone call at home from Denham saying I must return at once to the studios to meet representatives of a company called Technicolor.

I wasn't in the best of moods, having to drive back to Denham after a hard day's work. When I arrived all the other Denham operators were there. It was explained that one of us would be chosen to go to America to learn all about this new colour system as production would soon begin in England.

Those first interviewed came out of the office looking considerably shaken. Apparently, the questions had been highly technical. One operator came out with the fixed stare of a sleepwalker muttering the law of inverse squares; another staggered out in dazed bewilderment: 'Lux, flux, Lumens, lamberts?' Then came my turn. The office desk had several stern-looking gentlemen sitting around it. I expected to be asked, as in the painting of the child being questioned by the Royalists, 'When did you last see your father?'

They started the questions: education, photographic school if any, and then they got to the lumens bit. I interrupted them firmly and with as much dignity as I could muster told them I was hardly the man they wanted as I knew very little about technical equations. In fact I was a mathematical dunce. After a shocked silence I was asked what I thought made me a good cameraman? I felt that my answer – always studying the many forms of light in houses, trains, buses, etc. at various times of day, and analysing the lighting used by the Old Masters of painting – was hardly what they wanted to hear.

They looked at me in silence. One of them asked me which side of the face did Rembrandt have as the key light? I was on slightly firmer ground on this one and said it was the left side. The questions continued. Which painters did beautiful interiors? That was easy. 'Vermeer and Pieter de Hooch. I believe they used a camera obscura,' I added, showing off. I enthused about the educative value of the candle lighting of Georges de la Tour. I started to warm to my subject, but they cut me off in my prime and I was ushered out of the office feeling somewhat like a late Picasso.

The next morning I was told I had been chosen. I couldn't resist a giggle. I'd been chosen for telling them I knew nothing about technical photography. I'd been chosen because I knew about painting.

I can't remember when I first noticed a painting. As a child nomad, I knew nothing about art galleries or museums. And nowhere would I have seen a picture on a wall – certainly not in the extremely modest environment of vaudeville lodgings.

As a very small child I scrawled something in chalk on a pavement in Manchester and squatted down with my cap upturned for money as I had seen beggars do. I remember a few coins being thrown into my cap, but my pleasure was cut short when my horrified father came by, wiped my inspired art away and took me home.

One day, out of all those hundreds of weekly schools I went to, our class was actually taken to 'see art'.

We traipsed inside a grey provincial building and entered into what was for me a wondrous new world: painting. Rows and rows of brilliantly coloured dreams. The curtain had risen on a new source of enchantment and I was resolved to see more paintings from then on.

In our showbiz travels, museums were rarely encountered, but when my parents were resting in London I was able to visit the National Gallery or the Tate and on these occasions I was in transports of delight. As a youngster's hobby might be collecting stamps, bird-spotting, or cigarette-card celebrities, my heroes were painters, and pretty soon I was able to recognize instantly most of the great ones. Nothing recondite about that. The vast differences in painters' styles are obvious to everybody, even from a distance.

Perhaps, though, because of my consecrated dedication to paintings, I looked that much more closely and studied deeper. But sometimes I didn't have the courage of my convictions.

In an antique shop in Eton High Street, I noticed an unframed painting on the floor, leaning against the wall. I said to the owner, a veritable dragon called Mrs Cox, 'Isn't that an Ingres?'

'No,' she sniffed sourly, 'it isn't. If you want it you can have it for five pounds.'

As it was only a rather dull portrait I declined her offer and left, in spite of my visual vibes.

Some months later I revisited the formidable Mrs Cox who gave me a most peculiar look. 'Young man, after you left, I took that painting to London. Experts confirmed it *was* an Ingres and I sold it for ten thousand pounds.' And she didn't give me anything. Not a sausage.

One day, gazing at a roomful of paintings, I realized something starkly obvious that I'd never noticed before. Light! It was light that was the all-pervading element in painting. No matter how creatively a painter composed a picture, whether it was a portrait, a landscape, or even a bowl of fruit, it was light that dominated the subject and brought the canvas to life.

Now I gave all my attention to the way painters used light and also began the habit of analysing the light all around me: in rooms, buses, trains – everywhere. How light plays subtle tricks, bouncing off walls, how its various reflections and changed light sources can reveal much insight into the character of a face.

It excited me to see how painting had made progressive use of lighting through the centuries and how photography had made similar advances. And here I made an interesting discovery: that both primitive painting and the earliest film photography, although hundreds of years apart, had progressed at a parallel rate.

Early fresco painting, before the Renaissance, was flat, with hardly any three-dimensional effects of light and shade. And so was early film photography.

The flatness of early painting was probably induced by mosaics. In fact, Cimabue and his pupil Giotto in the thirteenth and early fourteenth centuries had worked in mosaics before going on to fresco painting, where watercolours had to be laid on to wet plaster before the plaster had dried, so that there was little time for speculative attempts with light and shade.

And there were equal difficulties during the birth of the cinema, when the film emulsion was so insensitive that a great deal of light was needed – whether it was the sun flooding through the windows or the strong standing lights on the floor – so that the light by necessity had to be frontal and flat. Those close-ups of the early film stars – Bessie Love, Lillian Gish, Theda Bara – show blanched shadowless faces, curiously like a fresco painting.

Over the years, painting and film photography made simultaneous progress. The glorious Renaissance masters, Michelangelo, Leonardo, and Raphael, brought life and depth to their work; the flat look disappeared in films due to the innovative genius of D. W. Griffith – in partnership with his great cameraman, Billy Bitzer, who was arguably the first to use strong backlight (no one had dared to shoot into the sun before). Film lighting began to show something of the chiaroscuro used by the Old Masters.

My passionate study of painters and light helped me immeasurably as a lighting cameraman. Rembrandt, Vermeer, Pieter de Hooch and the mighty Turner were my idols.

But if the Old Masters have been my inspiration, the Impressionists inspired me still further. I became more aware of pure colour and the effects of reflections from their work. For instance, if the sky was bright blue, I would make my top lights blue as though from a reflection from the sky. Of course, it's subtle, and the man in the street wouldn't even notice, but I knew they were there and felt good about it.

But the trip to America to learn about Technicolor was not to be. Plans were changed. Technicolor came to England and built a laboratory, and as a consolation prize I was assigned to their first colour production on this side of the Atlantic – *Wings of the Morning* – and I had time to make another trip to my lady Paris.

I was so lucky to have first experienced Paris in the thirties, before the Second World War. Now, something of the boundless ebullience has gone. In those days a newcomer could stroll down the Champs-Elysées and marvel at the Parisian atmosphere. Now enormous car showrooms and airline companies predominate and McDonald's has settled in. Several perfume shops are now overpowered by the smell of Chinese food. Nevertheless, Paris is still a wonderful city. The theatres are still fun – the Lido is magnificent – but in the thirties I think it was more outrageous. The *Folies Bergère*, for instance. Imagine over a hundred people on the stage in heavy velvet costumes and large feathered hats, all giving voice with operatic gusto to a deafening crescendo and then, on a climactic note, every single costume and hat disappearing in a flash (apparently by wires), and the entire company left stark naked.

I never saw anything like that at Golders Green Hippodrome. I did see at the *Folies Bergère* the great Mistinguette with Maurice Chevalier, and the superb Josephine Baker – what a performer! What legs!

At a small club in Montmartre there was Madame Patachou, a pretty, dignified-looking woman who sang ballads, tender and sad, but so outrageously rude that even my French friends were jolted in shock. There was always a bawdy chorus you had to join in and if you didn't, she would rush up to you with a large pair of scissors and cut off your tie, just below the knot. Those in the know used to wear old ties. There were hundreds of ties hanging down from the ceiling as a further incentive to sing. She sang with a soft melancholy, and as my French wasn't good enough to follow the sophisticated subtleties, I had to rely on my friends' translations. One of her ballads was about her wonderful lover who made love to her all through the night, and then (sighing so sadly) would sit outside on the stairs playing with himself. All in that low sad voice, even with the bawdy punchline, it was worth a tie or two.

Going further down the scale, there was a show in the boulevard de Clichy called *Cabaret de l'enfer* which had all the *fin de siècle* gaiety – and the faint aura of evil – of Toulouse-Lautrec's time. The entrance had a gaping fanged mouth and manic eyes, and there were full-sized plaster nudes falling down into hell. Inside was a long bare room with seats for about fifty people. At one end was a crude proscenium and curtain which parted to show a nude lady posed on a small dais with her body seemingly enveloped in flames.

The audience was mostly tourists, pretty high on the awful cheap champagne served on the premises. My training in special effects made it easy for me to see how this illusion was achieved. A faint whirr of a projector gave it away. The projector was hidden off-stage and the image of flames was projected on to a sheet of glass angled at forty-five degrees. *Voilà!* One barbecued nude. The curtain comes down and volunteers are called for to experience this 'fantastic' illusion. 'Go on Dad, we're in Paris, let's have fun.' Dad is persuaded to mount the dais to thunderous applause and his giggling family prepare to see him enveloped in flames. But the naughty *patron* has changed the reel in the projector. *Tiens!*

It was really quite clever. Dad's head is clearly seen, posturing jovially to the audience and his family, but now a naked male body has been substituted for the flames, matching perfectly below Dad's grinning head and masturbating furiously.

Dad's family freeze in a tableau of horror, Mum swoons and the audience fall about, amid cheers and wild applause. *Très* naughty, très French.

4

Technicolor Adventures – Exteriors

British Technicolor was born in a stable. One casual day as I passed the old stables at Denham I saw crates being unpacked and was introduced to half a dozen Americans with wonderful hats who had that resolute pilgrim look: George Cave, head of the camera department, Ray Rennahan, chief cameraman (for whom I was to operate), Henry Imus, chief camera technician, Dick Jones, engineer, and last, but certainly not least, Natalie Kalmus, wife of Technicolor's president, Herbert Kalmus. Natalie Kalmus *was* Technicolor. She had complete control of the colours of sets, costumes, and everything to do with colour on the film.

At the stable nativity I marvelled as the first Technicolor camera emerged from its packing case with an air of proud, sleek beauty. It was painted bright blue and its shining chrome fittings reminded me of a brand new Rolls-Royce.

This is how a Technicolor camera works. It's called a three-strip process because it runs three films through the camera at the same time. One film runs behind the lens in a normal film gate and the other two films are run together in a second gate at right angles. Behind the lens is a square prism which has a partial mirror set at forty-five degrees which allows 25 per cent of the light to pass through on to the single gate and reflects 75 per cent of light to the second gate, which is at right angles to the prism. There are also filters involved which separate the three primary colours, but that's the main principle of the system.

The vital part of the camera is the prism. It's actually two forty-five-degree prisms cemented together to form a cube; one of the faces is coated with the partially reflecting surface of gold. It is an object of optical perfection and has a special mounting so that it can be removed and replaced without affecting its near-perfect accuracy. Naturally enough, no one was allowed to handle it until fully qualified by training and practice – even my most able assistant Henty-Creer had to practise with a wooden replica for some weeks. The training actually included softening a possible fall to the ground with one's foot!

The camera assistant had to stay close to the camera at all times and, should the camera go on location, had to keep the camera in his bedroom. Every three days on location, the camera assistant had to 'read register', using a short length of special film made of brass. Five tiny holes are drilled – domino fashion – and placed in the two gates. By peering through a powerful telescope one is able to check if the prism has shifted – and the working tolerance is only eight ten-thousandths of an inch.

Over the next quarter of a century, until the advent of single-film Eastmancolor, which tolled the death knell of the three-strip camera, I used this superb Rolls-Royce of a beauty all over the world in all kinds of dangerous situations: in steel foundries (inches away from molten ingots), in battleships in wartime seas, on top of erupting volcanoes, in burning deserts and steaming jungles, and diving on to the Colosseum in Rome in an old Italian bomber. On *Western Approaches*, the camera sank underwater for half an hour before it could be rescued, still undamaged in any way.

The coronation of King George VI was a highlight of Technicolor's early success in England. The obvious advantage of colour for such glorious pageantry was a delight to both the nation and the outside world. Seeing all the exalted nobility in their scarlet robes, noble insignia and dazzling tiaras, I couldn't help feeling that they were film extras, hired for the day. But they were real all right: the Duke of Norfolk was testily ordering we Technicolor serfs to get a move on – you don't get that kind of talk from film extras.

Then came the great moment when our camera was trained on the future King. It was a couple of days before he was crowned, and there he stood, in the sunlit garden of Buckingham Palace, with Prime Minister Stanley Baldwin. It was such a scoop for Technicolor that the heads of the company were all there helping to assemble the camera equipment so we could capture this important scene as quickly as possible. I attached a large tape-measure to the camera and ran swiftly to the face that was shortly to be on millions of postage stamps, the soon-to-be King of Great Britain and Northern Ireland, head of the Church of England and the British Commonwealth, and what do you think I did? I hit the King on his nose.

In crumpled horror I apologized, but the King laughed and, making indulgent gestures, turned to Baldwin with a grin: 'We could send him to the Tower for that, couldn't we?' Baldwin nodded with mock grimness: 'That we could, sir.' And, as I measured the distance to Baldwin –

taking care not to repeat my boxing trick – he said, 'No side pockets, please,' which remark sent the King into fits of laughter again.

I had the impression that King George VI was a really likeable human being. I wasn't aware at that time of the behind-the-scenes dramas: his unpreparedness for ruling the nation so suddenly after the abdication of Edward VIII, his stammer problems and the fears his wife and children had that his stamina might not be equal to the gruelling demands of being King. His reaction to my accidental blunder convinced me that kindness was second nature to him and that his family must have loved him very much.

On the day of the Coronation my camera was one of several covering the royal procession from Westminster Abbey to Buckingham Palace. I was perched on the roof of a tiny house at one of the entrances to Hyde Park. My assistant and I had been there all night because of the enormous crowds. In the early morning there was a complete dress rehearsal. The procession of all the fairy-tale coaches, painted and heavily gilded, was heading my way like something from a Disney spectacular. The sun was out, in brilliant celebration of a new page of history. So I photographed the rehearsal. Why not? As I was in longshot I couldn't see inside the coaches. I seem to remember there were people in some of the coaches, but nobody could see who they were. It looked so beautiful, so I photographed it, although the actual procession was not until some hours later.

The weather, fickle as ever, changed just before the real procession started, and rain poured down derisively. Imagine the puzzlement of the Technicolor hierarchy when they saw the rushes, with all the other cameras leadened with depressing rain. I was the only camera to show the whole procession in brilliant sunshine.

It seems appropriate to tell a Noël Coward story about the Coronation procession of Queen Elizabeth II. Because of the heavy rain all the open Landaus were closed, except one. Queen Salote of Tonga became an instant heroine of the rain-soaked crowds by leaving her Landau open. She was an enormous woman, at least six feet four inches tall and broad as a huge barrel, her ebony face glistening dramatically in the rain as she happily waved to the cheering crowds. Opposite her was an incredible antithesis in size – a tiny man, perhaps four feet six in height, a non-stop fountain of water cascading from the brim of his high top hat into his lap. Noël Coward was watching from a balcony with several friends, one of whom said: 'Good God, who is the little man?' To which Noël replied: 'Prrrobably her lunch!'

*

Wings of the Morning was the first Technicolor film to be made this side of the Atlantic. It was a romance concerning gypsies and horse racing, and starred Henry Fonda and the captivating French actress Annabella.

Before shooting started the director, cameraman, production manager and I went on a recce to Marseilles in the South of France to see a large gypsy camp which figures prominently in our film. We left from the old Croydon Airport in a tiny single-prop plane and flew to France where we had a magnificent bouillabaisse before visiting – really just visiting – a brothel to entertain our American friends who were most impressed, except when one of the girls sat, quite naked, in the production manager's lap. He was acutely embarrassed until we extricated him with much amusement. Next day we saw the camp and then flew back to England. Over northern France, the pilot asked us if we would like a beer. Of course we would, so he promptly put down in a field adjacent to a country bar and we sat in the French sunshine enjoying our beer before taking off again. Oh, glories departed.

It was, of course, a completely new experience to work on a feature film in colour. The lights were different; all strong arc lamps, and the dictates of the Technicolor hierarchy meant that the general tone had to be flat. Dark shadows were frowned upon and every light had to be measured meticulously to have the right level of illumination. Considering these limitations my cameraman Ray Rennahan did a splendid job, getting the requisite level of soft front light, then highlighting with strong cross lights and back lights.

I heard that when Marlene Dietrich was being tested in Hollywood for her first Technicolor film, *The Garden of Allah*, she refused to be lit with several lights and insisted on a single high key light. The Technicolor boys were unhappy but Dietrich insisted and got her way. The result was, of course, highly successful and from then on cameramen started to light Technicolor films with their accustomed chiaroscuro.

Henry Fonda was hilarious to work with. When he wasn't required in a scene, he would disguise himself and change jobs. Ray Rennahan would be lighting the set and would ask for a lamp on the spot-rail above. The lamp would come on and, to Ray's astonishment, swing about all over the place; when Ray and his electrical gaffer demanded to know what the hell was going on, a strange electrician in an old trilby hat and looking oddly like the leading man would shout gibberish down at them.

Fonda's presence made working a non-stop enjoyment, but God

played the best joke on us. In the film our gypsy horse wins the Derby. We used a genuine racehorse in the film for the scenes leading up to the real Derby, and Steve Donahue, one of the greatest jockeys of all time, rode him as though in the actual race. All we had to do then was to show the real Derby winner as it passed the winning post and the audience would assume it was our film horse. Trouble was, our horse was a chestnut and, for the first time in donkey's years, a white horse won the Derby. In the end we had to fake it in close-ups.

In the autumn of 1936 an enormous Cadillac coupé drew up at the entrance of a factory just outside London. There was little sign that this depressing building was the home of 'glorious' Technicolor.

The occupants of the Cadillac were Count von Keller and his wife, who were ushered into the office of the managing director, Kay Harrison, where they made a most unusual request. On their world travels they had so much enjoyed taking pictures with their 16 mm camera that they now wanted to hire a Technicolor camera and a cameraman so that they could travel the world in their car making professional travelogues.

Kay told me later that the naïvety of this request had rather taken his breath away. He had explained gently, that it wasn't quite as simple as that. A Technicolor camera has to be carefully maintained by a minimum crew of two and travel with many auxiliary cases in a well-upholstered van. And he doubted that any cameraman would be too happy sitting in the boot of a car with the Technicolor camera on his lap. The Count and Countess, although taken aback, agreed to everything, and a regular travelogue unit was put together: Hans Neiter (director), John Hanau (production manager and extra director), myself and my two assistants, Chris Challis and Ian Craig.

We had a large van for our equipment which included a tracking dolly with rails and in Rome a huge camera crane was used. Our company was called World Windows. Each travelogue was to be of ten minutes' duration and was to be released by United Artists.

Count von Keller was quite out of the ordinary. Six feet five inches tall with a persuasive Teutonic air of authority, he had been a high-ranking officer in the German army but hated the Nazis and had escaped to America. He was definitely a *Boy's Own* type, loving adventure and inducing others to like it too. He was a crack shot and had a slight limp from a bullet wound sustained in a hunting accident.

For me this assignment was a great slice of luck after years of yearning to see the world. Adventure was on the horizon – and education too.

Cowper put it nicely: 'How much a dunce, that has been sent to roam/ Excels a dunce that has been left at home.'

Our first travelogues were in Italy. My impressions of Rome were those of any tourist: a city of contrasts; raucous crowds, and the perpetual snarl of traffic, clashing against the silent Roman ruins – once the nerve centre of a mighty empire, battered by time and plunder, but still aloof from the modern world.

This first visit was another seminar in my late education, seeing such a profusion of beautiful things. The creations of Bernini, for instance, which glow all over Rome. I would often pass through the Piazza Barberini, and salute Bernini's Fountain of Triton held aloft by four dolphins. Fountains were one of his more obvious contributions to the Roman scene, and I wondered if he got his initial interest from his father, Pietro, who created the fountain of the Baroccia at the foot of the Spanish Steps – that rather incongruous boat of stone in the act of sinking, with water pouring out of its bow and stern, only yards away from where Keats and Shelley once lived, indulging in prosodic comment – or just having a giggle . . . who knows?

I was able to study Bernini's fountain of the four river gods in the beautiful Piazza Navona from a most unusual vantage point, perched high on a camera crane, with my Technicolor camera drifting over the powerful statues which symbolize four great rivers of the world, a hollow creation of rock that miraculously holds a huge marble obelisk aloft as effortlessly as if it were a fountain pen. Floating above it, I was able to study closely the figures and fantastic animals which seem to move in the whirling water. And all part of my working day.

Another delightful fusion of work while furthering my love of the arts was when I photographed St Peter's. When I tracked my camera round the famous colonnade in St Peter's Piazza, I was able to appreciate more fully Bernini's poetry in architecture. Those slim, statue-topped columns set in a circular embrace: a loving cradling of the pious, or a pair of pincers to entice you into the Catholic faith? Whichever way you look at it, it is another example of Bernini's creative virtuosity.

Inside the basilica itself I was presented with what seemed to be an insurmountable problem. The sheer immensity of the place – 700 feet square and 400 feet in height – would need a battery of powerful lamps to provide enough light for colour photography. (In those days the emulsion speed of Technicolor was very slow; I needed 600 ft candles at full aperture – f1.5.) All I could muster on the travelogue budget was fewer than a dozen small incandescent lamps. I tried a mad experiment.

The Technicolor camera had no regular cranking handle, only a tiny handle at the back which was used for threading the film when loading. I placed the few tiny lamps as artistically as I was able, then slowly turned the loading crank until twenty feet of film had passed through the camera. That took about ten minutes. Then I reversed the direction of the film until I was at the beginning again. I now laboriously repeated this process, using the same twenty feet of film, for what seemed like hours.

Days later, when the film was processed back at the English laboratories, the result was surprisingly perfect. I had photographed the interior of St Peter's for the first time in Technicolor and with practically no light.

Lighting these wonderful creations – Michelangelo's *Pietà*, for instance – I placed my lamps so carefully, like a caress of veneration, until I felt I had achieved the most effective modelling of the marble as the sculptor himself had seen it, hundreds of years before. When I lit the thirteenth-century bronze figure of St Peter, I stood for some time looking at the right foot, which was worn away by kisses of the devout. Imagine! A large piece of bronze worn away by kisses. How many millions of pious lips could it have taken to do that?

I didn't realize then how lucky I was to have the freedom of that great place to myself as I moved my camera and lights from one hallowed spot to another. I also didn't realize that the Pope himself had been watching from up in the gallery. He had seen me invade the most sacred places, and probably closed his eyes when he saw me tripping up the marble steps to the *confessio*, and scurrying over his high altar.

The Italian directors on these travelogues were extremely artistic and stimulating to work with. They wanted the camera to glide or dart in and out of the multitude of Roman splendours with the agility of an inquisitive gadfly. My Technicolor camera equipment at that time was heavy to work with, and quite inadequate for their elegant techniques.

On our first film of Rome, we were supposed to start with an eagle flying in the air and then, as it dived, the camera was to dive in a plane – as if from the eagle's point of view – straight down into the Colosseum. Just like that. The only plane we could get hold of was an old Italian bomber. My camera was well-secured looking out of the bomb bay and I was strapped in so that I would not be tossed out. The heavy battery for driving the camera was placed at the rear of the plane – and stupidly I hadn't thought to tie it down. The first time the cumbersome old bird went into a reluctant dive, I heard a sinister swishing noise and turned my head just in time to see the battery hurtling towards the hold like a shell from a gun. Only by luck was I able to stop it from braining some luckless tourist below.

The ancient Italian bomber was certainly no Spitfire. It dived like a drunken porpoise, lurching ponderously downwards, and by the time it had got up any speed, it was perilously close to the floor of the Colosseum. I managed to get some effect in the end – but I must confess, my heart and my stomach weren't quite in it.

The shots of our captive Roman eagle soaring against the sky were even more disastrous. The symbolic bird looked magnificent with its nasty hostile glare, and a menacing flap of its wide wings. The only problem was that it had apparently never flown in its life. It just squatted on the ground, and glared at us balefully, not moving an inch. Someone had the idea of placing it on a higher tower and just pushing it off. This we did – about twenty times. Each time, the wretched bird screeched and flapped frantically as it fell to earth like a stone. The director swore eloquently in Italian, and had to settle for the hope that little portions of each take could be cut together to give the illusion of the great eagle in flight. Surprisingly, it worked – but it was hardly a moving experience!

One of my favourite streets was and is Via Margutta; long and narrow, it runs parallel to the Via del Barbuino. Nearly all the buildings are antique shops which have been there for hundreds of years, and there is an unmistakable aura of the many treasures that have passed hands through the centuries.

In the early nineteenth century Cardinal Fesch – an uncle of Napoleon – was rummaging in one of these antique shops and saw an old trunk. On the wooden lid was a painting of an old man, but the head was missing, sawn out of the panel. He was intrigued enough to buy it. Many years later, he saw – in a cobbler's shop – the missing head painted on a wooden panel. By a million to one chance a lost work by Leonardo da Vinci was thus rescued from oblivion. Today, this painting hangs in the Vatican. It is merely noted as 'Gerome by Leonardo'. There is nothing written underneath to tell of its fantastic adventure.

One day when I was returning from Hadrian's Villa, I could hardly get to my hotel in the Via Nationale, as the street was packed for a procession. I was curious and stood on a large case that held my Technicolor film magazine. I was just in time to see Adolf Hitler and Mussolini pass by in an enormous Mercedes, their arms stretched out stiffly in the fascist salute, and the crowds Heil-ing like mad. It was another ironic contrast. In this noble city with beatific art wherever one looked, I was gazing at pure evil.

Without warning, I was yanked off my perch on the magazine case by three husky secret police who arrested me, being under the impression that the case contained a bomb. I finally convinced them that I was not going to assassinate the Führer and Il Duce. But if only I could have!

Our next travelogue was prosaic enough: an Italian foxhunt in country-side pleasantly sprinkled with Roman ruins. Then we went to Naples.

The main idea of this travelogue was to show the sparkling serenity of the towns around the bay of Naples threatened by Vesuvius which might, at any moment, spew out enough molten lava to bury these towns completely, as it did to Pompeii and Herculaneum in AD 79. I think we would have been happy enough just to show the sinister mountain looming behind all our scenes of carefree Neapolitan life and left it at that, but when we arrived and saw voluminous smoke coming from the volcano we knew we had to photograph as close to the crater as possible.

The mountain of Vesuvius is over 3,800 feet high. It has had hundreds of eruptions since the catastrophe in AD 79, but none anywhere near so violent, except in 1631 when 3,000 people were killed. We were told this present eruption was not a major one, so we decided to go up as close as possible. We drove as far as the winding road went, to a small plateau about a quarter of a mile from the summit, and with thirty guides made our ascent to within a hundred yards of the crater.

It wasn't pleasant. The ground was fossilized lava and was so hot we couldn't stand still. From the crater itself clumps of molten lava spurted out occasionally, falling uncomfortably close; we had to be ready to dodge these as we worked. 'Work' meant three of us clutching the camera on its tripod, someone else hauling our battery, and stumbling over the frighteningly hot ground through smoke and sulphur to a place as close to the crater as possible, pointing the camera for a few seconds before the heat became too much, then retreating to a less hot area.

There were patches of ancient lava out of which fresh red-hot molten lava was haemorrhaging; it was hot enough to melt most things on Earth, but its dull red colour and snail-like moving speed was hardly dramatic. I calculated that if I ran the camera at half speed – twelve frames a second, instead of twenty-four – it would make the lava appear to emerge faster, and if I deliberately didn't compensate the exposure for shooting at twelve frames it would over-expose and make the wine-red lava more orange hot. The old lava ground was jet black so I couldn't over-expose that anyway.

We certainly got some exciting material that day – but at a price. One of the guides fell in the heat and was taken to hospital. The tripod legs were burnt as were the soles of our shoes; the valuable prism in the camera was damaged by the heat. I could guess Technicolor's reaction to that.

We tried again the next day, but this time at a safer distance. The volcano was still sending up dense spirals of smoke, but we were able to incorporate some artistic ideas. Incredibly, we were allowed to take out of the museum several 'bodies' of those trapped in the eruption two thousand years ago – plaster casts from the lava which had encased the victims, their corpses withering away over the centuries to leave moulds in the rock, frozen inside the lava encasing them in poignant positions of terror and death to be discovered two thousand years later. We placed them on the ground dramatically and, through whirling smoke, tracked through them. We would certainly never get permission to do anything like that today!

We sent the exposed film home to Technicolor with a letter from me explaining the difficulties we had encountered capturing the eruption and apologizing for the damaged prism and burnt tripod legs. I received a very stern cable forbidding me to repeat such a foolhardy act. A few days later I received another cable. They had just seen the rushes and said it was the most exciting material they had ever seen. Congratulations all round.

Our film included the ruins of Pompeii – so fascinatingly evocative of the past. Our Italian director, Pietro Francisca, had very creative ideas and was a joy to work with. At that time all the Roman artefacts were in situ and it was stimulating to photograph them. Now, so many of these beautiful works – statues, mosaics, even the best wall paintings – are in museums. We were lucky to have been there at that time, when everything was in its rightful place. We were even allowed to visit the two-thousand-year-old brothel – its location indicated by a penis incised on a nearby pavement. The walls are covered with sexually explicit paintings, showing that little has changed in two millennia.

Many years later I was at Pompeii again on a film: *The Last Days of Pompeii*. It was sad to see how bare it looked, stripped of so many interesting artefacts, now in museums. Somebody said museums are the graveyards of art. I realize, of course, that if these artefacts were left outside they would soon perish in today's corroding pollution, but surely the tremendous advance in technology would be able to protect these works of art in the open air instead of the lifeless atmosphere of museums?

After Rome we went on to Palestine. By boat of course. In those halcyon days, except for short trips in Europe, we always travelled by boat, with its attendant holiday atmosphere, good food, swimming pools, dancing and new friends. Sad how this relaxed pace has disappeared from our working lives.

We sailed into the harbour at Haifa with the morning light sparkling a warm welcome. Our ship was crammed with Jewish emigrants thrilled at the sight of their promised land. For a few days we stayed at a small hotel on Mount Carmel. In spite of fiery Elijah of the Old Testament, I still remember the intoxicating smells of wild herbs, redolent with innocence and peace.

How did I ever equate peace with turbulent Palestine?

When our little film unit arrived in Haifa in 1936 the newspaper headlines were grimly explicit: TERROR STRIKES HAIFA, TWENTY-THREE DEAD, JEWS STABBED TO DEATH, FOUR ARABS MURDERED BY ARMED BRIGANDS, TENSION AS DEATH TOLL GROWS.

The newspapers weren't kidding. We endeavoured to look and act like British tourists and not to go on buses (where the occasional bomb was hidden). I was invited to dinner by a pleasant Jewish family but just before I left my hotel I had a phone call cancelling the dinner as their daughter's throat had been cut. The Holy Land?

Somehow the Jewish people survived as they have done for thousands of years. What was most noticeable to me was the different persona of Jews in Palestine. They were not the well-dressed business types, but vigorous, open-air people in shorts, with tanned faces, working hard on their new country and happily living rough in kibbutz settlements (always strongly guarded with round-the-clock sentries).

Von Keller was much concerned with the danger of our situation and thought it wise for us to carry guns. I had a 9 mm Beretta which I carried in a holster under my left armpit. I'm ashamed to say this, but carrying a gun gave me an extraordinary feeling of pugnacity. It was years before the James Bond films, but I felt I could stand up to anybody and stand no nonsense. Thank God I never used my gun except to shoot at bottles for target practice.

Haifa was our organizational base, but we were glad to leave and go on to our first travelogue: Jerusalem. Von Keller told us that on every film, he would like us to work like demons to finish the job in a few days; then, when it was over, he would give us a wonderful time: parties, swimming – anything we wanted. And he kept his word. After each film we would relax and enjoy a delightful holiday while the next film was being prepared.

We worked hard in Jerusalem, but how could anyone complain when the nature of the work was so fascinating? Jerusalem is a thrilling sight even from a distance: perched on a high hill among the sun-bleached mountains of Judaea, with the Kedron valley below running right on to Jericho and the Dead Sea.

The great walls surrounding the old city have been destroyed many times, in countless invasions when everything was laid waste. They were rebuilt at new positions over the centuries, and the archaeologists have been arguing about wall positions ever since.

Inside the walls, thousands of years of historic Jerusalem lies under-foot. The Jerusalem of the time of Christ was already rooted in past destructions and all the succeeding Jerusalems since the Gospels lie on one another like so many layers of compost, enriched with the bones of carnage. Phoenix-like, the city has always risen from the ashes of destruction; there is something splendidly defiant about old Jerusalem.

Walking through the narrow, dark, traffic-free lanes of the old quarter, one is magically transported to biblical times. The bustling crowds in their timeless clothes, the heavily laden donkeys, even an occasional camel – the scene is wonderfully unchanged. Only my Technicolor camera was out of harmony, but the light was 'heavenly': shafts of sunlight, sharpened by the dust which penetrated the shadowed air like golden swords.

The modern part, outside the walls, jolts you into the present with its cars, traffic lights and modern clothes. But here too are overpowering ghosts of past greatness: the mighty Herod's temple, where the one remaining western wall became the 'wailing wall' for the Jews, who at one time were allowed only one visit a year to mourn their temple's destruction.

It was stimulating and educative for me to work in such surroundings. Although von Keller had asked us to finish each film as quickly as possible, the very nature of the situation set a more relaxed tempo; there was always time for me to talk to someone accompanying us and, as we moved around the various locations, I learned much from the occasional Rabbi, Zionist or local.

I photographed the Via Dolorosa, where Jesus is supposed to have carried the cross, and the Holy Sepulchre, the most sacred Christian site in Jerusalem – a disturbing tangle of fact and fancy. The facts are hardly substantial, floating mistily through two thousand years of non-stop battle, plunder and, more than once, total destruction.

I reflected, as we worked, how much in Jerusalem is revered through faith alone. The Mount of Olives is higher than Jerusalem. In the far distance can be seen the smudge of blue that is the Dead Sea. Behind rise the purple Mountains of Moab. As I was setting my camera, I was told that Jesus knew this view: he would have gazed at it when he came over the hill from Bethlehem. This I believed at once, without question. This was real. Not a reconstructed monument of unproven speculation, but unchanged earth and space, with a view as the eyes of Christ saw it.

One day, after work was over, I was descending the ancient stone steps from the walled city when I experienced an extraordinary manifestation of spiritual beauty. An old man, blind, with a fine face and white hair, was slowly climbing towards me. He was being led by a boy about seven years old – probably his grandchild. The boy was impatiently tugging the old man's hand to go faster, causing him to stub his bare toes painfully on every step. One would expect a sharp rebuke at the boy's thoughtlessness, but when I saw the old man's face I felt a surge of emotion and wonder. The sightless eyes were stitched tightly against his interior thoughts but his face was creased in a smile, so wonderful, in his tolerance and love for the child, that tears sprang to my eyes. I had that glorious feeling, a stab of insight, that life possessed purpose and beauty. It was a perfect epiphany.

For the first time since I had arrived in Israel I experienced a numinous detachment from earthly existence, without that ache of doubt which pervades those dubious 'holy' places where so many have made piety a lucrative business.

Soon afterwards, we were humping the camera over the enchanting beauty of the Garden of Gethsemane. The olive trees were huge – many with enormous girths and obviously extremely old. Some say that some trees are from the time of Christ, but I doubt it: every tree in Jerusalem was cut down by the order of Titus in the siege of AD 70.

As we worked I felt more guilt than reverence. Here was I walking about looking for a good camera position, when all about me was the spirit of cataclysmic events that made this small place the most poignant theatre in the world. On this hallowed ground we were making a film, trampling perhaps, on the very spot where Jesus was arrested by the high priests: blasphemy.

We moved on, heading for Amman. En route we stopped to bathe in the Dead Sea which, at 1,200 feet below sea level, is the lowest place on earth. It's dead all right; although looking like any other sea, there isn't a particle of life in it. The 30 per cent salt content – ten times that of ordinary sea water – means that one cannot possibly sink in it. We took photos of each other lying on our backs in the water, reading news-papers. If a splash goes in your eyes it's pure agony, and it tastes like a hot toddy of vitriol.

On the road by the Dead Sea, we passed by something nobody knew existed at that time. I might have glanced through the car window at the wild, craggy landscape, and perhaps looked curiously at a group of strongly shaped rocks, hundreds of feet high, resembling monster's claws, with some holes near the top like black snake's eyes; I could have remarked that they were probably caves. They were indeed caves and, if only we had known, inside those caves were what became known as the Dead Sea scrolls, one of the most sensational discoveries of the twentieth century. They were discovered by a goatherd in 1947, ten years after we had passed by. Quite nearby, the ruins of Qumran were buried under the earth, also awaiting discovery. Qumran was the monastic settlement of the Essene sect who wrote the scrolls and who hid them in the nearby caves when the Roman legions were heading their way after the latest razing of Jerusalem.

That first scroll's discovery led to further exploration in adjacent caves and many more were discovered, some of them dating back a thousand years before the oldest biblical scriptures then known.

Our next base was Amman, in the mountain capital of Transjordan, from where we would sally forth to photograph the Arab bedouin in their desert habitat – a wilderness so savage that we sometimes wondered if we would ever find our way back to base. We had invaluable help from an Englishman whose name is now a legend in the Middle East: General Sir John Glubb, known as 'Peak Pasha'. The Arabs venerated him and he was considered a greater man than T. E. Lawrence. Peak Pasha was in command of the then British-mandated Transjordan's Arab Legion's Desert Patrol, some of whom escorted and protected us on treks where the natives might not be quite so friendly.

Glubb's famous camel corps was a delight to see, loping along at a surprising speed through the stone-littered deserts and twisted foothills.

The terrain was impossible for a car. We drove as far as we could, then manhandled the camera over loose sands and rocky gullies until we reached our location.

The bedouin live a nomadic existence, unchanged for thousands of years, with their black goat-hide tents, and the barest necessities of life. They wear the same flowing robes and headgear – the keffiyeh – and carry at least one curved dagger in their belts.

I felt like Dr Livingstone in darkest Africa when I saw their reaction to the portable wind-up gramophone we played to them. They couldn't have been more awestruck if Allah had descended from the sky.

On one occasion we were invited to a bedouin lunch. I dreaded it, for I knew the food would be goat, but we had to respect our host, a proud patriarchal sheikh with a hawkish nose and a full beard.

For the lunch we had to sit in a circle with crossed legs – something I've never been able to do without extreme discomfort – and our hosts (all men) stood around us with arms folded, watching us eat. The wives had all been bundled back in their tent.

I knew we had to eat with the right hand only – *de rigueur* in the East – taking a portion of goat from the large circular tray and munching away, pretending we liked it. As I feared, it was horrible, but I fought back nausea and did my duty. When we'd finished there was a pile of gnawed goat and bones on the tray. We now rose, and our hosts sat down in our places and ate our leftovers heartily. We could hardly believe it as we pretended to admire the scenery.

Our hosts now got up, leaving their remains, and clapped their hands for their wives to emerge from the women's tent and finish off what was left in the tray! We then sat nearby for coffee, made from desert plants and terminally bitter. I forced myself to drink a cup, but my ordeal wasn't over. Four times the coffee jug came around, my desperate efforts to decline ignored. I was approaching a state of panic when, luckily, someone who had noticed my plight told me that if I didn't want any more coffee I only had to wiggle my cup sideways and that, thank Allah, was the last time I drank bedouin coffee.

Once we had to spend the night with the bedouin as we were too far away from our base to return that day. We filmed a session round a camp fire where there was singing, and the bedouin performed a mock battle, very convincing against the leaping flames, after which we moved into a goat-hide tent to sleep. The tent stank, and I was rather glad we had to rise well before dawn in order to photograph the sunrise in the desert. The air outside was fresh and clean and the wide, yawning sky was a bruised purple, which made it all well worthwhile.

Usually the task of taking our exposed film to Haifa for transfer to London was entrusted to one of my camera crew, but one evening von Keller suggested that he and I took a break and drive to Haifa ourselves.

We set off from Amman in his powerful Cadillac, stopping for dinner at the King David Hotel in Jerusalem, and left there at about midnight – speeding down the main street at a hair-raising sixty miles an hour.

Just outside Jerusalem there was a long stretch of road that was dangerous at night. Cars had often been shot at by terrorists hidden behind the gullies on either side of the road. Stupidly, I dropped my briefcase out of the car and von Keller had to stop while I scrambled out to find it, a tense few moments knowing that a bullet might rip into me any second while I searched in the darkness, but I found the briefcase and dashed back to the car, ignoring the look von Keller gave me.

The road became more winding and mountainous. There was no sign of life in the inky night. It became apparent we were lost. What had started out as a fun trip to Haifa was now a depressing chore. I was sleepy and bored, not having a clue where we were, and it was now two in the morning.

Ahead of me and to my left I could see dim figures moving about in the darkness, about fifty yards off the road. I turned to von Keller: 'Shall I get out and ask them the way?' At that moment there was a loud crack of rifle fire and a bullet went clean through our windscreen midway between von Keller and me. Our reaction was surprisingly slow, considering. We had driven on for several seconds before we showed our shock and von Keller said shakily, 'Jack, I don't think it's a good idea to ask them anything.' A few minutes later we came to a junction with a sign: 'Nazareth 2 miles' and to our left 'Haifa 45 miles'.

Haifa was deep in slumber when we arrived and stopped outside a building. No lights were visible. I asked von Keller where we were, but received only an enigmatic smile in reply as he motioned me to follow him up some steps to a doorway. As we entered music greeted us and a dozen glamorous girls came forward, escorting us to a large table. There were waiters bowing obsequiously and the girls were smiling enticingly. I believed I had fallen asleep in the car and was having a lovely dream, but it was real all right. This was a night club and von Keller had ordered – at considerable expense – that the place should stay open regardless of when we arrived.

I sat down in a daze as champagne arrived and the girls surrounded us with beguiling charm. They were all European and very beautiful. The next few hours were better than a dream. We danced, and ate a superb buffet supper – or was it breakfast? – and after that took several girls in the Cadillac for a dawn ride to the sea.

Later that day at our hotel Count von Keller told me he had phoned the police about us being used for target practice. He had to go out to order a new windscreen and asked me to stay in the hotel as an intelligence officer was coming to ask questions about the shooting. The intelligence officer arrived and I gave him all the information I could. I noticed he was carrying a Mauser automatic like I would carry an umbrella. He was the sort of British officer who immediately gave the impression of the utmost competence: lean, with intelligent eyes, seemingly casual with the occasional amusing comment but very much alert to the situation. I told him about the junction with the 'Nazareth 2 miles' road sign; it was obviously important to him.

Next morning, the intelligence officer told us the men in the hills, Arab terrorists, had all been captured. The intelligence officer's name was Captain Wingate – yes, that's right, *the* Captain Wingate, later General Orde Wingate, the hero of World War Two who led the Chindits in the Burmese jungle against the Japanese. Apart from the many decorations he received for his brilliant actions in the war, he also received the DSO for his part in leading guerrilla forces in Palestine during the Arab revolt.

There were more absorbing travelogue journeys: the gigantic ruins of Baalbek, with its massive pagan temples starkly set against the snow-wrapped mountains of Lebanon; Palmyra, mysteriously isolated in the Syrian desert, far away from the tourist tide. What had been a bustling centre of a trade route in Roman times, with caravans emanating from all over the East, was now only rows and rows of skeletal columns, sticking up like bones in the sand, and nothing else in sight – just avenues of columns and occasional arches stretched to infinity as in a Salvador Dali image.

But the best was yet to come. Petra. It runs south over difficult terrain. When I was there, the journey was nothing like so easy as it is today; but even today, everyone still has to enter Petra by a narrow gorge. You must go by horseback unless you are energetic enough to walk a rough one and a half miles through the stony gully. Of course, we had to abandon our cars, and our equipment had to be carried by mules and porters.

The scenery around Petra is decidedly spooky. The dark, grotesque mountains, so split by millions of sinister crevices that passage is impossible except for the one small cleft in the face of a mountain: a narrow gorge hundreds of feet high that winds in varying widths – sometimes the width of a truck, sometimes so narrow a horse and rider can only just squeeze through. Surely, the most private city on God's earth.

As I rode through on horseback I noticed, with some astonishment, occasional lengths of lead piping which I later discovered had been put there under Roman occupation.

It was all rather uncanny: the clattering of horses' hooves echoing in the cold gloom of the twisting gorge with the sky a narrow ribbon of light high above. Then came the moment I had heard about but was not quite prepared for.

Rounding a bend, I stopped suddenly, robbed of breath. Close before me, miles from any sign of civilization, was a large temple carved like an exquisite pink cameo out of the mountain itself; the surfaces smooth and perfect as Chartres or St Peter's. The contrast between the rough wilderness of the mountain and the pristine baby pink of the temple was evocative of a Disney cartoon. I know of nothing more astonishing than this sudden unexpected sight. What was its style, its age? Classical, yes. Corinthian columns, broken pediments, capitals. Was it Roman? Hellenist?

The experts dated this façade – and others in Petra – as second-century AD, but there is still so much mystery about the place. In general it is a city of tombs, with huge façades cut into the surrounding hills, but the temple I was gaping at was called Pharoah's treasury and the Arabs believe there is treasure hidden in the sandstone vase on top of the façade. This vase is pitted with rifle shots from those who hoped to release a shower of jewels from it.

Further on, we made camp. We were the only ones there. Tents had been erected for our travelogue crew of five, plus a guide, and we had dinner under hissing acetylene lamps.

Our guide was well informed on Petra. Yes, the 'modern' buildings were second-century Roman, but some artefacts, flint tools, arrow heads, etc. went back to palaeolithic times. He admitted that little is known about pre-Roman Petra. The Nabataeans had been there. There were theories that Petra had been the home of the Horites, who were driven out by the Edomites, who were in turn defeated by a king of Judaea who slaughtered survivors by throwing them off the highest rock ('You'll see it tomorrow'). But he said Petra was still something of a mystery. The last person who was active here was Lawrence of Arabia.

There was a slight drama when a scorpion was discovered under our camp table. It was killed before it could perform its lethal overarm bowling. Our guide made us feel a little uneasy by advising us that if bitten by a scorpion or a sandsnake – 'and there are quite a few here' – the best thing to do is to take a sharp knife and cut away the flesh around the wound as soon as possible. When we retired to our camp bed I gingerly poked down under the blankets with a stick to make sure I hadn't got company.

Next morning we started work, exploring a city lost to history for fourteen hundred years and only discovered during the previous century.

I was on horseback most of the time; Petra is that big. The Rose Red City is not really red – although roses have so many colours one could easily find one to match. The predominant colour is salmon-pink, but the sandstone façades and buildings are veined with fascinating variegated hues: purple, russet brown, pinks and ochres – it's as if a studio painter had been in a hurry to finish the set and had let the colours drip over the rocks.

We marvelled at each extraordinary sight. The wide basin surrounded by mountains could be a vast sports arena. The surface is uneven with mounds – all that is left of older cities. Rows of façades are superbly carved out of the high cliffs and there is an amphitheatre, a market place, a forum, paved streets and sometimes steps that now lead nowhere but once accessed places long since gone. And labyrinths of terraces with tombs, all carved from the rock face. There were fields that were packed masses of dazzling pink oleanders as far as one could see, another equally full of kniphofia – 'red-hot pokers' to you and me.

On my suggestion we did a 'double take' with the camera, panning over a background that was untouched by human hands, continuing the pan past some steps, then jerking the camera back to the steps as if a discovery of something made by man.

I enlarged on this idea. There was a magnificent view of a temple called El-Deir, the largest temple of all, sculpted out of a mountain. It is enormous: only eighty feet less in height than London's St Paul's Cathedral. From the distance I was photographing it I could, by going very low with my camera, hide the temple behind a foreground rise of earth. I wanted to start low, then rise up with my camera to reveal the great temple, but I had no crane. Why not improvise? We managed to borrow two wooden tent posts which we sunk into the ground, tight against the sides of my camera. A kind of rope pulley was fitted on top of the posts and *voilà!* – the camera rose revealing the temple as a dramatic surprise.

Each day after we finished work there was little to do. No restaurants, theatres or anywhere to visit. I used to wander about in the gathering dusk looking for artefacts, and eventually I found one, a small Roman oil lamp which is one of my most cherished possessions – at least I know it's genuine!

While we were waiting at Beirut for the boat to take us home we took advantage of von Keller's exhortation to have a good time now that shooting was over. Today Beirut is a grim ruin, almost completely destroyed by endless internecine war, but in those days it was an exhilarating mixture of the Côte d'Azur with a spicy tang of the Arabian Nights. There were endless parties, swimming, water skiing, night clubs and very little sleep. And it was during this heady round of pleasure that I met Sylvia. She was eighteen, spoke several languages fluently, and was a swimming champion. Furthermore, she was going to England on the same boat as myself. On the voyage we stopped off at Cairo, but Sylvia and I eschewed the hotel and spent the night in the moonlit splendour of the nearby Pyramids. There was a dreamlike theatrical quality about it all. Somewhere in the shadows a soprano was singing wonderfully.

We lay on the timeless sands of Egypt and gazed at the winking stars – billions of them – and saw the rosy-fingered dawn sneak over the weary stare of the Sphinx as it had been doing so many years before Homer had been born.

It was all pure Noël Coward romantic corn. We got engaged, and some weeks later we were married. The day after our wedding my cousin and first love, Julie, phoned me. Her marriage had foundered and she was separated and alone. She was seventeen when I first met her. I was a year younger. She was standing by a lamp post in a suburban street, waiting for my arrival by bus from Elstree. Although we were cousins, we had not met before. It was a family get-together, and she had been sent to the bus stop to escort me to the Christmas gathering. Her eyes were a gentle violet blue and her face cuddled in soft blonde curls. I didn't know about pheromones then, but there must have been a lot around that day at our first meeting. She stood there in the quiet dusk and said with a nervous seriousness: 'You are Johnny.' 'Yes, and you are Julie.' I spoke clumsily, for I was instantly in love with her. However, there was a painful shock awaiting me. She was engaged to be married. Her fiancé was much older and was a salesman of some sort. Of course I hated him and spent that Christmas in misery. A song going the rounds was called, 'My Heart Belongs to the Girl who Belongs to Somebody Else' and I felt it had been composed just for me.

I told Julie I had just been married the day before. She congratulated me and wished me every happiness. I felt a certain pang the way things had worked out. I'm sure Julie knew I had been in love with her years before, but now I was married and that was that.

The marriage to Sylvia was a disaster. Short and sour. I was certainly to blame to a large extent by taking my young bride with me on location to the Sudan on *The Four Feathers*. This was no easygoing travelogue, but a tough and exhausting movie. Our home for three months was a tent in the desert with the temperature at a hundred and fifteen degrees.

We quarrelled every day, made love, and quarrelled again.

The British army also camped with us, represented by the East Surrey regiment, who wore Victorian uniforms and fought the native 'fuzzy wuzzies' in mock battles with convincing realism. I was one of two cameramen on this location. Osmond Borradaile, a friendly Canadian (who had worked in Hollywood the year I was born!) was the senior cameraman, but we both had full crews. Wilkie Cooper was my operator – he photographed my first film as a director – and Geoff Unsworth was the assistant. Geoff was to become a great cameraman, winning two Oscars for *Cabaret* and *Tess,* on which film he sadly died. My number boy was Wally Beavers who became the head of England's wonderful matt painting process which was to help me win an Oscar for *Black Narcissus.*

The few of us who were qualified dined every evening with the army brass and, in spite of the heat and the desert conditions, we had to dress up every night in black tie.

Zoltan Korda, the brother of Sir Alexander Korda, was the director. He was suffering from some kind of skin disorder and wore a blazing red flannel mask that covered his face, with holes for his eyes and mouth. He also wore white gloves and a large hat so there was very little of him to see, but he made up for this sinister anonymity with a voice that surpassed any bellowing sergeant-major. His savage rages curdled any sympathy one might have had for the discomfort and pain he might have been suffering. Every day was pure hell. We all got a blast, and I received several for daring to bring my wife with me.

But there were a few nicer days. We journeyed up the Nile on a houseboat all the way to Abu Simbel, with its four awesome gigantic statues of Rameses II hewn out of the rock cliffs; it made all the location miseries bearable. Years later when Abu Simbel was, incredibly, moved to accommodate the building of the Aswan High Dam, I was able to see it again in its new home – we shot scenes there for Agatha Christie's *Death on the Nile.*

Exciting and quite frightening was the big scene in the desert where the wild, legendary Sudanese attack the British who had built a *cheriba*: a protective wall of thorny branches.

The British were issued with period rifles and, of course, blank cartridges. The Sudanese had their own razor-sharp daggers. They were told it was all a harmless friendly game. Nobody would be hurt and it was all 'pretend'.

The Sudanese were magnificent, hurtling themselves through the walls of prickly bush and, with the most terrifying screams, made pretend combat, going right up to the serried ranks of the British soldiers, who fired their blank bullets without pause. The Sudanese fought closer and closer until they were 'pretending' at very close range indeed. That was when the trouble started.

A blank cartridge is quite harmless, but at a range of a couple of feet it stings like a thousand wasps. Some natives, yelling with pain, thought they had been shot by actual bullets and started to fight in earnest.

For a moment it looked as though a genuinely horrific battle would go on unchecked with several lives at risk, but our assistants and the Sudanese interpreters dashed in bravely shouting that the battle was finished and a serious slaughter was averted.

But there was no saving my disastrous marriage. On the boat going home we occupied separate cabins. In England we tried again, but fate decreed that I had to spend some months working in India, and this time we both agreed that it was unwise for Sylvia to accompany me. She went back to her mother in Syria and I never saw her again. Eventually, I married my first love, Julie, and together we had three fine boys.

In India we made more travelogues for Count von Keller's World Windows, starting at Bombay and journeying 22,000 miles by car all over India, going right up to Darjeeling and then back to Bombay. Having waited so long to see the world I was seeing it, and would continue to see it many times over.

Today, when air travel to distant places is easy (and boring), it doesn't impress anybody to have worked in Egypt, Japan, India, Australia, Africa, China, Mexico, etc., but in those days travel was wonderfully exciting. Instead of sitting down in a crowded plane I travelled in all kinds of boats, trains, buses, on horseback – even by camel.

Arriving, after days on dusty Indian roads, at Agra where the seventeenth-century white marble tomb, the Taj Mahal, had been built for Shah Jehan's wife, I gazed at this incredibly beautiful structure in the moonlight and, just as I had marvelled at the Sphinx in the moonlight with a woman singing in the shadows, there was also a woman at the Taj Mahal singing unseen in the garden. The jasmine blossoms were in full bloom. It was, as Noël Coward said in *Private Lives*, 'A sort of dream', but never in my wildest dreams did I imagine I would one day know Coward personally. It was many years later when I was living in Switzerland that we met as neighbours and became friends. I was often invited to his mountain chalet, Les Avants, with its theatrically beautiful view of Lake Geneva. He had that wonderful gift of great men: a natural egalitarian graciousness, never patronizing. It was as if we had known each other for years. He came over to my apartment in Vevey to show Julie and I his new small sports car. He played on my piano and told me some stories I must include. He always had that clipped, flamboyant way of talking, waspish and witty. It was a joy to listen to him. Beatrice Lillie, who was then sixty-two years old, had a boyfriend who ranted against Noël at a stage rehearsal and called him a senile faggot. Noël, furious, gave Bea's age away. Her boyfriend said, 'Beatrice Lillie is only starting life now.' Noël said, 'Well she's left it rather late.'

Noël was engaged to play a Hungarian role opposite Bill Holden and diligently practised a Hungarian accent based on Alexander Korda. When rehearsal started the director stopped him in horror. 'No, Noël – please, no accent, we want *you*. Play *yourself*.' Noël was taken aback for a moment, then decided to play his part laughing at every line he spoke. Bill Holden fell about and called him a canny son of a bitch.

He was very interested in my paintings but on the way out he stopped in the hall and peered at a Picasso drawing. 'Who did that?' 'Picasso,' I said. 'Serve him right,' said Noël briskly as he departed.

The Taj Mahal was indeed more dreamlike in the moonlight and I wanted to photograph it that way. In those days, however, Technicolor film was too slow for night exposure so I made an attempt at day-for-night photography. I placed two poles either side of my camera just out of picture, and thin wires – which wouldn't show – were stretched across at various heights from the ground. To these I attached pieces of Plasticine the size of pin heads – speculating at the positions of the stars – and stuck silver paper on each piece of Plasticine. Then I positioned reflectors behind the camera which reflected the sunlight on to the area of my stars. By turning each piece of Plasticine until the silver paper caught the reflected sun I was able to have many bright glints of 'stars' in the background. A pale-blue filter on my camera plus the usual underexposure for day-for-night changed the sunny day into a starry moonlit night.

Driving across the multifarious continent of India, we were able to make several attractive travelogues. We went south to Mysore for a jungle episode, travelling by car convoy with mattresses strapped to the roofs so we could sleep in the isolated 'guest houses' at various points along the way.

The roads were dirt tracks populated mostly by monkeys – although I once nearly ran over a leopard sleeping on the road. Von Keller, true to form, had his Cadillac fixed up with swivelling lamps with which he and I went hunting tigers at night. I was usually the one who swivelled the lamps hoping to catch a tiger in the rays while von Keller readied himself with his twin-barrelled rifle. It was hilariously unsuccessful. I would slowly swing the lamp around until eyes were seen, reflected like twin torchlights in the darkness. Von Keller would shoot and we would discover, not some fearsome tiger, but a jackal. After several night forays we gave it up. Von Keller then made arrangements for a proper tiger hunt, and he asked me to go with him. In those days we were far less enlightened about the folly of killing animals, and in my callow youth I was keen to appear 'manly' and enjoy the thrill of hunting a wild animal in the jungle.

In the end, the tiger hunt was something of a fiasco. For a start, von Keller actually bought the tiger for a tidy sum from the maharaja who owned the area. And we didn't actually hunt anything. For three successive nights, young buffaloes had been tethered to a tree in the jungle and inevitably devoured by the tiger who, of course, became accustomed to this sacrificial offering. On the third night, von Keller and I were lying on the ground waiting for the tiger to drop in for his usual meal only fifty feet from where that night's dinner was tethered. We had a couple of bushes over us as camouflage and we both had 12-bore rifles which the maharaja had lent us. Two Indian hunters were hidden nearby in case there were 'problems'.

We waited in the half-light, with dwindling excitement. An hour passed. I had brought a book with me and read in bored silence. I was sure it would all be a waste of time. Only the usual noises were heard: birds screeched in the distance, a monkey scampered by. It would all be over soon, I believed. The young buffalo would be released and we could go home.

Von Keller looked more and more disappointed, staring ceaselessly around in the gathering gloom. Then I heard him gasp, and he gripped my shoulder in a tense silence. I followed his fixed stare and saw the tiger, just visible in the dark foliage, hunched and still, peering at the young buffalo like a cat stares fixedly at a mouse.

Then it sprang. It hurtled over a span of at least twenty feet, awesome and magnificent in its effortless power. The buffalo was killed instantly; gripped by the neck as it sank to the ground. The tiger prepared to enjoy his evening meal. Now came the funny bit.

A small lamp with a dimmer control had been rigged in the tree where the buffalo was, fed by a battery and run to where we were hidden. I was to turn the light up slowly until the scene was well-illuminated. As the light came on, the tiger looked up with some puzzlement at what must have seemed to him a very early dawn. Von Keller raised his rifle and I saw, incredulously, that he was shaking violently. This high-ranking commander of the German army, whom I knew to be a dead shot, was so excited that his rifle was shuddering like a pneumatic drill. The panic was contagious, so trying to steady myself, I raised my rifle and aimed at the tiger's heart, waiting for von Keller to shoot first as was his right. He shot, and the tiger stiffened and slumped. I then issued the *coup de grâce* and the tiger stayed on the ground. Von Keller was utterly breathless, and so was I. I had experienced my first tiger hunt. I wouldn't want to do that again.

The Indian temples were much more peaceful than the savage jungle – although one temple I photographed actually worshipped monkeys, who were the sole occupants of the place and scampered about their holy shrine with absolutely no piety for their god Hanuman. Architecturally, the temples were fascinating. Tall, fragile spires, barrel-shaped domes in a variety of styles, with amazing intricacy of carved detail: an abundance of voluptuous figures illustrating the folklore of everyday life, sacred gods and goddesses, often in very erotic attitudes, showing a complete freedom towards sex that might seem outrageously wanton, but it was explained to me that nude images suggest the sensuality of the spirits of fertility, and the perfection of a woman's body is emphasized by abstract exaggeration. Most of these deliciously sensual forms were carved many centuries ago and I reflected that this glorification of natural sexual relationships was such a contrast to the ethics of Christianity.

As late as 1954, Pope Pius XII rebuked the subversive views of those who 'so exalt marriage as to rank it ahead of virginity'. Whoever believed that should be cast away on a desert island with at least ten hungry virgins.

We filmed an Indian durbar-a-levee (official reception) at Alwar, a town close to Delhi. The maharaja, young and pleasantly uninhibited, was venerated by the small population like a pop star and the durbar was an occasion of glittering pageantry. Even the elephants were painted and dressed in coloured finery and the locals loved it.

The reason for their happiness and the town's prosperity was not the result of the young maharaja's wise statesmanship. Everything – the economy, laws, taxes and general order – was run by a quiet, unassuming Englishman named Captain Jones. The maharaja could bask in the locals' idolization but Captain Jones, a modest little man in a small office down a side street, and a most proficient servant of the British Empire, looked after everything perfectly.

There was more filming at Benares on the Ganges, the great holy river where millions of devout Hindus bathe in the sacred waters hoping to be cured of their ills. Those who don't survive their illnesses are publicly cremated downstream on wooden pyres. I photographed the ceremony as we passed by boat, braving the fury of the men who set the corpse alight by his holy ponytail.

Finally we drove all the way to Darjeeling, seven thousand feet up, on the borders of Tibet, and marvelled at the sight from our bedroom window of the reeling majesty of Mount Everest. Von Keller actually hoped to organize a party to make our way up it, but mercifully it was the wrong time of the year and we drove back to Bombay to sail home.

5

Technicolor Goes to War

In the summer of 1939 I was in Sicily working contentedly on a commercial for Cadbury's milk chocolate. It seemed a long way from the machinations of Hitler and the inexorable advent of war.

One evening after work I was having a drink in the town square with a Sicilian colleague and was introduced to a quiet, respectable-looking man with grey hair and glasses who could have been a bank clerk.

In fact, this ordinary-looking man was Lucky Luciano, one of the most famous gangsters in the history of crime. I wondered why he was sitting comfortably in a Sicilian café instead of being in an American jail. I learned later that while serving a ten-year sentence in the States he had been deported to Sicily to help organize the Mafia to destroy Fascism in Italy.

We chatted for a while. His manner was courteous and friendly. I stared at him, fascinated. It was hard to believe that this disarmingly modest man had been responsible for the drug-induced suffering of so many people.

A church bell chimed six. Lucky smiled and said easily: 'You must excuse me, I have to report to the police station at this time. Arrivederci.' And he walked away. I looked after him. Arrivederci? Not bloody likely.

The gentle bucolic ambience of a farm just outside Sardinia was shattered when our production assistant brought a telegram from Technicolor ordering me to return to England immediately with the Technicolor camera as war was imminent. 'Bring the camera at all costs, even if you have to jettison the rest of the equipment.'

This posed a problem. Our Italian production manager, Blazio, had left £2,000 as security with the Italian customs which he would recover when the camera equipment was checked out through the normal channels. This usually took a few days, but we couldn't wait that long in the circumstances. It looked like the Italian production company would lose their deposit.

Blazio was adamant. He stuttered quite a bit which made him hard to understand – especially when he spoke Italian – but we got the message. We could not take the camera away with us, it must go through customs.

There was only one thing to do. Chris Challis and I decided on a secret night departure. Blazio was very nervous that evening and watched us suspiciously until we retired for the night. At 3.00 a.m. we crept out of the hotel carrying the heavy camera, having secretly arranged for a car to collect us just round the corner.

Perhaps Blazio couldn't sleep that night. He must have looked into our bedroom for he scurried out of the hotel in full chase. A cops-and-robbers comedy ensued, with Chris and I speeding through villages and Blazio hot on our trail.

Somehow we gave him the slip. I believe he was sure we would use our air tickets from Sardinia and when he lost track of us, he headed for the airport, but Chris and I went to the docks instead and luckily we were able to sail away on a small boat to Marseilles. Poor Blazio. Still, I expect he got his money back in the end.

At Marseilles railway station we ran into trouble at customs but Chris, who was in the Territorial Army reserves, declared he was an army officer (showing his membership card) and that I was his batman; the two of us had orders to go unhindered to England. Somehow they believed us and we travelled by train to London with our precious baggage.

During the war the voluptuous Technicolor camera, bred in Hollywood's dream factory, was used surprisingly often by the army, navy, and air force. It was found to be useful for camouflage, for instance. I did a lot of photographing of secret sites from small planes, showing camouflage from the air. Technicolor was also used on military manoeuvres, target practice on ships, and many other war-time activities.

One of my less-pleasant experiences was facing heavy-calibre machine-gun fire, set up to miss my camera by a few inches. I was protected, of course, by thick steel sheets, but to face heavy bullets coming towards me and penetrating a thick railway sleeper with the occasional nerve-shattering and very loud near miss was uncomfortable, to say the least.

Of the many revolting horrors of war, those who suffered terrible disfigurement by bombs in the Blitz were the most despairingly sad. Sir Harold Gillies was doing wonderful work in plastic surgery, repairing and reshaping faces half blown away or mutilated beyond description. I had to go down to Basingstoke where Gillies was performing these miracles to record, in picture and sound, various stages of his work.

It was difficult for me to keep composed, seeing such dreadful disfigurement. Those who described their experiences were fascinating examples of triumph over tragedy.

There was a young girl of about sixteen whose face was half blown away and who now had several new features, including a nose taken from the flesh of her back, and nostrils and new eyebrows taken from her scalp. Other parts of her face were patches of skin lifted from her body.

The touching part of it all was the complete faith they all had in Sir Harold Gillies. The young girl was cheerfully saying how lucky she was to have such wonderful surgery; everything was going well and she was looking forward to going out to parties again and meeting boyfriends soon.

How could anyone tell her that in spite of Gillies' brilliant expertise, it would take more years than she realized before she could look the way she imagined? For technical reasons her eyebrows were half an inch wide; her face looked like a wax model that had melted in intense heat.

A little boy of seven had lost most of his arm. Several inches of open bone had been left as Gillies was going to graft a part of the boy's body flesh on to this bone. And there he was, cheerfully waving his little arm with the naked bone sticking out, like a half-eaten chicken.

My assistant on this macabre photography was Jimmy Wright. He was only nineteen and the horrible injuries made him physically ill. Shortly after this there was a most incredibly tragic twist of fate.

Jimmy was unusually good looking, with delicate features, gentle brown eyes and wavy black hair. He could have been a young film star, but his fervent ambition was to join the Royal Air Force in which his father had been a distinguished officer in the First World War. Jimmy was too young when the second war started, but soon after he managed to join up and train to be a combat pilot. His plane was hit by enemy fire and Jimmy was terribly burned, losing his sight and most of his face.

He was transferred to Basingstoke for long-term plastic surgery. After the war, Jimmy often visited us on film sets. Sir Harold had done all he could, but he couldn't make new eyes.

Western Approaches was to be a prestigious war film as a tribute to the Merchant Navy. The Crown film unit was in charge of this documentary-style film. It was to be done in Technicolor, which had never been used before by the British government.

It sounded exciting and I hoped fervently that I would be asked to photograph it, but the Crown film unit had their own cameramen so I didn't think it likely. Luckily for me, none of the cameramen had any experience of Technicolor and I was assigned to the film.

It had a dramatic story. Survivors of a torpedoed merchant ship spend fourteen days in a lifeboat in the Atlantic. One of the seamen is wounded in the head. A German U-boat has spotted the lifeboat, having picked up its distress signals. Realizing that the signals might bring a British ship to rescue the lifeboat crew, the U-boat commander decides to wait underneath.

A merchant ship is seen on the distant horizon and the lifeboat crew fire distress rockets while the men gaze at the ship in happy expectation. A wounded seaman sees a periscope right nearby and shouts a warning but the crew thinks he is delirious. A tortured debate follows. The captain decides that it is possible a U-boat is underneath them and they might be used as a decoy. He tries to signal the ship, reflecting a biscuit tin in the sun. He is only partly successful. The ship dodges the first torpedo, but the second torpedo hits her.

The ship's master orders his crew to the boats, but he remains concealed with his gunner on board. The U-boat commander, believing the ship abandoned, surfaces to finish her off with explosives, but the captain rakes the U-boat with machine-gun fire. In the duel which follows, the gunner is killed but the U-boat is sunk. The story is fictional, but all the cast were men of the Allied navies.

The director was Pat Jackson. Young, intelligent, and with much courage as I was about to see. We became fast friends, and are to the present day. The film was scheduled for six weeks. It took over a year and was the most despairingly difficult ordeal I have ever known.

We started with the lifeboat sequence and this alone took six months. Our base was at Holyhead in Wales. The scenes were all with sound, of course, but the idea of using our Technicolor sound blimp in a lifeboat was comical. (To those who have never seen a Technicolor blimp, I need only compare it to a four-foot by three steel safe for the joke to be apparent.) We had to use an auxiliary one-piece lightweight blimp; for the most trifling operations and adjustments the whole thing had to be removed – fiddly enough on land, but well-nigh impossible at sea in a rolling lifeboat.

Everything about this film had to be authentic. Studio requisites like make-up, model shots, matte shots, etc. were anathema to the documentary world. It had to be a real lifeboat, a real sea and bona fide seamen.

There were countless problems to overcome, but at last we went to sea to start work. In our lifeboat were crammed the director, myself, my assistant, the sound man, script girl, camera and sound gear, portable radio transmitter, water barrel, boxes of sandwiches for the day, and a flapping sail which swung murderously around when you least expected it. And one other item: twenty-two merchant seamen. All this every day for six months!

Our lifeboat was towed by a massive drifter. Charlie, our sound recordist, was the only one not in the lifeboat. He was ensconced deep down in the hold of the drifter with his equipment. Like the lifeboat, the drifter rolled about all day and Charlie, not the best of sailors, had to have a bucket by his side constantly.

Sea-sickness soon became a deadly burden. Even some of the veteran seamen were sea-sick at times and most of us went through the ghastly misery of nausea every day. The Irish Sea in winter was really rough. Our crowded lifeboat would bob up and down like a ping-pong ball. Sometimes, the lifeboat looked as though a machine-gun had raked the crew. Every wretched victim would hang inert over the side, heaving spasmodically like captured fish in a net. Our director, Pat, was one of the heaven blessed – he was never sick – but it must have been unimaginably difficult for him when so many were pathetically *hors de combat*.

I was regularly sea-sick while looking at my camera to check that nothing except sea and sky were in my picture, for we were supposed to be in the Atlantic, thousands of miles from land – difficult enough in the Irish Sea in war-time, with ceaseless convoys, aeroplanes, thousands of seagulls, buoys, mine-sweepers and, most ridiculous of all, hundreds of thousands of oranges which were floating around us from a ship that had been torpedoed! Another headache was weather continuity; trying to intercut bright blue skies and radiant sun with stormy skies and dull winter light that made our seamen unrecognizable silhouettes. I was forced to rig up a couple of small lights in the packet boat using a small generator in the drifter so that we could at least recognize faces.

We tried shooting out of sequence, letting the weather dictate that day's action. This worked until beards started to grow, providing another continuity headache. The seamen were supposed to be adrift for fourteen days with beards growing up to an inch long, so if we were forced by weather to shoot an early sequence, the seamen had to be shaven clean, and their chins smudged with dirt until their beards had grown again.

There were hardly any sunny days that winter. I made an interesting experiment. We had to shoot an important close-up of the captain which had to match a sunny sequence already shot. There had to be bright sun and a blue sky, but in December it was raining thinly under a leaden sky; the sun was behind dense clouds. One of my lamps was incandescent (i.e. orange). The lamp had a blue filter to correct it to daylight. I took the filter off so the captain's face was bathed in a very orange light. Now I over-exposed the negative which bleached the grey sky into white, and instructed the Technicolor laboratories to correct the orange light by printing it much bluer and, hey presto, the overcast sky became a bright blue and the captain's face healthily sunlit. This technique paid dividends since it meant we didn't always have to wait for correct weather conditions.

Although our camera equipment was covered with waterproof canvas, salt water and the salt atmosphere permeated everywhere, corroding viciously. Nearly every day the pungent smell of smoke from our cables and plugs shorting meant that we had to dry the connections with matches or lighters or clean them under a waterproof cover while spray splashed derisively.

The camera's prism had to be set to a fraction of an inch, so it was with tense caution that we placed it into the camera, trying to keep a perfect balance while doing so. This meticulous operation was a sight to be remembered in a lifeboat on stormy seas, and reloading the camera with fresh film was always a nightmare when the lifeboat was rolling about wildly, throwing gallons of water over us as we staggered drunkenly about, lifting off the sound blimp and threading up the film somehow under a flapping tarpaulin.

One day everything went perfectly from the start. The weather was right, and so was the sea, the wind, and all the rest of the ever-changing conditions. It was so perfect that it was all rather uncanny. Our nautical gremlins must have taken the day off. I checked the light reading from my photometer and set my exposure smugly. One rehearsal and the actor seamen were magnificent. Pat Jackson and I looked at each other a little nervously. Drawing a deep breath Pat said, 'It's too good to be true. Let's put the sail up.' We both grasped the halyard and pulled exuberantly until the sail billowed gustily in the breeze; we hung on until it was made fast by a seaman. Suddenly, the mast snapped loose at the base and the sail and mast were blown over into the sea with Pat and I clinging to it over the side in dazed bewilderment. We went back for the day in silence with set faces.

Being towed in a stormy sea was also not without the possibility of sudden catastrophe. On one occasion our lifeboat was swept savagely round, crashing into the side of the rearing drifter and very nearly underneath it.

At one stage the seamen were on the verge of mutiny. One in particular, who was always making trouble, threatened to beat up Pat Jackson unless we returned to port but Pat courageously stood up to him, and the mutiny was quelled.

One day we received permission from the Admiralty to use a German submarine which had just been captured intact. 'But only for one hour', we were told. All Pat Jackson wanted was to see the submarine emerge from the sea for a few moments. A simple enough shot, we said. With Royal Naval efficiency, an exact sea rendezvous was made for the following day. The German submarine was to come to the surface at a precise longitude and latitude so all we had to do was station our drifter ready to photograph the Nazi sub as it surfaced. I was set up with my camera well in advance of zero hour, which was 11.00 a.m. precisely.

As the clocks counted down the seconds to zero we were holding our breath with tension. More seconds, then minutes ticked by, and no submarine. The sea was rolling quite a bit so I had to be ready to adjust my viewpoint, although we had instructions to be pointing to ultra-fine compass exactitude.

Still no submarine. The skipper of our drifter began pacing nervously about the deck muttering, in a thick Yorkshire accent, 'Ah don't like this. Ah don't like this at all. Ah don't.' And suddenly the submarine rose out of the sea, not hundreds of yards away as planned but only a couple of feet. I had the impression it would scrape the paint off our drifter. It was a shrieking nightmare. This gigantic mass of sea-dripping metal – twice the size of our rolling drifter – rearing up high above us on a huge wave, and so very close, amid screams of panic. Then the submarine thundered down in the wave and nose-dived under the sea. We never saw it again.

We didn't get permission to use another submarine until just before the end of our shooting when we were able to have another Nazi submarine for a whole day.

In this scene we had to show the Nazis (our own seamen dressed in German uniforms) jumping into the sea from the sinking submarine which had just been shelled. Much against the creed of documentary realism, we later shot the interior of the submarine as a set at Pinewood studios.

To simulate the submarine sinking the commander had to set his sub at the most acute diving angle possible and then stop the dive, leaving the stern just out of the water. My Technicolor camera was tied on to the extreme tip of the stern – and I was operating it!

The commander had declared positively that he could arrest the dive at an exact depth so that the camera would show the submarine apparently sinking, and then he would stop the dive with the stern safely three feet above sea level.

I had to believe him. I didn't even ask him if his brakes were in good order. I turned the camera. The Nazi seamen jumped from the doomed submarine as it sank from view under the sea. It was a great shot, but the commander was two feet out in his calculations. The sea nearly engulfed my camera, stopping one inch under the lens and right up to my anxiously stretched neck. But it really was a great scene.

That, mercifully, was the end of the lifeboat saga.

The one sequence we had to shoot at Pinewood Studio was not entirely without mishap. We had to show the interior of the stricken submarine with water bursting in and the panicking Germans trying to escape. The submarine was built in a large water tank fifteen feet deep. My idea was to put the camera in a small wooden booth with a glass window to shoot through, which would be placed in the tank and show, just above water level, the seamen engulfed in the water; then I could wind the camera down on a unipod to show the seamen under the water.

It was calculated that several heavy weights must be placed on the base of the booth to equalize the buoyancy. With the tank half-full of water, the booth was lowered into the submarine, but we found it was still too buoyant. We kept putting more weights into the booth until I could only operate my camera with crushed difficulty, but there was still too much buoyancy.

In the end, heavy planks were laid across the top of the open booth and several stalwart stagehands stood on them. At last we shot the scene. And what a scene it was, the German seamen threshing about above the water, then, as the water rose, I turned the handle of the unipod so that the camera descended until we were shooting through the water seeing the seamen struggling for their lives. The assistant director called 'lunch' and then the drama – or rather, the bathos – occurred. The stagehands walked off the planks. The booth leaned over majestically, then toppled right over on its side, immediately immersing our priceless Technicolor camera and myself eight feet under water.

I had a certain difficulty extricating myself from the weights which had slid across the booth, but even as I surfaced several of the crew had dived in to help unscrew the camera from the unipod and bring it out of the water. It was several minutes before the camera was brought out, placed in a bath of oil, then rushed to Technicolor to be taken to pieces. Luckily, no harm was done. More extraordinary, the exposed film in the magazine, which of course was soaked in water, was developed and found to be quite unharmed.

Now came the big stuff, photographing the convoy of merchant ships crossing the Atlantic, and the battle between our cargo ship and the U-boat. Being a government film we had no difficulty getting permission to join a convoy going to New York. There were over a hundred ships in the convoy. It was a glorious sight.

I had to use a different camera for this trip. There were only four Technicolor cameras in Europe at that time, and with U-boats lurking all over the Atlantic, using Technicolor was too big a risk. Instead I took a single-film camera called a Monopack, which was much inferior to Technicolor, having a decidedly blue bias necessitating correction in the lab.

Shooting the Atlantic sequence was quite a different adventure. From working in the confined space of the lifeboat, we were now on an enormous cargo ship with only three of us; Pat, Denny Densham (my new assistant) and myself, operating. We worked newsreel style, showing the vast armada ploughing through the Atlantic rollers, and this time it was real. We knew U-boats could always attack to prevent merchant ships from bringing vital supplies from America, and that kept the adrenalin flowing.

Half-way to New York we had to photograph our own merchant ship alone in the Atlantic and we slowed down to let the convoy get ahead out of sight. A light cruiser escorted us and when we had shot our scene we had a message from the cruiser's commander to come over for a drink. A launch took us over and we climbed on board. It was exhilarating to see at close hand such bristling efficiency. It was packed with men (there were 800 on board) showing the powerful sinews of a Royal Navy ship in war-time. The bustling energy, rapped commands as seamen worked on their gun equipment, the roving radar, messages being sent – it was all highly uplifting.

The officers welcomed us cordially. It was all evocative of Noël Coward's *In Which We Serve*. They were calm, cheerful and intelligent, and had that indefinable British sly sense of humour. We had our drinks, said our goodbyes, and were launched back on our cargo ship. Some days later, we were told that this cruiser had been torpedoed and sunk, with all hands lost. The shock was close to that of losing a relative. I still think about it after all these years.

This was my first time in New York. It was the stuff of dreams to see the cloud-capped skyscrapers and so many lights everywhere – more poignant after the black-out of war-time Britain.

The *New York Times* recorded our arrival on its front page. A whiff of fame perhaps, but hardly for me. The caption underneath the picture stated: 'Pat Jackson, the director, with one of the seamen . . .'

Anyway, the few days in New York were a whiff of rapture. To say that the natives were friendly is an understatement. We were invited – sometimes by strangers – for a drink or to parties, perhaps as curiosities from war-ravaged Europe, but it was most pleasant. Someone would come up to us at a party; 'I make hats: what size is your wife's head?' and next morning there would be a box of hats sent as a present. This happened with perfume and even silk stockings.

We sailed home from New York early one evening, and watched the myriad lights sink deeper into the black night. This time our great convoy – 110 ships – was packed with incredible cargo: trains, tanks, explosives – an awesome floating arsenal. We were told that cases of fourteen-inch shells were right underneath our cabins. I reflected that if a torpedo hit us there would be a spectacular firework display. In my small cabin – made even smaller by boxes of presents – Denny and I started to load fresh film. At 9.30 p.m., Denny and I were still busy loading film when there was a loud hammering on my door and a voice shouting something in a thick Irish brogue. This had to be Paddy, a young Irish seaman who often gave us morsels of news gathered by the ship's radio together with the latest rumours. 'Go away Paddy,' we yelled, 'we're loading film, come back later!' but the hammering and the inarticulate shouting continued, much to our annoyance, as we were in complete darkness with valuable film in our hands.

Then we heard a dull, but very powerful explosion and knew what Paddy had been trying to tell us. We hastily jammed the film back into a tin and unlocked the door. Outside, although late at night, the sky was a brilliant glaring red like an overdone sunset. We saw in stark horror a ship close on our port quarter ablaze and rolling over on its side with its cargo of tanks toppling into the sea as the ship sank. There were many bodies in the water. Another ship passed terrifyingly close to us turning help-lessly in circles as its rudders had been blown away. This wasn't a scene in a movie. This was real and quite terrible. What had happened, we found out later, was that the ship in front of us had been torpedoed and was heading, out of control, straight towards us. Our captain had yelled 'hard to starboard' and this immediate response saved us from colliding.

Four ships were sunk that night and over a hundred lives lost. I photographed what I could, although we couldn't use it in our film. It was sent to the Admiralty instead. The entire convoy kept going at full speed. If ships had slowed down, they would have been sitting targets for the U-boats; the survivors in the sea were rescued by the escorting cruisers who had also been dropping depth charges all around us – and these were also terrifying as they made an extremely loud smacking noise below the ship's waterline.

The depth charges were frequent from then on and every time we came under attack, which was quite stomach churning. Denny and I slept in our clothes that night (although I don't suppose it would have helped much if a torpedo had made our acquaintance) and continued to do so until we reached England, feeling we had awakened from a bad dream. Then I realized how foolish I was. We had made only this one trip, but the merchant seamen were doing it every few days, always with the strong possibility of being blown to oblivion. They were the real heroes.

The final weeks' shooting were by no means easier. We went on various warships all over the Mediterranean to get more real action. Sometimes we were in very old ships loaned to England by President Roosevelt on lease lend. They were known as 'four stackers' which rolled and lurched almost as much as our lifeboat had done.

It crossed my mind that the lifeboat sequence seemed cosy by comparison with recent horrors but no, not even the threat of being blown in pieces was as soul destroying as that lifeboat. One of the lifeboat seamen had said, quite seriously, that he would rather be torpedoed and really be adrift in a lifeboat than have that experience again.

1 My father on stage. At a command performance King Edward gave him a cigar saying, 'The entertainment was capital. I have never seen dancing like that in my life.'

2 Could there be such a thing as a glamorous angel? Well, my mother was one.

3 Typical stage 'pros' on tour. My father holds me in the front row and my mother is immediately behind.

4 The seaside al frescos were in between shows. I am sitting to the left of my ebony-faced father.

5 My first film as a camera assistant aged fourteen.
Yes, cameramen did wear caps back to front in those days!
The woman in the centre is Anna May Wong.

6 The crew enjoyed Marlene Dietrich being naked in the bath
almost as much as she did.

7 Marlene learnt much about photography from Joseph von Sternberg.
Here she is watching a rehearsal through my camera.

8 Petra, before package tours, was an arduous journey, mostly on horseback. No cosy hotels sixty years ago; only tents and scorpions.

9 *Western Approaches*. We filmed in this lifeboat every aching day
for six months. Most of us were seasick all the time.

10 Pat Jackson and I swore we wouldn't shave until the end of *Western
Approaches*. This picture was on the front page of the *New York Times*
with the caption: 'Pat Jackson, the director, with one of the seamen.'

11 With Michael Powell on location.

12 Setting up on *A Matter of Life and Death* (*Stairway to Heaven* in America). Note the enormous Technicolor camera.

13 Doing some wild camera movement on *The Red Shoes*.

14 I was noted for my frequent huddles with players during which
I would explain my photographic problems. Crouched beside my
Technicolor camera, here I am chatting with stars
Robert Helpmann, Moira Shearer and Leonide Massine.

15 Accepting my Oscar for *Black Narcissus*
from Jean Hearsholt and J. Arthur Rank.

6

Technicolor Adventures – Interiors

When a film unit has finished the main shooting on a set, any odd, unimportant bits left to shoot – a close-up of a cigarette smudged in an ashtray, a letter – all these dreary minutiae are left to be done later, by a very small crew, perhaps only the cameraman and his assistant. It's obviously expensive to have a highly paid film crew hanging about while a visiting card is being photographed, so these little extras are left for the humble.

It was achingly dull work – like housemaid's chores, sweeping the crumbs off the table after the great feast.

But I was employed by Technicolor and this was a job to do. I had a lot of photographic experience behind me, but mostly exteriors, and there's a wide gulf between exteriors – where Nature has already set the lights – and interiors, which call for sound knowledge of light and the creative use of it. I already knew, from my work on 'Handle' and the odd lighting jobs I had had on commercials, that I could succeed as a lighting cameraman on a big feature. The problem was convincing others I could do it.

Michael Powell was nearly finished with *Colonel Blimp* and I was doing inserts for this picture on another, tiny, stage. This particular insert was more interesting than usual. It was a drawing-room wall, on which there was a collection of stuffed animal heads, all with large branches of horns. It was difficult to light without casting multiple shadows, and I spent more time than usual arranging the lights.

Looking through the camera, I heard a voice say 'Interesting', and there was the great Michael Powell gazing quizzically at the animal heads, one arm propping up his chin. Was his attitude thoughtful or critical? He turned slowly to me and said, with a kind of casual politeness: 'Would you like to photograph my next picture?'

I tried to hide an enormous gulp. 'I'd like that very much, Mr Powell.' 'Right,' he said briskly, 'we start shooting in six months.' And he was off, striding quickly off the stage. My excitement faded rapidly. In six months he would have forgotten all about it.

Several months later, I was in Egypt working the exterior second unit on *Caesar and Cleopatra*. I wasn't brimming over with happiness. The work was dull and routine, endless shots of sullen Egyptian soldiers, made to dress up in ancient Coptic costumes, and I kept thinking of the dream Michael Powell had fashioned which had now faded like the mirages seen every day in the shimmering desert heat. I was also going through the misery of gyppy tummy.

In my hotel room I had the irrepressible urge to vent my feelings. I strode to the open window and bellowed out at the top of my voice: 'Fuuuccckkk Egypt!' After a few seconds, an unmistakably British voice wafted up from a window below: 'I say, did you say Fuck Egypt?' 'Yes,' I grated. 'Yes, I did.' 'What a good idea,' the voice ascended. 'Let's shout it together, shall we, one, two, three,' – and the unknown voice and mine combined in a fortissimo yell that flung our feelings out into the moonless night.

Now more windows were opening, with increasing enthusiasm for a more concerted effort. In moments the anonymous voices had multiplied to about twenty, and our combined cathartic bawl must have been heard on the other side of Cairo. Next morning I received a cable from Michael Powell: 'Where the hell are you? We start in four weeks. Regards Michael Powell.'

Phew! Had my anguished howl from my hotel window sped like a psychic telegram to him? I was able to get permission to return to England immediately, leaving the remaining work to Ted Scaife, and there I was, on my first big feature film, as chief cameraman. It was indeed a watershed. There is no doubt, I owe my career and subsequent success to Michael Powell.

However, it wasn't that easy to get my big break. Michael had to make what he calls in his memoirs 'a painful decision': he had wanted his cameraman Erwin Hillier (who had made such a triumph on *A Canterbury Tale*) to share the photography of *A Matter of Life and Death* with me – which also meant sharing the credit. Erwin had asked for a couple of days to think it over. At the same time, Michael had asked me whether I would work with Erwin on the same terms. I agreed, but Erwin declined so, as Michael writes, 'I gave the whole job to Jack.'

So this was my big break at last, and a paradox: I had worked for Technicolor for ten years and had more experience of the problems posed with Technicolor than anyone else in Europe, yet this was my first major feature film.

And what an exciting first feature to photograph! There were huge, wonderful sets to light. The 'Stairway to Heaven' (its title in America) was a towering engine-driven escalator which had taken three months to build, with a hundred massive steps, each twenty feet wide.

Quite early on, I had said casually to Michael Powell, 'Of course heaven will be in colour, won't it?' And Michael replied, 'No. Heaven will be in black and white.' He could see I was startled, and grinned: 'Because everyone will expect heaven to be in colour, I'm doing it in black and white.' Then I asked him, 'Michael, do you make films for all types of audiences, or just for yourself?' Michael shook his head vigorously. 'I make films for myself. What I express I hope most people will understand. For the rest, well, that's their problem.'

So here I was, not daring to tell anyone I had never photographed in black and white before, and faced with having to create great aurora borealis effects in a heaven (a colossal set) that seemed to stretch to infinity – it was in fact a hundred yards long – with great pinnacles of rock where the counsels faced each other, surrounded by thousands of extras.

No one could have had a better environment for his first big film. Michael Powell had a powerful team around him. Alfred Junge was one of the most accomplished art directors in the world and his department shimmered with artistic talent, including the costume designer Hein Heckroth, who was later to triumph as the production director of *The Red Shoes*. My operator was Geoff Unsworth, and my focus puller was Chris Challis, a staunch friend from the travelogue years who became another top cameraman. In fact, Chris had already photographed a black and white feature film for Michael Powell, *The End of the River*. Understandably, Chris was disconcerted at being downgraded to focus puller, but I persuaded him. 'Chris, you know Micky and he knows you. I bet you anything you'll be promoted in no time at all.' And he was. Within a few weeks he was photographing the second unit. Later he photographed a film I directed, *The Long Ships*.

Right from the beginning I realized that Michael was a cameraman's dream. He nearly always accepted any ideas I put forward with enthusiastic support. He very rarely dithered or had doubts about things. Like all good minds he possessed a nervous vitality. He hardly ever just walked; quite often he leapt, or took great strides. If a problem arose he would cradle his arms, ponder deeply for a few moments than pronounce his decision with utter finality – before leaping away.

Working with him, I was able to use colour ideas I hadn't been able to use before. For instance, in one scene David Niven and Kim Hunter are playing table tennis. An officer from heaven appears and magically freezes the scene so he can talk to David as time stands still.

I usually use an amber filter on arc-light sunshine as the carbon arcs are too blue. But on this occasion I used a lemon filter – unreal, of course – but it created the magical atmosphere the scene was meant to have.

Sometimes I had to combat the dictates of Alfred Junge who was a little autocratic, wanting me to light the set his way. I respected him as a great art director but I wanted to do it my way and I succeeded in this, although Alfred certainly kept me on my toes.

David Niven was great fun to work with. He was a bracing raconteur with richly funny stories of his career in Hollywood. He told me of the time he played Edgar Linton in *Wuthering Heights*. His wife Cathy (Merle Oberon) was dying and David had to bend over the bed and cry in close-up.

'I can't do that,' he said. 'I never cry. It's impossible.' The director told David not to worry, there was no problem; the make-up man would place a little menthol in his nose, and all he had to do was strain slightly and his eyes would flow with tears.

This was done. The camera rolled, and David bent over and strained. And strained harder. Suddenly a glutinous green clot flew from his nose on to the dead Cathy who was suddenly resurrected with a piercing scream.

David frequently talked of two directors he had worked with: the inimitable Micky Curtiz, the Hungarian director of fractured English, who on *The Charge of the Light Brigade* gave the order to 'Bring on the empty horses' (which David used as the title for a volume of his autobiography), and the Russian director Gregory Ratoff, who also had fractured English.

I was to meet Ratoff years later when he ruined my blossoming friendship with Maria Callas. He had phoned me in great excitement. He planned to film the opera *Carmen*, Maria Callas was considering the lead role, but she felt nervous about the way she would look on screen. Everyone knew that nature had been rather over-generous with her nose, although I thought she had great character in her face. Ratoff told her he would get Jack Cardiff to photograph her which would prove how good she would look on film. She agreed and I was invited to have dinner with her, which was a huge success. I felt it was the beginning of a warm friendship and she even told me she was going to send me some special recordings of her operas.

I made the test at the Technicolor laboratories to keep it all secret and the result was excellent. I was sure she would be happy. Maria had already left for Rome so Ratoff – who was delighted with the test – left immediately to show it to her. He phoned me in London telling me she liked the test, but his next statement took my breath away. He had told Maria, 'Jack says that all you have to do now is to have an operation on your nose and everything will be fine.'

I was furious. I had never said a word about her nose and told Ratoff what I thought of him. 'Don't worry Jack,' said Ratoff, 'she'll do it for you, she likes you very much.' Of course I never heard from her again.

Black Narcissus was next on Michael Powell's list and this time there was no question about me photographing it. *A Matter of Life and Death* had been a big success. It was the first film to be chosen as the royal command film and in America it was also among the top ten best-photographed films of that year.

The story of *Black Narcissus* concerns an order of British nuns stationed in Calcutta who travel to a remote village high in the Himalayas, and open a school and hospital in an old Indian palace. The palace had originally been used by a libertine Raj to house his concubines, and the paintings on the walls bore witness to the erotic life enjoyed there.

The Himalayan wind blows constantly, day and night. The wind and the altitude have a disturbing psychological effect on the nuns who bravely fight these problems, but in the end it is the sheer pagan beauty of their environment that defeats them. After one of the nuns goes insane and dies, they return to Calcutta.

Alfred Junge was again the art director and Hein Heckroth the costume designer. The cast was interesting: Deborah Kerr, David Farrar, Sabu, Jean Simmons, Flora Robson, and Kathleen Byron.

Naturally, we all expected to go on location to India and were greatly surprised when Micky told us that the entire film would be made at Pinewood Studios, with the exception of just one day of exteriors at Horsham in Sussex, where there was a garden filled with sub-tropical plants and trees. It was a wise decision. It gave us greater control. With Junge's sets and backings, and the magic of 'Poppa' Day's matte paintings, there were many more artistic opportunities unencumbered by the usual problems on a far-off location. The great Poppa Day looked quite venerable with his long white hair and steel glasses, but he was truly a wizard with painted glass mattes for all kinds of trick photography. His work on this film was so realistic, I'm sure many people thought it was my photography, and perhaps I wouldn't have got the Oscar if they had known Poppa Day had painted the beautiful matte shots!

Micky agreed emphatically with me that the nuns shouldn't have any facial make-up. It would obviously look ridiculous, particularly lipstick. How many times have we seen Joan of Arc or Mary Magdalene with lurid eyeshadow, artificial eyelashes, plucked eyebrows and bright red lipstick. Funnily enough, some of the nuns' natural lip colour appeared too red in Technicolor and I had to ask for their lips to be toned down with flesh colours to make them look natural.

Many film people don't realize that when *Black Narcissus* was made in 1946, most of my lamps were arcs, even the smallest of which was big and unwieldy. Incandescent lamps are small enough to be hidden behind a table or chair, but to hide an arc lamp was out of the question. For candle effects or small table-lamps, a soft 'inkie' was easily adaptable to create an illusion, but an arc light had to be heavily diffused with tracing paper and the dimmer shutters used to get any sort of an effect. Then there was the arc light's smoke and its noise, because of which ninety per cent of our interior shooting had to be dubbed.

Still, the hard arc lighting certainly helped to suggest the crystal-clear mountain light, and the dramatic atmosphere needed for this fabulous Himalayan world.

One of my main worries were the backdrops seen through the windows. No matter how beautifully they were painted, it was asking a lot to expect a perfect realistic effect, especially when they were sometimes only twenty feet away from the camera. I suggested to Alfred Junge that we try photographic backings. In those days these were not used in colour films. They were only available in black and white and made by huge enlargements from a 10 × 8 still camera. Alfred agreed, but wanted to paint lightly over them. Here I disagreed and managed to convince him that pastel chalk rubbed in small quantities over the black and white print would hint at colour rather than intrude. It worked; we rubbed blue pastel in the sky and various ochres in the mountain shadows, letting the body of the print make the illusion. It really did look like a real exterior.

Michael Powell was right behind me, always. In order to enhance the dreamlike strangeness and sensuous beauty of the nuns' environment I exaggerated my effects, sometimes using more blue than usual in the shadows; in the dawn sequence where Sister Ruth goes mad I used soft greens in the shadows, not only because this coolness is always evident at dawn, but because the juxtaposition of green and red is uncomfortable and suggestive of tragedy – like Van Gogh's billiard room at Arles.

When we shot the exterior dawn sequence in which Sister Ruth falls to her death from the precipice of the palace, Michael insisted it must actually be shot at dawn. At that time Pinewood had a Works Committee who vetted everything we did for greater efficiency. The Committee was absolutely against us shooting an exterior at dawn, saying the English weather was unreliable at such an early hour, but Micky overrode them. The Committee reluctantly agreed, with veiled threats about what would happen if we lost a day's shooting.

But the gamble held a darker threat than the Committee's. It was Deborah Kerr's last contractual day. If we had to shoot an extra day with Deborah, it would have cost a lot of money and the Committee's caution would have been gleefully justified.

The day dawned beautifully. The sun came up with an indulgent flush and we blessed our luck. Just before we shot the first scene I suggested using a fog filter to help the dawn effect, and Michael agreed at once. Fog filters were never used in Technicolor in those days. I was still an *enfant terrible* who used all the effects, filters and lights which were taboo – but I saw no reason why I shouldn't make a slightly misty dawn.

We shot the dramatic scene with Deborah and it looked great. Next day there was a phone call from Technicolor. They said everything we'd shot at dawn was no good and should be retaken without the fog filter. They were coming over with the rushes right away. I felt very sick as we sat in the theatre and the rushes started. Apart from letting Micky down, this could be the end of my career. Micky was quiet and polite with the Technicolor chiefs who had come over specially for this disaster; I knew he had so much to lose if the scenes had to be retaken. The moment the first scenes came on the screen, I felt a rush of relief. They were good. They were bloody good.

Micky's voice came clearly over the rushes: 'Marvellous Jack, well done.' There were tears in my eyes in the dark. The relief! When the lights went up Micky spoke in that tone I knew so well: a calm, casual flippancy that belied his anger. He told Technicolor that what he had seen was just what he wanted: why on earth had they made such a fuss?

The big-wigs were worried that my fog effect would seem out of focus in some cinemas, particularly drive-in cinemas in the States. 'Rubbish,' said Michael. 'Black and white films have had much heavier diffusion than this for years and no cinema has complained. You really must allow Technicolor to have some art.'

There was one moment during filming when one of my bright ideas caused a whole scene to be axed, and how deeply I regret it.

The final scene of the film takes place in the Mother Superior's study in Calcutta with Deborah explaining why their mission had failed. It was a great scene. Deborah, sitting upright, speaks with calm self-control and a kind of cold dignity, telling the Mother Superior of the many difficulties of the Himalayan environment – the constant wind, the altitude, the resistance of the villagers . . .

Nancy Roberts, who played the old Mother Superior, had a wonderful face. Lined with a long life of experience and closeness to God, she sits still as a sphinx as she listens. Deborah hardly glances up as she talks but, towards the end, she falters a little and looks at the grim old face to see there a smile of compassion and understanding.

That does it. Deborah breaks down completely, sobbing her heart out, and the real reasons of failure are wrenched from her in a painful catharsis. The erotic beauty of the place; how she remembered the man she loved in Ireland, how she loved him, but he went away. The Mother Superior embraces the sobbing Sister Deborah like a child. She had feared for her cold-hearted control; now she knows Sister Deborah is a vulnerable human being. Fade out; end of picture.

Not only was it a wonderful scene, it was my best photography on the entire film. The Indian rains had come and ran in rivulets down the panes of glass. My lighting was close to black and white and the shadows of the rain on the windows ran all over the walls and on the taut faces of the women; the shadows were hard and black. Micky was delighted, so was I, yet this entire scene was cut out of the film!

Ironically, I was responsible. One of the very last scenes we shot was the rains starting, as the nuns slowly go away on mules. There were huge rhubarb leaves around us and I had the brilliant idea to have a close-up of a leaf on which just one drop of rain fell, then more and more until the rains pelted down as we tilted up to see the stream of nuns going sadly away. 'I like it!' said Micky, and I sat on a small ladder with a cupful of water, flicking drops on to the foreground leaf.

Next day we saw the rushes. Micky adored it and said he would end the film on that scene and cut out the entire scene of Deborah with the Mother Superior of which I was so proud.

I was stunned. I still am.

During the last days of filming *Black Narcissus*, Michael Powell said to me, 'What do you think of ballet?' Was ever an answer so stupid and callow as mine? 'Not much,' I said. 'It's so precious – all those sissies prancing about.' Micky's ice-blue eyes showed more amusement than outrage. 'Have you ever been to the ballet?' I grinned a shamed touché. 'Not since I was a child,' I admitted.

'Well, you've got a lot of catching up to do,' Michael said crisply. 'Our next production is all about ballet. It's called *The Red Shoes*, and I want you to soak up ballet as if your life depended on it. You'll be given tickets to go to Covent Garden – practically every night.'

I didn't realize how lucky I was at the time. I thought it would be a boring chore.

My conversion was hardly Pauline. I was made uncomfortable by the air of lofty affectation. It all seemed suspiciously spurious: the English dancers having Russian names, for instance; the French jargon for choreographic positions – it seemed such an esoteric world, one to which I was alien despite coming from the film business. I had learned in films that good acting was achieved by understatement. Ballet was a complete contrast: no dialogue, mimed gestures, dancing on points – it was obviously a shock to my sensitivity to overacting.

But in a very short time I was well and truly hooked. Ballet was certainly over the top, but I realized it was an escapist's delicious dream world. And, unlike the chaos of dreams, ballet had order. The choreography and music were disciplined by long tradition and good taste. I became an ardent balletomane.

Not only did I have free tickets nearly every night, but I had the privilege of going backstage. My early life had been theatre, and backstage my nursery. The nostalgia was acute: paint, glue, canvas; the pot-pourri of make-ups, all the perfumes of memory. But backstage at Covent Garden was quite different from the provincial theatres of my boyhood. This backstage was vast. The cavernous space evoked resonances of so many great evenings of opera and ballet, the very floorboards were laminated in theatre history. I read books on ballet, trying to remember those tongue-twisting Russian names – Karsavina, Preobrajenska, Riabouchska. How refreshing, in contrast, was the name Moira Shearer!

I visited Madame Volkova's classes, seeing how the dancers at the barre, who had all seemed so glamorous on stage, were now scruffy and unromantic in their practice clothes – drab pullovers, thick woollen stockings with an old rag round the head; and I marvelled at their stoic exertions as they sweated and grunted under the merciless drilling of Madame Volkova.

One morning a woman entered quietly from the back door, took off her coat and went to a barre right at the back of the room. It was Margot Fonteyn, the undisputed queen of the Sadler's Wells Ballet, if not the world. The night before I had seen her taking umpteen curtain calls from a rapturous audience, trying to hold so many bouquets of flowers. Most prima ballerinas would have made a sweeping entrance and taken a position right in front of the class as was her right. But not Margot. She exercised at the barre between young girls who were obviously acolytes, whose laboured movements and heavy breathing seemed grotesque against the pliant ease of Fonteyn. It was a revelation to me of humility.

These 'chores' I had to do for pre-production were proving extremely pleasurable. There were tea-parties at Michael Powell's house, where I met Leonide Massine and Moira Shearer to discuss the forthcoming film. I could see that Micky and his partner, Emeric Pressburger, were obviously thrilled to be realizing their dream of making *Red Shoes* come to life. Years before, in 1937, Emeric had written a script of *Red Shoes* for Alexander Korda, who wanted a ballet vehicle for Merle Oberon, but it was never made. Micky and Emeric had managed to buy the script from Korda and had revised it, incorporating an actual ballet for the first time. Having Moira Shearer playing the lead part was a master stroke.

From the moment I met Moira I knew she would be perfect for our picture. It was rare for a virtuoso ballerina to have such stunning beauty. I had seen her in *Symphonic Variations* and *La Boutique Fantastique* and marvelled at the grace of her dancing, with her blue eyes, radiant carrot-coloured hair and lithe body, all rare and wonderful to behold. She was rare in other ways. She was offered international film stardom, but was not all that interested. In fact, it took a great deal of persuasion to get her to play in the film at all. She wasn't awed or intimidated by the glamour of show business and was permanently dedicated to her world of ballet.

I introduced her to Sir William Russell Flint at Peel Street, who did several drawings and a large painting of her. He told me later that Moira was often critical of the way he had painted her. It was Scot talking to Scot: 'I don't think you quite got my nose right Sir William', or 'I think the legs are wrong'.

From the moment she started work on the film she became an instant favourite with the crew. They all adored her. No big star attitude from her. She actually came up to Chris Challis and I and asked us if we would like her to get us a cup of tea!

I thought my cup of happiness was quite full, but suddenly it was madly overflowing as though Dionysus had added a jeroboam of wine to it, when I received news that I had won the Oscar for my photography on *Black Narcissus*.

Congratulatory cables were flying in from everywhere and the phone was humming with happy talk. Someone from the Rank Organization said I absolutely must have a swell party. 'This will set your career for life,' they said. 'Show off a bit.' So I did.

I hired Harrods to provide a buffet supper and I cleared the decks for a big show-off, inviting anyone who was remotely connected with my film world. I didn't count the people who turned up, but there must have been over a hundred. There were two policemen to control the cars outside which almost filled the street.

All through those halcyon days our production preparation was going on with more than the usual enthusiasm. I was surrounded by talent. Hein Heckroth was the designer; we were already close friends and worked well together. Brian Easdale, who had done such beautiful work on *Black Narcissus*, was composing the music. Robert Helpmann was doing the choreography for the dance sequence and also acting in the film, but the great Massine would create his own choreography.

Leonide Massine. What an extraordinary man. He had danced with the famous Diaghilev Ballet (now the Kirov Ballet), and created world-renowned ballets on his own. He had worked with Picasso, Derain, Matisse, Dali, Ravel, Stravinsky, and Fokine. He had known Nijinsky and Karsavina and here was I, working with him, a man established in ballet history for all time.

He was slight, not tall, dark, and I would say very handsome – even at over fifty. His face had a quiet dignity. He would have been offended if I had told him he reminded me of my father. There was the same stern seriousness in his dark eyes that would light up when humour arrived. One thing is certain: when he was on the screen you couldn't take your eyes off him, such was his magnetism.

On the set, he was something of an outsider. Perhaps his Slav temperament prevented gregarious relationships, but his reserved manner kept him outside the fun and dramas of movie-making. He would always be there at least half an hour before the crew arrived, practising at his barre. Helpmann used to make snide comments: 'Poor old thing, he's feeling his age.' But I believe Massine was the fittest man on the set.

Micky allowed me to make tests on my own. I marshalled a tiny unit of dancers and made experiments to determine various camera speeds and other things technical. I had a gadget made to change the camera speed during a scene so I could go from normal speed to double speed

(48 frames a second). This was used to great effect when a dancer leapt in the air and, just before the apex of flight, I slowed the action for a fraction of a second, so that they appeared to hover in the air.

I could imagine ballet purists going purple in the face: 'How can we judge a dancer's talent when his awesome elevation is aided by camera tricks?' Well, obviously film ballet must be on a separate basis from the theatre. I had no qualms about this and neither, as it turned out, had anyone else.

It was fun having a go at choreography on the tests; I had a male dancer jump off a six-foot platform and shot it using a very wide angle lens and at about five times the normal speed so that he would appear to float down quite a distance. I changed speed with pirouettes so that a dancer would start off at normal speed and then, as I changed the speed to only four frames a second, she would whirl faster and faster until she was a spinning blur. This became highly successful in what was called 'The Paper Dance' with Moira. Micky was very pleased with my tests but, much to my dismay, he told me that he and Emeric had decided that the actual ballet sequence had to be limited to seventeen minutes. The music would be composed first and we must work strictly to every bar of the score which would be on a playback on the stage. I had to accept that many of my filmic ideas had to be abandoned.

Obviously, we had to have a spotlight for the ballet sequence. As the speed of Technicolor was slow in those days, this spotlight had to be really powerful. We ended up with a specially constructed water-cooled arc lamp of 300 amps. It was wonderful, a piercing ray of glory like a shaft from heaven, and it became a vital part of the authentic atmosphere of ballet.

The make-up for ballet is always greatly exaggerated. Anyone seeing faces backstage might recoil in terror or revulsion: thick black eyeliner, Cox's orange pippin cheeks and hot boot-blacking for lashes (they melt it in a spoon over a candle flame and, with an orange stick, separate the lashes, which look like monster spider legs). Close up, it was as grotesque as a Fauvist painting but from the auditorium it looked quite natural. I remember my father used to make-up in a similar way to heighten the facial expressions at long distance. I took our make-up man Ernie Gasser to Covent Garden as he had never seen ballet before. When we went backstage he was amazed: 'It's like a caricature!' he said. 'So crude, men with beards painted on their faces.' But from the audience the make-up looked just right.

I sold the idea to Micky of having two make-ups on the ballet actors – one for distance and one for close-ups.

Some weeks before shooting started there was another pleasant chore for me to do. I was sent to Hollywood by the Rank Organization – to whom I was under contract – to go around the studios and study their technical equipment in order to improve production methods in England. I met Peter Mole of Mole Richardson, famous in the industry for lighting equipment. He told me he had just made a powerful lamp which he had named a 'brute'. It was 225 amps with a wide beam and much more power than the 150-amp arcs I had been using in England. I was shown the two prototypes which had been made. They were wonderful and I yearned to have them for *The Red Shoes*. I somehow persuaded Peter to let me have these two prototypes shipped over to England. And so *The Red Shoes* used the first two brutes ever made. Now brutes are used all over the film world.

We started shooting *The Red Shoes* in my beloved Paris and then went on to Monte Carlo, where Micky packed the key people in his open-topped Bentley and roared round the Grande Corniche checking locations.

From the beginning there was an atmosphere of excitement. We all felt we were making something special. Micky had addressed the crew on the first day of the shoot and told us that we were about to embark on a great venture. 'We'll be doing things that haven't been done before, we'll have to work very hard – but I know it's going to be worth it.'

It was certainly an unusually happy unit in the South of France. We worked hard indeed, but in the evenings there was always a party or a sparkling dinner. During daytime shooting at Cap Martin we would have the luxury of a swim before having lunch. The actor Esmond Knight, who was almost completely blind (having been serving aboard the *Prince of Wales* when it was torpedoed in the war), always insisted on joining us for a swim and after we had guided him over the slippery rocks he would dive in with abandon. An incredibly brave man, and a riot at parties.

After one day-for-night shoot at Villefranche, the whole unit enjoyed a fabulous dinner party, with hilarious fun till dawn. Finally, after more shooting at Monte Carlo, we returned home to Pinewood Studios where the real work began.

The exhilarating thing about working with Micky was the way he was able to instil his own enthusiasm in you. He was the most stimulating director I ever worked with. He'd encourage me to go ahead with any idea I had, however wild and experimental. Nothing was too risky for Micky and I always knew if I tried something daring he'd back me up – as he had done over the fog filter on *Black Narcissus*.

We had our own corps de ballet. Ninette de Valois had turned down Micky's plea to use her super élite corps, but as it turned out, we couldn't have had a better troupe of dancers. How hard they worked! There's something holy about young ballet dancers: they are as dedicated as nuns; they earn so little and have to pay for their own shoes, which are under constant repair; and they devote all their important years to ballet.

Because of the punishing physical nature of ballet, female dancers tend to be flat-chested. Our wardrobe department was instructed to pad up the girls' breasts with cotton wool. To those who protested, it was explained that it was for the American market; 'The Americans like to see women with boobs.' The English corps de ballet – flat-chested or not – hated the cotton wool padding and slyly got rid of it at every opportunity. As if the imposition of artificial breasts were not enough, the girls had to suffer being hooked and laced into their costumes with such constriction that they could never indulge in more than a nibble of food at lunch time. An even more painful ordeal was the hardness of the concrete studio floors which, although overlaid with boards, were very hard for point work. The girls were on tiptoe most of the day, with no cushioning in the floor to absorb the force of jumps. There was a heat wave at the time and this, combined with the immense heat from my lamps, made it unbearable for them.

One day the girls were given five minutes' rest with their shoes off, but that humane gesture brought about a worse problem. The girls' feet were so swollen that once the shoes were off they couldn't get them back on again. That lost us two hours' shooting. We soon made up for it. Our pace of shooting was fast. Our film was charged with such confidence and enthusiasm that we forged ahead like a well-trained circus act. Not only did we have a film unit to organize, there was the corps de ballet to practise the dance sequences, and of course there was Moira, Massine and Ludmilla Tcherina who had much dancing to rehearse.

All this was ably supervised by Alan Carter, a Sadler's Wells dancer and choreographer who also had the job of keeping the peace between Helpmann and Massine, who had not realized that he was choreographing only his own part as the shoemaker and that Helpmann was choreographing the ballet sequence itself. This hardly made for easy relations. There were no flare-ups – they were both professionals – but it was always a delicate situation.

As the shooting progressed I had interesting talks with Massine. He answered my question about Nijinsky's famous entrance in *Spectre de la Rose*. 'Yes, it really was extraordinary,' he said. 'The leap out of the window was more incredible than his entrance. You actually saw him going up as he disappeared through the window. You didn't see him begin to come down. Diaghilev's servant used to catch him.'

On 1 September filming stopped for a two-week holiday period (an impractical and short-lived practice). I proposed to Massine that I make a short film of *La Boutique Fantastique* during the holiday period. Massine was enthusiastic. My idea was to hire a theatre for three days and just photograph the ballet with three cameras. We approached Moira and she agreed to join in. It was a thrilling prospect. With Massine's help I was able to get the performing rights to Rossini's delightful music and organized the costumes. Massine took me to the British Museum to study the score and other things connected with the ballet. I was puzzled at this but he told me that Diaghilev had impressed on him the importance of study at museums. Diaghilev apparently spent much time in museums studying everything concerning a new project.

I thought my little enterprise would be a piece of cake, but it wasn't. I had to have a corps of dancers familiar with the choreography. The Sadler's Wells girls were perfect, having performed *Boutique* many times. But Ninette de Valois turned it down flat. She apparently hated films and said she would try to persuade Moira not to participate. She did, and that was that: no *Boutique*. Oh, well.

The holiday idea was most effective, however. On nearly all films there comes a period towards the end, when everything gets a little stale and a certain amount of zing goes out of things. But when the unit came back after their holiday, sun-bronzed and happy, we all started work again with enormous vitality.

Soon after we resumed shooting a rather fantastic thing happened which more than compensated for my disappointment in not being able to make *Boutique*. Ludmilla Tcherina, who had a smallish part in our picture, was not only a dancer of distinction in France, but was also beautiful and charming. She and her husband, Edmond Audran, also a ballet dancer, became friends with me and my wife Julie. We discovered that Ludmilla and Audran shared our love for Tchaikovsky's *Romeo and Juliet* ballet. To my astonishment they offered to dance the entire ballet in my London house. (I had a very large drawing room, thirty-eight feet long.) 'Could you really do it?' I asked. 'The whole ballet?' Yes they could, and in no time the carpets were taken up and they were actually dancing to my gramophoned Tchaikovsky.

They danced brilliantly. Being so close to them as they whirled about the room gave an intimacy and power not experienced in any theatre. It was a wondrous evening. I never saw Nijinsky jump out of the window, but to have a complete ballet performed in one's drawing room was a spectacular compensation.

The curtain came down on *The Red Shoes*. It was sad for everybody. We had a farewell lunch in the Pinewood restaurant and Micky made a speech, in particular thanking the Sadler's Wells people, and we all went home euphoric, convinced we had made something special. We didn't foresee that *The Red Shoes* would have a Cinderella-like ordeal in the shifty marketplace of movies – even from the ugly sisters of the Rank Organization. The final cut film, with music, was shown to the top executives at Pinewood. Micky wasn't there, but Emeric was. The film was run in icy silence and when the lights went up J. Arthur Rank, John Davies and the executives just walked out – without a word to Emeric or anyone.

They all thought that *The Red Shoes* was a complete disaster. Micky and Emeric were curtly informed there would be no première. The film would just go out on ordinary release, as it had no hope, they said, of commercial success. Publicity and advertising were practically non-existent and it opened unheralded, unknown and unloved at the Gaumont Haymarket.

The critics were really baffled by the whole thing: no publicity, and a ballet in the middle of a film drama. There were some who liked it in a cautious way, but most reviews were awful, encapsulating all the conceit of critics who like to display their cleverness:

> Now, Mr Pressburger, if you do introduce a new ballet, presumably intended for the stage, is it then fair to have your ballerinas dancing in a set with the combined dimensions of the Grand Canyon and Salisbury Plain? And must it attempt to rival Walt Disney in everything but elephants with green polka dots? (Milton Schulman)

> *The Red Shoes* is a long and boring film: I suppose it had to be long in order to cram in as many clichés as possible. (Richard Buckle)

> This film wins my Oscar as the biggest and loudest and Technicolorest film-about-ballet-which-doesn't-quite-get-there-to date ... Perhaps somebody will now try with a modest script, a choreographer who believes in the cinema and about one-tenth of the money. (A. V. Cotton)

The London reviews were much better. They even attached superlatives. C. A. Lejeune said, 'The wedding of movement and colour is almost perfect'. Dilys Powell in the *Sunday Times*: 'An extreme pleasure . . . brilliantly experimental'. W. A. Wilcox thought it 'The nearest thing to a dope-addict's dream . . . a brilliant wedding between Covent Garden and film craft.' The *Daily Mail*'s Fred Majdalany described how the film 'flames into life with a twenty-minute ballet that is one of the most enchanting dance sequences ever filmed'.

Bad reviews can put off the public going to see a film, although some are saved by 'word of mouth', but if the final criterion is supposed to be the public's judgement there wasn't time. The film was soon taken off and there were fears it would be as much of a calamity in America. Since *Variety*'s London correspondent said it would only attract a limited audience in America, the Rank Organization had written it off as a turkey and were not going to push it any more there than they had in England. It seemed certain that *The Red Shoes* was doomed.

Then a little magic happened. Cinderella's prince arrived in the person of William J. Heinman. He was vice-president for distribution at Eagle-Lion, a company owned by Pathé on loan from Universal, where he had been supervisor for British imports for the Rank Organization. He loved *The Red Shoes* and so did his wife and children. In spite of the pessimism of just about everybody around him, he put *The Red Shoes* on in the tiny 500-seat Bijou Cinema in New York for an experimental run. It ran to full houses for over two years.

His faith and enthusiasm were infectious and somehow it all caught fire. *The Red Shoes* was given a road-show treatment – release at selected theatres only.

It had gala shows all over America, launching an incredible change of fortune which more than compensated for the film's miserable début at home. Proclaimed at last with all the fanfare denied it in England:

> Never before has there been a motion picture so drenched in beauty, so lovely in the poetry of colour and rhythm of form and design as this drama of the world of ballet. With *The Red Shoes* the Technicolor motion picture reaches its noblest level.

> *The Red Shoes* is one of those rare British films that revive hope in the motion picture industry as a source of artistic expression. It is beautiful in its rich use of Technicolor, beautiful in its dancing, and beautiful in its creation of living people in the ballet world.

> . . . an enchanting work of art worthy of a place among the best of all time.

There were many more like that, from all over America. *The Red Shoes* continued its triumphant march through Boston, Chicago, Cleveland, Baltimore, Philadelphia, San Francisco, and Los Angeles.

Records began to be set everywhere. As early as January 1949, *The Red Shoes* jumped into *Variety*'s top nine box-office leaders. By the end of 1949 *The Red Shoes* had passed the $2 million mark in rentals and finally earned a niche as one of the top totals ever amassed on Broadway. At a celebration party in Boston, Governor Denver personally congratulated J. Arthur Rank by telephone. I'd like to have seen Mr Rank's face . . .

The *Daily News* predicted Oscars: 'Without further ado, we hereby pronounce, at even money, that *The Red Shoes* will calmly walk away with the colour cinematography and Art Direction awards this March.'

Just about everybody I knew told me the same thing. I was absolutely certain to get the Oscar for *Red Shoes*. There was no possibility it could fail. No doubt at all they said.

But there was. I had a phone call from Lee Garmes who told me a sorry, and rather shocking, story. There had been a meeting of the American Society of Cameramen. It was agreed that *The Red Shoes* was a certainty for the award. But, as I, an alien, had won the Oscar the previous year, it posed a problem. If a foreign cameraman won an Oscar two years running it would put American cameramen in an inferior light. Bad for American prestige, they said. So the only way to prevent me getting the award was not to nominate me.

I should explain that the Academy has a department responsible for each of the five categories – acting, directing, writing, camera, sound. Each department nominates five potential Oscar winners which the entire Academy then votes on. As I wasn't nominated, I couldn't possibly get an award.

Some time later, when all the Oscars had been handed out, I was having dinner with Lee Garmes and a couple of other cameramen in Hollywood. Inevitably *The Red Shoes* came up. A cameraman I hadn't known before said, in a tone of patronizing joviality, 'Well, Jack, you can't win 'em all. I guess the labs did you dirt on that one. They sure screwed the colours up didn't they? It happens to us all.'

I looked across at Lee. He had gone scarlet with embarrassment. The others hadn't known that Lee had told me the real truth, but they must have known that *The Red Shoes* won the *Film Daily* award for the best colour photography of 1947. I put on a pleasant countenance although I didn't feel pleasant. 'Well,' I said cheerfully. '*The Red Shoes* didn't do too badly. It got three Oscars, including Best Art Direction, and Best Colour Design, so the selectors must have seen a better print than you did.'

Many years after *The Red Shoes* I was dining at La Gavroche in Chelsea and noticed Sam Spiegel at a nearby table with Rex Harrison. I recognized the great Nureyev with them. There was also a woman in the party who was making a noisy nuisance of herself, obviously the worse for drink. Spiegel used all his tact and charm to calm her down, but eventually gave up and paid the bill. They all stood up to leave. But the lady, now at the maudlin stage, was not for leaving, clutching a tiny dog defiantly and crying into her feather boa. Nureyev, with typical grace and power, lifted her masterfully aloft in his arms and carried her out of the restaurant, as in the last act of *Giselle*, to thunderous applause from all the much-relieved guests.

I saw him again at a party in my apartment in Switzerland. Of course, I was delighted to meet this truly fabulous dancer in person. He was, as I expected, a fascinating personality. We talked for a long time. I told him about a mad idea of mine. Just down the road from my apartment was Château de Chillion, where Tchaikovsky had composed *Swan Lake*. Supposing rostrums, approximating the area of a stage, were placed right in the lake by the shore, with the rostrum tops just half an inch under the surface – invisible of course – *Swan Lake* could be staged apparently on the surface of the lake, watched at night by thousands all around the bay. Could a ballet company dance on half an inch of water? Nureyev was fascinated and affirmed that it certainly could be done. Much to my regret I never pursued the idea. Perhaps one day ...

Towards the end of our conversation he casually mentioned his problem with arthritis. I was shocked. Nureyev with arthritis? He took off his shoes and socks and showed me the feet that had captivated millions. They were horribly arthritic; in a bizarre way it brought to mind the photographs of Renoir's cruelly distorted arthritic hands that had necessitated his brush being strapped to his arm. And when I worked on a film with Fred Astaire, I saw the famous feet similarly swollen and battered by arthritis.

What a penalty to pay for greatness.

From the enchantment of ballet to the freezing horrors of the Antarctic is just about the biggest contrast one can imagine. My next assignment was the story of Scott of the Antarctic. Actually, I didn't have to trek in Scott's icy footsteps; Ealing Studios provided real snow – made from an enormous machine – and a ten-foot wind machine to make the ambience as thoroughly unpleasant as the real thing.

Long before pre-production work on script and casting, and before I was engaged, Osmond Borradaile (with whom I had worked on *The Four Feathers*) went to the Antarctic with a Monopack camera and did a magnificent job, capturing the essence of the awesome remoteness of the coldest place on Earth. Unfortunately, the Monopack film had a pronounced blue bias and although Technicolor performed a miracle of adjusting the colour balance, the Antarctic still looked decidedly blue. Then another cameraman, Geoffrey Unsworth, was sent to Norway in the winter to get some more Antarctic-looking exteriors – this time with a Technicolor camera. But at that time of the year the sun was very orange and sat at a low arc on the horizon, with the result that the snowy landscapes were bathed in weak amber light. Later, in the summer, Geoff was sent to Switzerland; this time with stand-ins for the actors who hadn't been cast yet. Now the sun was hot and high overhead making the snow dazzlingly white so that the exposure made the sky ink-blue. Then I was called in to photograph the main picture, and all further 'exteriors' were done on a small stage at Ealing Studios. It was difficult enough making snow landscapes on a stage not much bigger than a tennis court, but I also had to match the colour and lighting to real exteriors that were so diverse in colour: overall blue, orange, and refulgent white snow with blue/black skies. A portable Moviola was always on the set so I could view the scenes to which I had to match the colour, often using filters to try to minimize the discrepancies.

For dull-weather effects I would tear cloud-shaped holes out of brown paper which, when placed on the arc lamps, would look like clouds; by superimposing these cloud effects on top of each other, I concocted a passably overcast sky.

The most scrupulous care was taken by producer Sidney Cole and director Charles Frend to represent the actual ill-fated expedition as realistically as possible. The original photos taken on the expedition were studied carefully so our sets and costumes would look exactly the same – even some original equipment, including cans of food that were actually used by the expedition in 1912.

Before I photographed the scenes in the small green tents that Scott and his party would have slept in, I went inside and closed the flaps to see the light conditions. Naturally enough, since the tent material was green, the light coming through the tent made faces look green, so when we shot the scene I used pale green filters on the actors' faces.

Next day our processed film rushes didn't arrive from Technicolor. We were told that something had gone wrong at the laboratories and it was being investigated. When our rushes arrived two days later we saw that the actors had no trace of green on their faces. They had spent the past forty-eight hours getting rid of my deliberately applied green tinge. 'You can't have green faces,' they said. But I could, and I got them.

The story of Scott's tragic failure is well-known. It was so faithfully portrayed that it was almost unbearable to watch. It had a Command Performance, but the heroes of the film were Technicolor, who did such a wonderful job matching the diversity of colour sequences.

7

Hitchcock and Hathaway

For Alfred Hitchcock, the success of *Rope* in 1948 was very satisfying. But for the money men who finance films it was much more exciting because Hitchcock had used a new technique that allowed the film to be made in a few days instead of a few months, thereby making huge savings.

Hitchcock's 'new technique' of a continuous performance without cutting, had a catch in it, though. *Rope* was all shot in one room. The technique was similar to television, moving the camera and the actors to many positions in a confined space. But very few movies can be made in one room. The average movie uses about fifty sets and there are always some exterior locations, so it would be most difficult – and rather crazy – to shoot every reel in one take as Hitchcock did in *Rope*.

But that's exactly what we did a year later on *Under Capricorn*.

It's quite likely that Hitchcock's success with *Rope* had gone to his head for on his next production, which I was assigned to photograph, a large composite set of a complete Australian mansion was built which filled the largest stage at Elstree's MGM Studios. As the camera was to track on a crane all over the place, we used the equivalent of an entire year's supply of carpet from the Granada cinema circuit to cover the whole stage so that we could track without rails through the many-roomed building from one end of the stage to the other.

That much maligned word 'challenge' was perfectly apposite. A cliché maybe, but this job was, for me, a daunting challenge indeed.

I had to light many sets in one go. The sets were mostly in sections which slid open electronically so that the giant electric crane could enter and exit. Sometimes I had lamps on separate dollies and electricians carrying lamps into positions and hurriedly scrambling out of shot or under a table as the crane passed by.

Here is an example of one ten-minute take/scene. The camera starts on Michael Wilding outside the front door of the mansion. He enters inside and we see a large circular hall with a winding stairway. He turns right and walks down a narrow corridor into the servants' quarters. After some dialogue he retraces his steps and passes through the hall again, going along another passage to a large drawing room. More dialogue and many more camera positions and then he exits, the camera following him back to the hall again. Now he mounts the circular stairs and walks down another corridor to a bedroom. He opens the door and enters, walking towards a large bed on which reposes Ingrid Bergman. She is asleep. As he and the camera approach her the bed itself tilts about thirty degrees towards the camera, so avoiding the need for the camera having to rise high on the crane for an overhead shot.

We would rehearse one whole day and shoot the next day. Good recorded sound was impossible: the noise was indescribable. The electric crane lumbered through sets like a tank at Sebastopol, whole walls cracked open, furniture was whisked away by panting prop men and then frantically replaced in position as the crane made a return trip. The sound department did exceptionally well just to get a 'guide track' (picking up dialogue above the din so that the correct soundtrack could be matched to it later).

When we had made a successful ten-minute 'take', everyone had to leave the studio except the sound people, Hitch, the script girl, and the cast, who would then go through the motions with dialogue without the camera. Amazingly, by sliding the sound tape backwards and forwards it all came together.

Perhaps the most incredible 'take' in the film was when the camera had ended up in a dining room where eight people were sitting at a long Georgian table. Hitch wanted to show the guests in a long shot looking down the table, then track in to a big close-up of Ingrid Bergman at the far end.

The Technicolor camera, in its enormous blimp, is over four feet high. To crane above the table over the candlesticks, the wine and the food, the camera would have to be very high up and looking down on the heads of the actors. To solve the problem, the table was cut into sections and everything on it firmly stuck down. Each actor had his own section of table. The camera was now positioned three and a half feet from the floor instead of six feet above the table. The start of the scene showed the guests sitting in their places and the table adorned with gastronomic delights. Now the camera moved forward, seemingly on an inevitable collision course, but at the last moment, each of the guests fell back on to a mattress clutching his section of the table with all the props stuck on it!

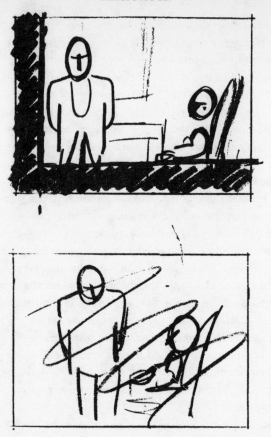

i Hitchcock's storyboards for *Under Capricorn*

To have the camera cleave its way through the collapsing guests, falling back like dominoes in rapid succession, was like a surrealistic dream, but it worked. I don't know how Ingrid kept a straight face seeing the actors parted like the Red Sea before Moses.

Almost all of Hitchcock's prodigious energy was expended on pre-production. The script was thoroughly re-examined in terms of narrative structure, combined with all his creative and dramatic ideas. Everything was worked out in detail and every page was timed. There would be high drama if a page was a few seconds out. It's fair to say that Hitch found the actual shooting of a film something of a bore.

He never looked through the camera, saying for example, 'Jack, you have the thirty-five lens on and you are cutting just below the knees, right?' And right he always was.

I watched him once, during a ten-minute take. He had his back to the actors, aimlessly looking down at the floor, and at the end, when he had said 'Cut', he made only one comment to my camera operator Paul Beeson: 'How was that for you, Paul?' On Paul's nod, he would signal his acceptance of the whole reel. More puzzling, he hardly ever saw the rushes of the day's work. The editor would keep him closely informed, but Hitch knew exactly what he was getting on the screen. From the moment he had drawn pictures of the camera set-ups, he had it all firmly in his mind.

I had been much more involved than usual in the pre-production planning. Usually I tried to dream up ideas for dramatic lighting, but on *Capricorn*, I had for the most part to work out how on earth I could possibly light so many sets at once! I worked more closely with the director than usual.

Practically all of Hitchcock's dramatic ideas were visual. If a camera-man is supposed to 'paint with light', Hitchcock painted with a moving camera. On his other films, using normal techniques, he was able to use his camera with such exciting bravura, cutting from one shot to another to obtain rhythmic emphasis.

And that's where *Under Capricorn* failed in the end. Despite Hitch's brilliant ideas on how to keep the camera moving, he was fatally inhibited by the inevitable loss of tempo.

Example of a normal film: two actors are facing each other. The camera sees them in profile, then cuts to another angle, looking over one actor's shoulder to see the other actor's face front on. Then one can cut to a reverse angle, seeing the first actor. Added to this, there can be single close-ups inserted in the editing process. On *Under Capricorn*, by shooting the whole reel without any cuts, the actors and the camera had to move cumbersomely all over the place in order to obtain the angles that the editor would have used in instantaneous cutting.

Joseph Cotten hated the new technique – and especially the electric crane. He was, with his stage training, a complete professional and never complained, but he told me that he could always sense the monster coming up behind him and was terrified it would crash into his back.

Ingrid Bergman also disliked the constant moving about in order to position herself. On one occasion when Joe and Ingrid were supposed to be facing each other, Hitch had positioned Ingrid slightly further back so that Joe had to turn his back to camera in order to talk to her. Some actors craftily move back like this – it's called 'upstaging' – but I don't think Ingrid manoeuvred herself with intent, although Joe might have thought so, for when the sound man asked what the set-up was Joe answered laconically, 'It's a Swedish fifty-fifty!'

Actually we didn't make the entire film in a studio. I had to go to Warner Bros in Hollywood for an exterior sequence. On Warner's back lot there was an enormous exterior set of an old town that could easily be eighteenth-century Australia. After the nightmare frustrations of those ten-minute takes, it was a balmy breath of fresh air.

I didn't see Hitchcock again until 1960, when I was in Hollywood after I had directed *Sons and Lovers*.

Hitch was pleased to see me, but he had a most peculiar expression on his face as we shook hands. He was staring at me in a kind of wonderment, and murmured slowly, 'I saw *Sons and Lovers*.' His look could only be described as puzzled. Then he said quietly, 'It was good. It was bloody good.' He obviously couldn't for the life of him believe that I, a mere cameraman, could have directed such a good movie. Of all the accolades I received for *Sons and Lovers*, Hitchcock's compliment – albeit given with such incredulity – was one of the most sincere.

A few days later, he invited me to his home just outside San Francisco, which he preferred to Hollywood because it had more of an English climate with its occasional fogs and colder seasons. Hitchcock's house was like his meticulously prepared scripts: in perfectly ordered taste, and well-organized for comfort and entertaining. On one bookcase wall was the complete set of the Everyman library, hundreds of those inexpensive little volumes that covered just about all the classics and novels ever written. Hitch and his wife Alma were pleasant and thoughtful hosts. Their home had a cosy English-type charm. It could have been somewhere in Surrey.

It was so relaxing to spend time with a director like Hitchcock without the weight of a film's preparation hanging over my head. Alma was a superb cook and Hitch's knowledge of food was as extensive as any chef's. He knew all the cuts of beef and kept them in a huge refrigerator. Because his massive weight tended to vary he had an extensive wardrobe, so if he went on a diet or put on pounds, he still had clothes to fit him.

The conversation was stimulating. He was a raconteur with deep irony and humour. He told the story of a joke played on Guy Kibee, the film actor, which involved the participation of many people all over Hollywood.

Guy was extremely worried because he was losing his hair. It was made known to him that an acquaintance had a brother who was a scientist working for the government in Washington and that they had, at long last, found the formula to make new hair grow. It was, of course, a top secret. Guy beseeched his friend to ask his brother to send him this special hair treatment, but his friend had grave doubts; the government would never allow it. However, some anxious days later a letter arrived from Washington saying that as Guy was well-liked in movies, they were making a rare exception and a parcel would be sent to him complete with instructions. But it must all be kept totally secret.

The parcel arrived with the magic bottle instructing him that a teaspoonful of the contents had to be rubbed into his genitals every half an hour. This Guy Kibee did, sometimes causing acute embarrassment. Now the joke got underway. People involved in the joke would meet Guy in the street or at a party and exclaim, 'Guy, what's happened, you look different – hey, you've got more hair!' This type of reaction was voiced by dozens of people from all parts of Hollywood, so it was little wonder that Guy believed it. In fact, he was combing hair he didn't possess.

Then came the drama. A telegram arrived from Washington saying 'Stop treatment immediately. Unforeseen developments. Letter follows.' The letter said that it had been discovered that the magic formula would make him completely impotent. A new bottle accompanied the letter with instructions that the only way to redress the damage was to smear the contents daily on his head, completely destroying the new hair.

And this Guy did with tears rolling down his cheeks.

Hitch's stories were well told, with bawdy cockney insight. Certainly the entertainment world, with its excessive craziness and its brilliant exponents of acting humour, is a natural milieu for funny stories.

Strangely enough, Hitch had never heard the tale of the hunting of the giant moose.

A man has waited years to hunt this mighty moose with the great hunter Jean Pierre, who lives in a log cabin by a Canadian lake. He knocks on the cabin door, which is opened by the son of the famous hunter who says his father will be returning shortly.

While they are waiting the excited hunter asks the boy how his father will track down the moose. The boy tells him that his father will row over towards the other side of the lake and half way across his father will make the mating sound of the moose (at this point the teller of the story must cup his hands and make the most blood curdling roar humanly possible).

Jean Pierre's son continues (with a French accent), 'The moose in the forest hears this sex call and crashes in the direction of the sound. Now my father makes the mating call again (another frightful roar) and the moose, now extremely excited, gallops faster and faster. Rowing quickly across the lake, my father sees the moose jumping up and down on the shore and again makes the call of love (another deafening roar). The moose is now in such a sexual frenzy that he jumps in the lake and starts swimming towards the boat.

'Again my father roars out and now the moose is swimming madly, faster and faster straight for your boat. He is really crazed now with great passion and you must be ready with your gun. My father rows straight towards the mad moose and when the boat is only a few feet away you must shoot him. But for God's sake you mustn't miss, otherwise he fucks my father.'

Hitchcock also told me some of his ideas, not so much stories, but brief dramatic situations that could be the basis for a story: a field of glowing white daisies; the camera tracks over the field and suddenly comes on to a patch in the white daisies of bright red blood . . . The police are chasing a Lascar in the London docks; the sailor slips and falls unconscious; the police examine him and see that his dark-brown colour comes off – it's make-up . . . He made a quick drawing showing the rear of a small van, with two small oval windows. Two men are fighting inside the van, and as they grapple and sway about the effect seen from outside is of two eyes rolling about in the oval windows!

I have the drawings and have proudly framed them. I told him I had cut out a newspaper item that could also be an opening of a movie. A man is driving in the South of France. He sees a girl in the distance, obviously hoping for a lift. He draws up and sees she is excitingly

ii   Hitchcock's drawing of the van with the rolling eyes

beautiful. As the car moves away he asks where she is going. The girl stares listlessly ahead and says, 'Well, it doesn't matter really, I've just taken a whole bottle of sleeping pills. I'll be dead in a few minutes.' And she slumps unconscious. He makes a frantic U-turn and drives furiously back to the village pharmacy, rushing in to tell the chemist who interrupts him: 'I gave the girl the sleeping pills. It was obvious what she was going to do, so I gave her a harmless sedative. She'll be awake in half an hour.' Hitch agreed it would make a great opening for a thriller.

I also told him about a time at Elstree Studios when the director Jack Raymond needed technical advice on how a pickpocket works his craft. By good luck a real pickpocket was being held at the local police station and he was allowed to come on the set under police escort. Jack Raymond told the pickpocket what he wanted and made the motions of picking a pocket himself. The pickpocket shook his head. 'Oh no, guv, I don't do it like that. I do it like *this*. I've just taken your wallet, sir.' Raymond jumped in amazement at being deprived of his wallet. 'And your wallet,' to another assistant standing near. 'And your keys, guv,' to another. There was positive awe seeing such sleight of hand, and the police were hugely amused at our reactions.

Hitch talked of the many subjects that he'd been unable to make into films for various reasons, usually because the story rights had been held too long and the overheads had become astronomically high. One in particular, of the Thompson–Bywaters murder in 1922, had been of special interest to Hitch ever since he was a lad of fourteen living in the East End of London. I knew the story well and had read the book *A Pin to See the Peepshow*, which told the tragic story of Edith Thompson who was hanged – dragged screaming to the scaffold – on the much-disputed technicality of being an 'accessory after the fact' to the murder of her husband Percy by her lover Frederick Bywaters. It would have made a wonderful film, but there were formidable legal objections by the family of the murdered man although, in fact, a play of the book was later made for television.

Another story Hitchcock tried to get was J. M. Barrie's classic *Mary Rose*, and a brilliant drama with a ballet background *Bullet in the Ballet* – both tied up by previous buyers of the screen rights.

What happens is this. A book comes out and someone takes an option on the screen rights. Then an unsuccessful script is written, and another, then there are more option payments made, and so on; so when someone else eventually wants to buy the rights they have to pay all those accumulated overheads – sometimes hundreds of thousands of pounds. There are consequently many wonderful stories gathering dust, unmade.

I told Hitch I had seen a play in London on television that I knew would make a great movie. I phoned a producer friend and urged him to switch on his set and watch it. He saw it and agreed it was an excellent idea and promised he would find out if we could buy the screen rights. He was too late. Alexander Korda had bought the rights for a tiny sum and soon after sold them to Hollywood for $25,000 – a big sum in those days. It became a massive box-office winner. The name of the film? *Dial M for Murder*, directed by Alfred Hitchcock.

The Black Rose in 1950 gave me the chance to work with one of the few genuine giants of movies: Orson Welles. The boy genius, *enfant terrible* of Hollywood. Since I had seen *Citizen Kane* and *The Magnificent Ambersons*, I had no doubt he was the most thrilling film-maker in the business, and I was overjoyed at the prospect of working with him, even though, in this case, he was only an actor.

The director was the formidable Henry Hathaway. Hal Rosson, the ferocious cameraman who had fired all his operators until I stopped the slaughter, was a benign angel compared with Hathaway. He had started as a prop man and, by all accounts, was a hellraiser – and a good one at that. He told me many stories of his struggles up the ladder. There had been a time when his studio had undergone a fierce period of economy, cutting working costs to the bone. Prop man Hathaway was told that there were too many trucks going on location, with too much equipment, and the new order was that only one small truck was allowed. And there, on the last scene of one movie, they were hundreds of miles from the studio in a vast desert. It was a classic long shot: dramatic mountains with the sun setting gloriously on the horizon. But there was an agonizing problem: the camera had to be placed high. The director, knowing the new studio order, was in despair. There were no rostrums.

'How high do you want to be?' Hathaway asked.

'At least twenty feet,' the director said sadly. Hathaway put his fingers in his mouth and made a piercing whistle. Round the mountain bend a huge truck appeared with rostrums. The director was overjoyed, but now the cameraman was up against it. The sun had left the actors in the foreground and he needed lights. Hathaway made a piercing whistle again and a colossal generator truck appeared loaded with beautiful lamps. The scene was magnificent and the studio was full of praise. Hathaway's laconic summing up was, 'Jack, always bring your equipment.'

Hathaway was originally the prop man who had to follow Cecil B. de Mille about, holding his chair behind him, so that when the great man decided to sit down, he just sat, knowing that Hathaway kept his chair right behind his noble posterior at all times.

Years later I saw for myself this megalomaniac at work in Paramount Studios. He no longer used the chair routine, but had a man follow him constantly holding a microphone on a long cable so that all de Mille had to do was speak quietly and his voice would thunder to every corner of the studio. De Mille was wearing his early western outfit with the legendary boots, and was strutting about, looking through a viewfinder, to choose a camera set-up. 'Bring a step-ladder,' he said, casually, but as imperative as God commanding Moses to bring him some tablets of stone.

A step-ladder was almost immediately placed at his feet, and de Mille started to ascend. Here was a terrible problem for the wretched mike holder who was stretching his arm higher and higher with increasing concern as de Mille slowly mounted the steps. Luckily, de Mille stopped half-way up to boom out instructions while the mike holder stood, arms outstretched to heaven, hoping his master wouldn't go up another rung.

Following his stint with de Mille, Hathaway became an assistant director working under some of the toughest directors in the business, known and feared for their grinding sadism, like Victor Fleming and John Ford. In the spine-chilling atmosphere of flagrant bullying Hathaway was well trained and soon became the archetypal tough-guy himself. He even fired a cameraman once – a rare act for an assistant director. He began directing cheap, one-a-week westerns. When he asked the front office for better films to direct he was turned down as being 'too uneducated'. He asked a friend what he should do. 'Read everything you can', was the answer. So Henry bought all the copies he could find of *Reader's Digest*. Reasonably, the bosses were still not impressed, so Hathaway used up his savings to visit Europe to 'become educated'.

On his return Paramount gave him a script to read and told him to report back on it the following morning. 'Can you make this film in ten weeks?' they asked. 'Quite definitely,' said Hathaway. 'And can you do it for under $200,000?' (a very low budget indeed, even in those days). 'Certainly,' said Hathaway. So he was given his first feature film to direct.

It took nearly a year to make and cost over a million dollars. The film was *Lives of a Bengal Lancer*, which made an enormous profit for Paramount and gave Hathaway a fat contract. 'When you get a really good script,' said Hathaway, 'don't let them rush you.'

We started filming *The Black Rose* in Warwick Castle. Tyrone Power was in a scene with Finlay Currie and it was falling apart because Finlay kept forgetting his lines. In spite of Hathaway's reputation as a bellicose Minotaur, he was always sweetness and light to the actors, and his rancour always served to protect the cast psychologically. For instance, he would not allow marks to be made on the floor indicating the actors' positions, because he knew that some actors are so scared of missing their marks that it disturbs their performance. Sometimes, the camera assistant has to tell the director that he can't 'carry' the focus and that an actor a few feet behind the foreground actor won't be very sharp. Hathaway would go mad if the assistant said this loud enough for the actor concerned to hear, who then knew he would be out of focus and whose performance deteriorated.

Sometimes the camera assistant has to warn the director that there is just enough film in the camera to do one take, so if there's a false start – as often happens – there won't be enough film to complete the scene. There would be another explosion from Hathaway. Now the actor who has heard the assistant expects the camera to run out of film during the scene, so the camera assistant always had to be careful to whisper these things to Hathaway or he'd be sent packing.

Finlay Currie continued to dry-up for take after take. Hathaway would cover his frustration with sweet talk: 'Don't worry, Finlay. No problem at all. Let's try again, shall we?' He would then glare balefully around, and if he saw someone not required for the scene he would blast them off the set venting all his frustration on the unfortunate crew member.

We continued, take after take. The atmosphere had become suffocatingly tense. Tea-break time passed unacknowledged. We knew how Hathaway would explode if a break for tea was mentioned.

In the scene Tyrone had to walk some distance to a castle door which was hidden from camera and, just before his exit, say one last line. We had got to take twenty-eight when Finlay remembered all his lines perfectly and behind the camera Hathaway was beaming with delight. We had got it at last. Tyrone walked to the door and, to our horror, forgot his exit line. He apologized profusely to Hathaway, whose beaming face was now crumpled like an empty tube of toothpaste.

What had actually happened was this. My junior camera assistant, Red Gemmal, thinking the scene was over, was about to enter with a huge tray of teas for the crew. Tyrone had opened the door and saw Red innocently about to stride in. He then did something that endeared him to the unit for ever, deliberately fluffing his exit line knowing that if Red had entered with the tray of tea, Hathaway would have fired him instantly. (Years later I told Hathaway the story. He gaped at me for a moment and then laughed, but grimly.)

Our location shoot was in Morocco and our 'hotel' was an abandoned Foreign Legion camp made entirely of mud. In my room there was a nest of starlings in the ceiling; I made firm friends with the birds who woke me every morning with their chirping.

On the day we arrived in our camp Hathaway had seen the British unit sitting down to tea. He hated the British tea-breaks: 'Goddam British, drinking tea all day.' To my amazement he pinned a notice on a board saying that in future the unit must drink their tea standing up. Then he said, 'Come on, Jack, let's look at the location.' As we got into the car I told Hathaway he had just made a very big mistake. The British unit had respected him up to now, but by putting that notice on the board he had lost their good will and nobody would obey that order anyway. Hathaway glared at me. 'You're full of crap.' He accelerated furiously for a few seconds then made a savage U-turn and drove back to the camp where he tore the notice off the wall.

My relationship with Hathaway was similar to other firebrands I'd worked with. I never showed any fear of him and expressed my opinions without fawning servility. British camera crews call the mat placed on the ground for looking through the camera on low set-ups a 'grovel mat', and grovel I didn't. Hathaway respected this and we got on reasonably well together, but he fired several of the unit in the first couple of weeks. Our assistant art director was making a sketch outside his hut and was stripped to the waist, humming a tune as he enjoyed the Moroccan sun. Hathaway fired him: 'This is not a goddam holiday camp.'

The plane taking the victims of Hathaway's rages back to England was called the Hathaway Special. The unit, as always, treated these dramas with their irrepressible British sense of humour, exemplified hugely by our assistant director, Bluey Hill. His humorous sayings were something of a legend in England. A bulky Australian, he had a stomach for drink as tough as Errol Flynn's. Hathaway never knew quite what to make of Bluey, but tolerated him because he worked hard and his high spirits helped the unit through the tough working conditions.

Any assistant director working with Hathaway was on a hiding to nothing. Everything that went wrong was blamed on Bluey. We were trying to do a scene in a Moroccan marketplace crowded with masses of Arabs and the noise was deafening. Hathaway was roaring to Bluey to get quiet and Bluey was roaring to an interpreter through a megaphone. Eventually some sort of quiet was obtained, except for a dog barking. 'Bluey!' shrieked Hathaway. 'Get rid of that goddam dog!' And Bluey yanked the dog away round the corner and tethered him to a post. We tried to shoot again, but now a baby was crying. 'Bluey!' screamed Hathaway. 'Do something, for Crissake!' Bluey picked up the megaphone and roared to the interpreter, 'Throw the baby to the dog!'

We had been working a couple of weeks before Orson Welles arrived. He was playing a Mongolian warlord travelling with gifts for Genghis Khan, a relatively small role but an important one. He had agreed to play this part on condition that he could wear a large overcoat which was lined inside with real mink. The producers argued that such an expensive coat lining would never be seen, but Orson insisted, saying he would *feel* right, and eventually the producers gave in. The unseen mink lining was a mystery until the end of Orson's stay when he took the coat with him, turned it inside out, and used it on his unfinished masterpiece *Othello*.

Orson's entry into our film was a tonic. He had a fund of stories and it was riveting to hear from his own lips the well-known drama that rocked America when *War of the Worlds* was on the radio and he staged a most realistic interruption with an actor-announcer cutting in on the programme saying that Martians had landed in America. There had been an incredible panic. Millions of people fled town and hid themselves in the country. Suicides were even reported. Needless to say the broadcast made Orson famous.

One day, amid the usual frenetic location work, Orson told me he had the idea of doing Homer's *Odyssey* (he called it by the Latin name

Ulysses) and would like to talk to me about it. That evening we had dinner and Orson asked me if I would be interested in photographing it. Would I! The *Odyssey* and the *Iliad* had stimulated me in my stumbling education, and Schliemann's discoveries at Hisarlik seventy years earlier made me spellbound at the probability that Troy was real. I yearned to visit the background of mysterious old Homer: Ithaca, Mycenae and, above all, Troy.

It wasn't until many years later that this dream was realized. Meanwhile, here was Prometheus sitting before me, freed from his chains – well temporarily – and offering me a job in Elysium. I studied Orson in the multishadowed ambience of the Moroccan restaurant. 'You'll play Odysseus, of course?' Orson's lips smiled as he nodded, but his eyes were unsmiling, 'And this time I shall finish the movie myself.'

I knew what he meant. Hathaway had told me of the travails of Orson on *Citizen Kane* and *The Magnificent Ambersons* which indeed was analogous to Prometheus chained to a rock, but instead of the eagle eating away his liver, it was the jackals of Hollywood. *Citizen Kane*, regularly adjudged by critics to be the best film ever made, was very nearly never seen. Cowed by the fury of Randolph Hearst – on whom the character of Kane was based – a group of scared Hollywood moguls offered RKO nearly a million dollars to buy the negative of the film so they could destroy it, but RKO bravely turned down the offer. Then there was a conspiracy to keep *Citizen Kane* out of the movie houses by crafty intimidation, but the film opened to rave reviews in spite of these despicable tactics. Another undisputed masterpiece, *The Magnificent Ambersons*, shared a similar fate. The studio didn't like the ending, and hired another director to shoot a totally different one.

Orson, understandably, didn't want to talk about the Hollywood piranhas; 'It's all behind me. I have no emotions about the yesterdays. One has to always look forward and say yes to life, like Joyce's Molly Bloom.'

We somehow got on to music and I saw at once that Orson's knowledge of the classics was toweringly higher than my own. I was happy enough just to listen. Then jazz came up and I was further surprised to find that Orson's knowledge of the early days of jazz was encyclopaedic. He knew all the old-time heroes: Pee Wee Russell, Charlie Parker, Jelly Roll Morton, Leadbelly – I forget the rest, but he knew them all. All I could offer was enthusiasm for Erroll Garner whom I had met, and Oscar Peterson whose surprisingly calloused hand I had once shaken.

Orson's role in *The Black Rose* was not very big, but every time he was in a scene he was magnificent. He didn't have the Falstaffian girth then, but his height and bearing lent majesty to his role. He had his tricks like all actors have; for instance, throwing away a line of dialogue he didn't like by reducing the delivery to a hurried – almost under the breath – nullity. There was a scene played in the Genghis Khan tent with Tyrone Power in which Orson had a very long speech. He told Hathaway he would never remember it all the way through and asked for the scene to be broken up into several cuts. Hathaway didn't want to do this and as we started shooting, I could sense I was watching a duel. Orson, after some lines of dialogue, would fluff to prove his point and we'd go again. Orson's ploy was obvious. All he needed to do was to fluff each time. Hathaway knew this and wouldn't give in. All Hathaway needed to do as director was to say, after each fluff, 'Let's go again.'

We went on, take after take, with Orson fluffing away. Hathaway was pacing up and down like a lion in a cage. Orson was deadly quiet, his actor's impermeability hiding the rage within. The unit was tense and silent, hardly daring to breathe. Sweat was running from Orson's turban over his pursed face, but the make-up man was too scared to run in and dab the sweat away – Orson would probably have bitten his head off.

At take thirty-six the physical part of the duel told. Orson was exhausted and must have felt as helpless as Sisyphus rolling the stone up hill, knowing it would always roll down again. Orson spoke the lines all the way through without fluffing, surrendering to the power of the director.

A few days later Orson left – with the company's mink coat and a few cans of unexposed negative film which would be useful on *Othello*.

As the years passed I saw Orson become the embodiment of a living ruin and what a pang I felt when he appeared in TV commercials advertising sherry. He was now a Pagliacci clown and I grieved at this abuse of such enormous talent. The list of his films that had fallen by the wayside shows many glimpses of unfulfilled glory: *Don Quixote, Salome, War and Peace, Heart of Darkness, Crime and Punishment, Ulysses*.

He did in fact, whilst keeping afloat on commercials, make a film which was actually finished and, for me, it is the most trenchant impression I have of Orson: the magician in *F for Fake*. His performance is superb and we see the real Orson. The years of cruel adversity seem to have germinated a burgeoning of acceptance to life's little games. His mouth twists and his eyes sparkle in sardonic acknowledgement of it all, and the message he conveys again echoes Shakespeare:

Let me embrace thee sour adversity,
For wise men say it is the wisest course.

We had a few more weeks' shooting on *Black Rose* after Orson left.
On one occasion Hathaway and I were looking for a camera position
from a hill overlooking an Arab village. Hathaway had the viewfinder
and couldn't decide which position was best. He kept grunting the pros
and cons as he peered through the viewfinder, slipping crabwise across
the incline of the hill, his cigar clenched with fierce determination in his
mouth. Having extolled his final choice he again had a change of mind,
and shook his head. 'Nah, this one is only sensational.'

Sometimes when I was lighting he would ask me to 'paint with a fine
brush', as he wasn't fully prepared for the scene; once we had to fake an
argument together to stimulate Tyrone's performance. Ty was sometimes
just too easy-going and relaxed. He had to kneel down, looking up at
the king of England as he taps his shoulder and knights him. The scene
obviously required some emotion on Ty's face: tension, joy, fierce pride,
but Ty's handsome features showed more the reaction of someone
watching a sleepy golden oldie on TV on a Sunday afternoon.

Hathaway gave me the signal – a wink – and told me to move a black
'flag' that was protecting a lamp's rays from hitting the lens. I duly
played my part:

'I can't move it, Henry, it's got to be there.'

'Jack, take the goddam thing away, I can't see the action.'

'You'll have to be the other side of the camera, I can't move that flag.'

'I said move it.'

'I cannot and will not.'

'Don't talk to me like that.'

By now Ty was quite angry kneeling on the stone floor all this time
listening to this ridiculous altercation; finally he exploded:

'Henry for Christ's sake . . .'

'Roll 'em,' Hathaway snapped, and we shot Tyrone looking up at the
king, his brows knitted together, his lips compressed, face slightly
flushed; he looked wonderful. Just like a man being knighted.

We were greatly honoured when the Sultan of Morocco invited half
a dozen of us to a dinner at his palace. As we entered through the impressive iron gates we marvelled at the procession of servants carrying
food on long litters across the courtyard. It looked enough to feed an
army. Then we saw a bus load of the Sultan's wives – about thirty of

them – so perhaps not all the food was for us. What an evening we had. Our first drinks on arrival were large tumblers of crushed almonds; there were so many delicious things to eat, small portions but each a taste of heaven. I lost count of the number of courses but it went on for hours.

Back at work next day we faced a problem. We needed a dozen women for a scene; difficult in desert territory miles from any town. Hathaway told Bluey to do his best and somehow find women for the next scene.

Bluey returned in an hour with a group of Moroccan women herded together in an open truck. Bluey signalled the women to jump down as he called out to Hathaway, 'Here you are, guv'nor, they're all apple charlottes, but they've got hearts of gold.'

'Apple charlotte' is cockney rhyming slang for harlot. We all stood staring, amused at Bluey's cheeky resourcefulness, and he was congratulated with applause. The 'apple charlottes' descended from the truck and as they looked around some of them gave happy cries of recognition: 'Hello Jimmy!' 'Oh, Charlie!' 'Hello, Tommy, big boy!'

Those named – electricians and stagehands – frantically tried to hide themselves as the unit erupted in laughter which not even Hathaway's glare could suppress.

8

La Belle France – Again

After the rigours of Hathaway I needed to get away from it all and what better holiday than to make another documentary with my preposterous old friend Jean Bernard in Paris.

Jean was short, jovial, with a large middle section and a tiny moustache like a cartoon Frenchman. As a teenager he had lived for a time in London, working as a garage attendant in Clapham. His English was broad cockney with a comically transparent French accent.

He adored his wife André, who was much younger and very pretty. She knew less English than Jean and would unknowingly use shocking expletives picked up from her volatile husband, unaware how unladylike she was being.

We had previously made a documentary about the Seine, called *Main Street of Paris*, in the course of which Jean took me to see a painter's studio on the river which consisted of two barges tethered together; one was the artist's living quarters and the other his studio. While having coffee in his living section I noticed, with a sick feeling of certainty, a human hand, severed at the wrist, nailed to the wall. 'That's not a real hand is it,' I said jocularly, covering my instinct to vomit. 'Mais certainement,' the artist affirmed brightly. 'C'est mon grand papa.' As he went to get some sugar, Jean whispered, 'His grandfather died last year. He was such a funny fellow. Always joking.'

I finished my coffee trying not to look at the less than humorous hand. The artist who, funnily enough, had a very serious mien, took me to his studio on the adjoining barge to show me his collection of drawings, while Jean returned to his office. We approached his easel which had a large drawing pad on it. He lifted up the cover and I tried not to show my shock at his first drawing which was a close-up of a penis.

The drawing pad was about three feet by two inches. The drawing was finely detailed: the veins and flaccid flesh perfectly lifelike; every single pubic hair coiled daintily as the hair of a renaissance cherub. I gravely studied the drawing for some moments, murmuring appropriate noises of praise. Then he flourished the next drawing which was another penis. There were more flourishes. They were all penises – about twenty in all. I ran out of praise. I mean if you've seen one penis, you've seen them all. The artist waxed eloquent: on the simple dignity of the limp phallus . . . the awesome fury of procreation . . .

I thanked him for letting me see his penises, and made my exit, keeping my head down in case I should see his grandfather's principle appendage nailed on a wall, and wondering if anyone would believe my experience, or if they would say it was a pure phallusy.

In the course of shooting *Main Street of Paris*, Jean obtained permission for me to photograph paintings and statues in the Louvre – a joyous occupation until disaster struck.

I had fun with the *Venus de Milo* and after that I set two lights on the *Mona Lisa*, each one at forty-five degrees to avoid reflections. The lamps were about six feet away. In those days that most publicized of faces in the world was not protected as it is today. Just a framed canvas on the wall.

While I was setting up the camera I smelt something hot. Lamps always give out a smell of heat, so I wasn't too worried, but an official was bearing down on me with dramatic speed and his hissed words went through me like a bayonet: 'Monsieur. You are burning the Mona Lisa.'

Out went my lights and out went I with my crew, feeling like Dreyfus on his way to Devil's Island.

This time it was to be a two-reeler of Montmartre, a place very close to my heart. Jean handed it to me on a platter. I wrote the script, directed and photographed it while Jean made all the production arrangements, such as taking my camera crew and I to the cheapest restaurants he could find.

I read up on Montmartre and Jean introduced me to fascinating characters on 'La Butte', that 'little city on a hill', whose stories helped me to form the narrative structure of the film; the more homework I did, the more excited I became.

By colossal luck, Jean discovered someone who had a collection of very early photos of Montmartre, most of them from the mid-nineteenth century. I was able to use them in my film, placing the Technicolor camera on the exact spot where the original photos had been taken. Then I made a long thirty-second dissolve so that the old sepia photo slowly changed into the present day. In some scenes huge tower blocks would slowly appear, surrounding centuries-old houses that still remained – an eerie and sad comment on 'progress'.

I also used this long dissolve technique in the Place du Tertre, a little square that millions of tourists visit every summer. First I photographed it in winter – the trees completely bare and the square deserted. To my great joy a dog walked into picture and peed against a tree.

The following summer I went back to the exact spot (marked with pencil on a balcony) and made a half-minute dissolve again, so that one saw the bright green buds slowly appear on the trees and then fully bloom; what had been a deserted scene in winter was now filled with strolling people and painters working under coloured parasols.

I discovered to my astonishment that Jane Avril, the legendary chanteuse who had been the toast of Paris in the nineties and immortalized by Toulouse-Lautrec's posters, was still alive!

I couldn't believe my luck and immediately made plans to photograph her at the Moulin Rouge, where I intended to track through the smoke and people dancing to a table where a solitary woman was sitting: a very old woman with white hair, gazing ahead, perhaps remembering her years of fame at the Chat Noir and the Moulin Rouge, her triumph in America, and all those posters by Lautrec.

The day before I was to shoot this scene Jean turned up – breathless – and told me that Jane Avril had just died, so that, sadly, was that.

There were plenty of exciting things ahead of me. Montmartre, the mount of martyrs, has hundreds of years of absorbing history, going right back to the third century when a man named Denys tried to convert the Gauls to Christianity and was beheaded by Emperor Diocletian. Denys is said to have picked up his own head and carried it some miles to a place that is now known as St Denis. This hagiographic legend produced many pilgrimages, churches were built and a painter was commissioned to paint St Denis recovering his severed head.

I wish I'd seen Montmartre when it was a village; a pastoral haven of windmills and vineyards and a refuge from the grand boulevards below. When I was there, it was much more urban but the atmosphere was still pretty rural and seemed a world apart from busy Paris.

The French have always had a leaning towards romantic fantasy, nowhere more so than in Montmartre, where make-believe flourishes amidst the freshness of the high air. Mimi Panson, for instance. A romantic legend, dear to the hearts of all France, she was invented by the poet Alfred de Musset. She was a seamstress – say the poets and composers of operettas – a pretty working-class girl and a friend to all artists. She is thought of with great tenderness. Her 'actual' house in Montmartre is as real as Sherlock Holmes's in Baker Street and her window box is always full of flowers.

Montmartre even has a make-believe town hall, with a president and mayor whom I met and who made me a citizen of the republic of Montmartre. The president's son, Claude Pinoteau, worked with me as my assistant director and later became a top director in France.

I started my film below Montmartre at Clichy, where the deafening traffic was being 'controlled' by a very excited gendarme who constantly blew his whistle and gesticulated frenziedly. I shot this at only eight frames a second so that the action was speeded up like a comedic nightmare; over this I placed 'The Flight of the Bumble Bee'. Then the camera leaves this bedlam and starts panning up the thousands of steps leading to Montmartre; at its summit there is complete silence until a woman is heard singing, with a rich, contralto voice, alone in a deserted street – a heavenly serendipity.

The narrow streets in Montmartre have so much history; many painters lived there in desperate poverty. Modigliani at one time lived in a shed in the rue Lepic. Van Gogh lived in the same street at number 54, thrilled at his first awareness of pure colours that Signac had revealed to him. Renoir lived in rue Cortot where he brought his little grisettes to pose for him and where he painted his monumental *Moulin de la Galette*. Cézanne lived there as did Picasso and Pissarro – not forgetting Utrillo who painted the Montmartre streets and gave most of his early paintings to bistros in exchange for bottles of wine.

Most of them would spend evenings at Au lapin agile, 'the agile rabbit' – a sort of cabaret-pub. It was originally called Cabaret des Assassins, but the caricaturist Gill painted a sign for it, a rabbit jumping into a pot and made the pun, lapin à Gill. The agile rabbit is now known all over the world. At the time of the original proprietor, Père Frede, there were paintings by Picasso on the walls, now long gone into the auction rooms.

There was the block of studios called Bateau-Lavoir (because it looked like a 'washing boat'). It could have been a film-set for a Dickens melodrama. The rent was extremely cheap, and no wonder – no water, no heating, no lights, and hardly any furniture! Ironic to think that the young artists who painted there included Picasso, Gauguin, Van Gogh, Juan Gris and Matisse, who produced paintings in such awful poverty that years later would be sold for so many millions of dollars.

Picasso's contemporary Georges Braque was there for a short time when he was twenty. There were poets like Max Jacob and Apollinaire who were of great assistance to the new breed of painters, and there were girls – grisettes, *demi-mondains*, all categories of the eternal woman – who were taken in by the painters as models, who would live with them for a time and then be passed on to other painters like library books.

Nearly all those noble titans had long departed – although Braque and Utrillo were still alive and I hoped to use them in my film. I did meet a few who, although nowhere near as famous, were exciting and very good artists. Some people called Gen Paul the last of the Impressionists, but he was more of a Modernist and although not a Picasso or Toulouse-Lautrec, is now hung in museums all over the world. His paintings of clowns and musicians, seemingly amorphous daubs, were very clever; you soon saw that the scattered shapes had authority and order. There was a hint of Soutine's savage Expressionist distortions, but Gen Paul had much more sense of humour and his racehorses were the most delightfully delicate I have ever seen. I watched him work and saw how carefully he thought out each stroke of his brush with devoted concentration, always with a Gauloise drooping from his lips. His studio had several brass musical instruments on the walls; trumpets, saxophones, trombones, and his 'palette' was a circular cast-iron garden table. He never cleaned it, and there was a thickness of about eight inches of old paint piled up from the countless paintings he had done.

One day I told him I had seen one of his rare drawings of a nude in a nearby house. He took me to the house to refresh his memory and then, back in his studio he drew a replica of it in about two minutes: a superb display of uninhibited and sure draughtsmanship, which also had the Gen Paul hallmark; a saucy turned-up nose.

Fernand Léger was famous all right, although not strictly Montmartre. His studio was down from La Butte and was a hive of activity with several students working there. Léger didn't look a bit like a painter. Tall, thick-set, with a labourer's broad shoulders and a rugged close-cropped head, he could have been a farmer or a boxer, never a painter. Nevertheless, he was highly esteemed by the art world, with his major paintings fetching big money.

I'm afraid his work didn't excite me. Where Renoir's paintings exude luscious femininity, Léger's work was intensely materialistic: a Brave New World of massive shining metal related to all aspects of urban life. Cars, planes, traffic lights, poster hoardings – all these he reduced to geometric shapes.

He fetched a painting from a corner and placed it on an easel for my inspection. I was trying to look interested when a student stepped in saying, 'Excuse me, Maître, you've got it upside down.'

Utrillo and Braque were being approached by Jean to appear in my film; I had my fingers crossed. Meanwhile I worked down from La Butte to the nightlife of Montmartre – the cabarets around Place Pigalle. At cabaret Eve I had to stick tiny wads of cotton wool over the dancers' nipples as topless women were not allowed by the British censors in those days. The cotton-wool-breasted girls thought this was hilarious, but I didn't. Try sticking cotton wool on twenty dancing girls' nipples and you'll see what I mean.

In another cabaret I photographed the can-can, perhaps the most exciting riot of noisy fun ever danced. The deafening volume of the music and the dancers' tremendous energy was madly intoxicating and I could readily imagine La Goulue, the greatest can-can dancer of them all, dancing at the Moulin Rouge to ecstatic cheering, with Toulouse-Lautrec busily sketching her in the audience.

The plump La Goulue had a dizzy rise to fame in the nineties but took heavily to drink and soon after was reduced to selling sweets outside the Moulin Rouge where she had been such a star. She ended up working as a servant in a brothel.

I now had the all-clear on Utrillo and Braque. First I visited the home of Utrillo, eighteen kilometres from Paris. Le Vesinset, in a tiny bourgeois district, was starkly different from the bohemian furnace of Montmartre. And here I was, shaking hands with a fiery legend, who had lived such an agonizing life and was, miraculously, still alive.

Or was he? Here was an empty shell of a man whose spirit had died years ago; now there was nothing left and he was quietly resigned to it. His face was etched with a lifetime's drunkenness, haunted and sad. His eyes, smudged like an error in a painting, seemed to have no focus; each iris was ringed with silver senility, reflecting nothing of his volcanic inner world.

Few could have had a more turbulent existence: his constant drunkenness; being jeered at as he painted in the streets; beaten up and left in gutters; beaten many times more by the police; always in and out of asylums and prison. All this was real, yet incredibly, those exploits have been enhanced by grotesque fabrications, by bistro gossip and by art dealers in order to get higher prices – for canvases for which they had paid next to nothing.

Out of all the phoney folklore some facts are solid enough. His mother, Suzanne Valadon, was the model – and in many cases, the mistress – of several celebrated Impressionists including Puvis de Chavannes, Renoir and Toulouse-Lautrec. Then she became a painter herself. Surprisingly Degas, a fierce misogynist, liked her tiro drawings and encouraged her. He called her 'that terrible Maria' ('Maria' was changed to 'Suzanne' on Toulouse-Lautrec's advice).

As she left home every day to model she would leave baby Maurice in the care of her mother, a solid provincial who, to keep her grandchild quiet at night, gave him a country broth with red wine in it. Thus, Utrillo became an alcoholic before he could walk.

When he went to school he often had a lift home on a workman's cart and when they stopped for a drink, Utrillo had one too, taking his alcoholism a good stage further until he craved for drink like a real veteran.

In his teens Utrillo became desperately ill from all this and went into hospital where a doctor suggested giving him something to take his mind off his craving for drink – drawing, for instance. Suzanne gave him a few lessons in perspective and soon he was painting, on cardboard, views of the Montmartre streets. But this didn't solve the drink problem. He was giving his paintings to bistros for a bottle of wine and would usually end up in either the gutter or the police station.

At last the authorities put him in an asylum for life, but a few influential people – including dealers, most probably – arranged his release on condition that his mother and stepfather never let him out of their sight. The constant supervision and tension must have made for a weary life for Valadon and her husband; Utrillo was always giving them the slip and getting violently drunk again.

In spite of his pitiful existence Utrillo continued to paint the streets of Montmartre – often from postcards – when he was locked in his room. Because of his notorious reputation and his aura of madness, dealers began to see that they were on to something – they began buying his paintings for practically nothing and selling them for ever-higher prices.

Modigliani died penniless at thirty-five. Utrillo was becoming rich, but was not allowed to touch a penny of his fortune, thus enabling his mother and stepfather to live like millionaires. (But at what a price – to be constantly watching Utrillo and suffering his drunken furies. Sometimes in the streets he would expose himself, shouting to the shocked passers-by as he waved his penis 'I paint with it.')

Then Lucy Valor turned up. She was the widow of a Belgian industrialist and she shrewdly set her cap at Utrillo who, strangely, was attracted to her. Strange because he hated women and would shriek abuse at them in the streets. Lucy Valor was very fat and it was said that Utrillo equated her large buttocks with the large bottoms of the women in his paintings whom he saw as 'laying hens'. Anyway she got him, after terrible scenes with Suzanne Valadon. She married him and his fortune and Suzanne and her husband were now without their enormous income.

Utrillo, after many years of constant parental supervision, must have felt he was now free of bondage but soon discovered he had just exchanged gaolers, this time for a voracious monster who took good care that her goldmine was kept under constant guard.

When I met him I was well aware of his outrageous background. Utrillo sat quietly on a settee with Lucy Valor, who did all the talking. I tried not to be influenced by the stories I'd heard about her, but the moment I met her I felt instinctively that the stories were true. Her over-bright affection and obvious insincerity made her repulsive. Jean had already told me that she had suddenly become a painter. He had spat: 'Dada she calls it! I call it *caca* – piles of *merde*!'

He was right. Her paintings were rubbish, and with colossal effrontery she had hung several on the walls mixed up with Utrillo's.

I photographed Utrillo and Valor together – she insisted on that – in fact I had the impression it was Lucy Valor I had come to see. She was the star and not Utrillo, whom she treated like a pet animal. Once she told him to look more cheerful and he obeyed her, giving a ghastly caricature of a smile.

Jean and I attempted polite conversation with him, but it was very difficult. Jean said afterwards we had been lucky. Apparently Utrillo would often explode like a volcano, screaming insults at a guest and terminating the interview. At least we were spared that.

Occasionally he would leave the room, Valor explaining that he had gone to his private chapel to pray. Later, when Valor was engaged in conversation with Jean, Utrillo got up and looked out of the window. I walked over to him and showed him a little book of his paintings I had brought with me. The change in him as he looked through the book was extraordinary. He was like an excited schoolboy who had opened a cupboard revealing wonderful toys. He chortled and gurgled like a baby, touching the photos of his work with nostalgic delight and he wrote in my book with pleasure.

After that it wasn't too difficult to persuade him to let me photograph him at work in his studio, a small room upstairs where there already was a partly finished painting on the easel: the famous *Moulin de la Galette in the Snow* which he had copied so many times. There were also, significantly, a few postcards of Montmartre in the room and I remembered the many pictures he had painted from postcards; in fact, when his paintings were first sent to America, the US Customs wanted duty paid on them as, they said, they were only postcards.

He dabbed away at the painting listlessly – almost as if a robot – while my camera recorded him. I watched the famous Utrillo actually painting before my eyes – and all I could feel was pity.

During the shooting of *Montmartre* I went to see my rushes at Francoeur Film Studios. Leaving the projection room and walking through one of the empty stages, I came across my assistant, Claude Pinoteau, chatting away to Jean Cocteau.

I was face to face with an awesome legend; a prodigious *enfant terrible*, author, poet, painter, opium addict, designer of ballet and opera, and an exceptionally talented film-maker. Such a genius was actually conversing with me. And not just exchanging polite formalities, but seemingly interested in prolonging the conversation. Well, yes, he had heard of me – the film business is like a village – he had seen *Red Shoes*; '*Ravissant*', he said and we chatted away like old buddies.

There was only one dismal snag. He was speaking to me in rapid French. My French had never been much beyond night-school standard and I was in an agony of frustration. To compound my panic Claude Pinoteau murmured an apology and left us alone, and there we stood, two figures on an empty stage, one loquacious in animated French, the other mumbling *in extremis*.

Then, like sun bursting out from storm clouds, I realized that Cocteau's French was unusually lucid, as well as being luminously accented by miming gestures, so that I could understand much more than I could have hoped, and, strangely, my wretchedly inadequate language improved. In my desperation to converse with this distinguished man, some kind of vocal adrenalin forced every dormant French word to the surface and I survived the crisis.

He had a sensitive face, a long aquiline nose, and sharp birdlike eyes; his hands, spidery and expressive, shaped his thoughts like a magician's wand. Sometimes he would break into English but not for long, as his nimble mind accelerated in his native tongue.

'I enjoy conversation,' he said. 'Conversation makes me free, and I use this freedom to examine everyone I speak to.' Talking to people helped him to fight boredom, which he called, with more mimetic gestures, 'the shapeless monster'. I told him I had worked with René Clair and Jacques Feyder, and discovered that my old Denham Studios friend Georges Périnal (who had photographed *Sous les Toits de Paris*, and with whom I had worked on *The Four Feathers*) had been Cocteau's cameraman on *Le Sang d'un Poète*. On that picture, Cocteau told me, they had been working all night. Eventually the early morning cleaners entered the studio and resolutely started cleaning up, making an enormous cloud of dust. Cocteau protested furiously until Périnal pointed out the wonderful effect the dust had made, and the scene was shot with much gratitude to the cleaners.

I told him I had done a similar thing on a travelogue in India, photographing a village in the early morning and obtaining a dawn mist effect by having a car move off at high speed in the background which raised an enveloping cloud of dust.

We talked on – or rather he talked on. My paucity of French didn't matter much because he did nearly all the talking, and wasn't I enjoying it! There was a large open door at the end of the stage and the sinking sun slanted long shadows as we talked. Sharp, dazzling rays of light pierced the smoke from his Gauloise.

Cocteau's conversation was so buoyant with ideas and observation that I could have listened to him for ages. I remembered Modigliani had painted his portrait and we talked about him. 'My God, he was handsome,' Cocteau said. 'He did the portrait in 1916 – four years before he died – I was very young – and although he had tuberculosis and was drinking himself to death he still looked like an Adonis. I paid only five francs for the portrait. I had to sell it later, and in 1939 it was sold for seven million francs.' His philosophic gesture said it all. 'Where is it now?' I asked. Another Gallic shrug: 'I've no idea.'

Cocteau enthused about his flirtation with films: 'Such a poetic medium for putting thoughts into images.' He regretted the enormous amount of money necessary to make a film and how it had to be an immediate success to get its money back. 'This is a terrible handicap,' he said. 'Art goes slowly; art must wait. Most great artists are dead before being recognized.' He sighed, 'Ah, but I adore the cinema. Dreams are very important to me and making films is very nearly a living dream. There have been many times when I had little money left and had to manage with old equipment, sometimes using a friend's 16 mm camera, but it is always worth it.'

I asked him about Picasso, whom he had known for many years. 'Yes, since 1916. Everybody is called a genius today. It no longer means anything, but Picasso is a genuine genius. He is also a genuine autocrat – he makes few concessions to fools. Even if he himself makes a mistake he has said, "I make mistakes – like God." But he is a good friend to me. He has tremendous inner strength. He is the only one of us who never tires . . .'

The orange sun had disappeared, and the stage was now dark. There were many more questions I wanted to ask him, but all things must end, and we parted. I never saw him again.

The next day I was in Braque's studio, at rue de Douanier, talking to him and blessing my luck. He was tall, with a full head of white hair, still handsome at sixty-seven, with eyes dark and serious. His bearing and manner had a gentle kind of wisdom. He spoke some English although, after my session with Cocteau, I felt much more confident with my French. Braque's studio was tidy and functional: a few calm green plants, some pieces of African art and a guitar – the *sine qua non* for a Cubist. His sailor's hat was on a table, a sign of adventure, although his stormy pioneering days were over, and he was now safely moored in the harbour of success.

Jean was there of course, but only for a short while, *tant mieux*; he could sometimes be a little too talkative and vociferous. I wanted to listen to Braque, not to Jean.

My invaluable assistants, Christopher Challis and Ian Craig, were getting the camera gear ready and the electrician was bringing a couple of lamps in, but to be honest I wanted to prolong this precious occasion as much as possible. Braque was relaxed and – perhaps a spot of *noblesse oblige* – seemed happy enough for conversation.

I gestured over the clean spacious studio and remarked how different it must be from the wild bohemian days of Montmartre: the singing and drinking at Au lapin agile, the incredible hardships of the Bateau-Lavoir.

Braque lit a cigarette and inhaled my question. 'Montmartre was a painters' ghetto,' he said. 'It was also a crucible. At the Bateau-Lavoir many wonderful things were forged; Picasso's blue period for instance, and don't forget, it was there that Cubism was born.'

Cubism: it turned the art world on its head, never to be the same again. Some argue that Braque was just as much the innovator as Picasso. Both were influenced by Cézanne, whose dictum was that all nature is modelled on the cylinder, the sphere, and the cone, and for Picasso and Braque this had set the ball rolling, so to speak. Oddly, Cézanne had never mentioned the cube!

Where Picasso had swallowed Cézanne up and galloped off in new directions, Braque remained loyal to Cézanne long after Cubism had spawned so many other 'isms'.

And now here was Braque painting before me.

I watched him work, calm and reflective. Utrillo painted mechanically, dabbing listlessly without pause and also without inspiration. Later, when I watched Kokoschka paint I saw how vastly different his approach was to Braque's: I was astonished by his acrobatic antics when he was painting. From six feet away he would suddenly prance forward and place a fleck of paint on the canvas with a loud cry of excitement. Braque had none of that hit-or-miss spontaneity. Every move was made after weighing each single brush stroke in his ordered, disciplined mind. He would gaze passively at the canvas, then make an unhesitating stroke with his brush.

The painting he was working on was far removed from the cataclysmic style of early Cubism, but it was still inherently Cubist. In his early collaboration with Picasso, neither had signed their canvases and it has been difficult – even for the experts – to decide who had painted what, but now, even I could see that Braque's work was quite different from Picasso's. It had a more elegant simplicity and somehow seemed more peaceful. He told me that the painting was one of a series called 'The Studio'. There was an easel, a bird in flight, and a white vase – like a cutout, sharply defined against jet black. It was tenderly poetic and gravely beautiful.

Had he enjoyed the brief Fauve period? Yes in a way, it was a new freedom and everyone benefited by it, but it couldn't last for long. 'One can't stay in a state of paroxysm for ever.'

During a break while Chris was reloading the camera, I asked Braque if he painted regularly these days or did he pause occasionally? He motioned me to follow him and took me to a cellar underneath his studio. As he switched the light on I gaped, open-mouthed, at what I saw. The cellar, which was about twenty-five feet square, was completely filled with his paintings; tightly packed like the pages of a book, rows upon row. By my rough calculation, there must have been over two hundred canvases.

I couldn't speak for some moments, while Braque regarded me with some amusement. I turned to him, 'But when is the world going to see all these paintings?' He shrugged: 'They don't belong to me any more. My dealer has complete control over them. Perhaps he will sell some soon, probably he will wait – maybe for years – when they will sell for higher prices.' I didn't ask the obvious. The dealer had surely paid Braque a substantial sum, to keep him in comfort for the rest of his life. (That was over forty years ago. In 1994 a Braque painting sold for over three million pounds. It seems that the dealer didn't do too badly out of the deal.)

Just before shooting was completed Jean told me we were running out of money and needed another two thousand pounds. He had shown a British distribution company some of my rushes and they were advancing the money on a deal whereby they were to have distribution rights in England. I couldn't argue, but felt that Jean was losing on the deal. I didn't know then that I was to lose much more.

It wasn't until later I discovered that Jean Bernard had re-cut my originally two-reel film into over five reels in line with the deal made with the English distribution company. Jean had used every inch of my film including all the NG (No Good) takes and the discarded scenes – everything – in order to increase the length of the film. I was furious and never forgave him.

In spite of this disgraceful act of artistic debasement, *Montmartre* was highly successful and ran for six months in London. Jean told me he'd left the film to me in his will and when he died I could re-cut it to its original size. He died a few years later and he had indeed left *Montmartre* to me, but, true to form, he had never signed his will, so my precious film went to a distant cousin in the French countryside and that was that.

On the last days of shooting Tyrone Power and his wife Linda Christian flew in from America and I was able to show them the fun of Paris at night.

When Ty and Linda left I realized that the late nights and the hard work on *Montmartre* had caught up with me. When I returned to my hotel and was preparing for bed I found blood seeping from my mouth. It didn't seem so dramatic, but it was obviously some kind of haemorrhage. I phoned Jean who came round and took me to hospital where I was X-rayed and put to bed. Next morning I was the subject of a technical argument between three doctors. Two said they couldn't see any sign of lung damage, the third was sure I had TB. Funnily enough, the awful significance of all this hadn't sunk in as deeply as one would expect. I was advised to fly home and contact a lung specialist at Guy's Hospital in London. The following evening the specialist visited me at my home in Palace Gardens Terrace where a bed had been brought down to the drawing room. The specialist had a black patch over one eye, which gave him a macabre appearance. He examined me with the usual stethoscope and finger-tapping, and then told me, rather airily, 'Yes, you have a spot on one lung, you'll have to have a pneumo-thorax operation that collapses your lung for two years,' and he left, leaving me stunned.

I looked round my spacious drawing room with its book-crammed shelves, its paintings; the place where Ludmilla Tcherina and Audran had danced the ballet of *Romeo and Juliet*; where so many famous people had crowded together at my Oscar party. It was now chillingly deserted and I felt that my exciting career – if not my life – was finished.

My wife Julie was with me. The children were asleep upstairs – perhaps I wouldn't be allowed to go near them for a long time – but Julie was being very brave and assuring me that it would be all right, that two years would pass quickly; but we both knew different. As always, I had lived beyond my means and I could not keep up a house and family for two years with no money coming in.

And after two years in a sanatorium – what then? Was I going to be a helpless invalid for the rest of my life, living in an eternal autumn?

The next day I wandered listlessly about the house – a condemned man awaiting execution. Julie and I talked about the situation as calmly as possible. I could sell things, she could go to work . . . it seemed all so unreal. During an aching silence, suddenly Julie said, 'Why don't we get a second opinion from Bischof?' This was our local doctor, a Canadian woman whom we knew had had TB – in both lungs, no less – but she was well now and working again.

Dr Bischof came next day and examined me most carefully. She was puzzled. 'Quite honestly, I can't be sure. It must be extremely slight. But I certainly don't think a pneumo-thorax is necessary.' She told us there was a young doctor who was making a name for himself in chest infections and I should get his opinion. His name was Kenneth Robson (he was later knighted for his outstanding work).

There have been several dramatic watersheds in my life, but without doubt meeting Kenneth Robson was the most felicitous. His examination took a long time and included peering through X-ray screens from several angles. In the end he said there was a very small spot on one lung, but agreed with Dr Bischof that a pneumo-thorax was quite unnecessary. He told me that the idea of TB patients living outdoors in huts was a thing of the past. Rest was vital. I could easily get that at home, but he advised it was psychologically better for me to go to Switzerland for a few months. So much depended on my mental attitude. If I fought TB mentally, I would surely win.

I felt I had woken from a nightmare. Kenneth Robson was younger than me but I trusted him as though he were Hippocrates himself. Robson advised me to go to Dr Roche, a highly respected Australian doctor at a sanatorium in Montana, Switzerland.

I had a most kind letter from J. Arthur Rank who offered to help me in any way. Many others wrote expressing their shock and concern and Henry Hathaway reassured me that 'All of us have had it to some degree.' When he was undergoing examination in America for cancer they found his chest was riddled with TB scars and that he'd had TB, but had never known it. He invited me to stay at his ranch in Oregon for complete rest with 'wonderful foods, cream butter, red meat, fruit, and everything you need'.

The Rank Organization helped me by making me technically redundant. They sent me my remaining salary from my two-year contract on condition that I promised faithfully to continue to work for them when I got well. That relieved my financial worries.

When I got to Montana I realized what Robson meant by mental aggression. In the room next to me there was a young man who was a musician, but he looked like a rugby player with his hefty physique. He wasn't seriously stricken, but somehow he hadn't the inner fight in him and he died. I saw a side of life that was extremely sad and perhaps subconsciously I was bracing myself to fight my affliction like a tiger.

It was fascinating to be present at Dr Roche's periodic lung inspections. All the patients who were not bedridden assembled in the X-ray room, which was lit only by a low-wattage red lamp, giving it the atmosphere of Hades. Dr Roche would turn up wearing dark red glasses to maintain his light sensitivity, then one by one the patients would present their chests to a large X-ray screen for Roche's inspection. He hadn't seen who was behind the screen but, extraordinarily, he would recognize each patient by their lung condition. 'Hello, Nicole, you're looking good this morning . . . Ah, Gerhard did you take the new pills? . . . Morning Françoise, you're doing splendidly.' It was all rather uncanny.

I don't think my lung condition excited Dr Roche very much. There were many patients who were in far worse condition than I was. In those days the two effective drugs were streptomycin and PAS – short for para-aminosalicylate, which I can never remember without looking it up – and it was PAS that I was taking.

Obviously, Dr Roche had to observe how I reacted to the treatment. The tubercular cavity had to contract slowly until it scarred over, but there was always the possibility it would re-emerge later according to individual resistance so I was still subject to Dr Roche's Argus-eyed surveillance.

After a few days I was allowed to go on walks of increasing distance and even did a bit of skating. There were two-hour rests in bed after lunch and sometimes film shows in the evening and always early to bed. I did an oil painting of the glorious Swiss mountains which I gave to a patient.

After six weeks I became fitter than I'd been for years. It was coincidental that just as I was yearning to go out in the world again I had a letter from my agent saying he'd been approached about me photographing a film with James Mason and Ava Gardner called *Pandora and the Flying Dutchman*. Could I do it?

Dr Roche thought about it, then said I could but I would have to take a two-hour rest in bed after lunch and not work too many hours. I had to be honest and tell him that the film business was not at all like that. I would be up very early every morning, work hard all day with a short break for lunch, and often work late at night.

Dr Roche stared at me thoughtfully and the moments hung heavily in the air while I waited for his decision. He smiled. 'Yes, I still think you can do it. Off you go.'

9

Ava

Ava Gardner greeted me warmly when I met her for the first time in her Savoy Hotel suite. The very first thing she said was 'Jack, I'm looking forward to working with you – you must light me very carefully when I have my periods.'

I gravely assured her I would be careful on those occasions. We talked about make-up and she showed me costume sketches for the forthcoming film.

As the press were always claiming, she was indeed one of the most beautiful women in the world. She moved with feline suppleness, using every part of her superb body as Hollywood had trained her; her voice was low and husky as befits a movie sex symbol. But behind all this, she was an ordinary, kind woman who, if she hadn't acquired that phoney Hollywood majesty called stardom, would have been an everyday American housewife, turning a few heads as she strolled down some midwestern main street.

Al Lewin was the producer/director and had also written the script. A tiny man – less than five feet – but with high achievements behind him; he had worked with Sam Goldwyn, King Vidor, and the great Irving Thalberg, producing films with Garbo, Norma Shearer, Jean Harlow, Clark Gable, Charles Laughton *et al.*

Most directors who have been around a while have that gaunt, soul-scarred look associated with fighter pilots who have survived a war, but Al showed no trace of mental massacre. His pink, cherubic face was always cheerful and his sky-blue eyes constantly sparkled with humour. He was almost deaf and carried his hearing aid in his waistcoat pocket. Half-way through the film we had a dinner party and played a rather cruel joke on him. We all gradually lowered our voices and Al, thinking his battery was failing, kept turning up the volume on his hearing aid. Soon we were only silently mouthing words and Al had turned the volume full up. Then we all shouted at once, causing poor Al to grab frantically at his hearing aid. Al, bless his heart, took it in good part – he must have known we were very fond of him.

Ava's co-star was James Mason, famous for that voice of his, as near perfect an English voice as can be. His intelligence was a bracing counterpart to Al Lewin's. A Cambridge man, with a nimble enquiring mind, he was good to listen to. Right from the beginning he and I formed a friendship that was to last many years, and it strengthened when we became neighbours in Switzerland. We used to play tennis several times a week and sometimes, when I had received a script to direct, he would read it aloud, in character, after which we would discuss the pros and cons.

On *Pandora* his then-wife, Pamela, was with him on our Spanish location with Portland, their baby of fifteen months, who, to the amazement of many of us, was permitted to stay up late with her parents. It was a theory of James and Pamela's that it would do no harm and would prepare her for the adult world.

I must say, it didn't seem right at the time, this tiny baby waddling about the hotel lounge until well after midnight, and when I heard later that she had a mink coat at eight, I felt she was going to grow up to be an archetypal Hollywood hussy. How wrong I was. I saw her again in LA when she was twenty, a stunningly beautiful woman with perfect grace and impeccable manners. So much for mouldering prejudice.

A couple of days before shooting started we all went to a local bullfight to see Mario Cabre, a famous Spanish bullfighter who played the same role in our film, and whose character was in love with Pandora.

We were in a holiday mood as Mario came out to cheers from us and we settled down to enjoy ourselves. After a few brilliant passes with the cape, we jumped in sudden horror as the bull caught Mario and tossed him high in the air. Our horror was not only because one of our important actors seemed about to be killed, but because Mario was already popular with us. He was almost family now. Luckily the *cuadrilla* rushed in and made a *quita* so Mario could be carried off. He wasn't badly injured, but his pride was hurt as he wanted to impress Ava, to whom he had taken quite a fancy off-screen too.

Later in the film he had to fight a bull, alone in a deserted ring, in front of Ava in the moonlight. This time he gave a wonderful exhibition with the cape. There was no crowd, only the director, camera crew and Ava. He ended his dazzling display with the *mariposa* – the butterfly – rarely used because it is deadly dangerous; the cape is held *behind* the bullfighter and is passed from side to side as the bull advances

One mistake and the bullfighter is gored in the stomach. Al Lewin shouted at him but he ignored us; there was nothing we could do except watch in tension and pray until Mario walked away proudly, looking to Ava for acknowledgement. She was impressed as Mario intended her to be, but not in any romantic way.

She was in love with Frank Sinatra and pined for him constantly. I mentioned to her that one of my favourite Sinatra songs was 'I Fall in Love too Easily', which I had heard on the radio. A week later, I received from Sinatra his version of the song signed by him on the label.

It had been said in the press that Ava had a wild affair with Mario Cabre, but I don't believe it. Frank was still legally married to his first wife, but he was very much in love with Ava and they were phoning each other constantly. When we were shooting in London, he flew over to be with her. Of course the tabloid press had a great time with Ava and bullfighters. They dreamed up another affair Ava was supposed to have had with the legendary El Cordobes, but again I'm sure it was all newspaper hype.

We started shooting *Pandora* at Tossa de Mar on the east coast of Spain. I soon realized I had a problem. Both James and Ava couldn't stand bright light shining in their eyes, a common problem with many actors. We had to shoot a love scene on a beach in the moonlight. Because of the extensive backgrounds it was not possible to shoot at night, and so it had to be done day-for-night. This meant using lights and reflectors to balance the actors' faces against the stark glare of the Spanish sun. I could see James and Ava squinting uncomfortably, and set huge canopies of black net over them which helped a bit, but there was also the white-hot dazzle of the beach so – and this is typically ridiculous – we had to spray paint on the sand! The scene didn't really work: apart from the difficulty of trying to act a tender moonlit love scene in the sizzling glare of the Spanish sun, there was such a roar from the surf that the low intimate dialogue was lost. In the end we confined our shooting to long shots and saved the close-ups for the studio.

Mario Cabre was crazy about Ava. He wrote poems about her in Spanish and would read them to her with much fervour. But Mario wasn't her only worshipper. Al Lewin was so entranced by her beauty he would shoot many more close-ups than he needed, gazing at her as if in a trance. Only with great reluctance would he say 'cut'. We shot so many close-ups from different angles that Angela Allen, our continuity girl, gave up trying to work out how they would fit into the sequence.

The scenes with Mario Cabre fighting a bull posed the usual problems of getting the camera – or the bull – in the right place. An actor can be asked to move a little to his left or right, but you just can't do so with a bull. Mario was very clever and was able to manoeuvre the bull to a certain extent, but it was impossible to do close work.

I had an idea which proved to be one of the worst ones I've ever had: use an ordinary tame cow, put fake horns on it and then get into the ring and shoot close-ups with a hand-held camera. My idea was accepted with enthusiasm. A pair of sinister-looking horns was placed on our pseudo bull and we started shooting. It was an utter disaster. A real pedigree bull almost always charges railway-straight, and a bullfighter can let the bull almost brush his body as it thunders by. A cow, on the other hand, is altogether different. Our one frolicked all over the place like a drunken sailor, turning round in circles and kicking her legs like a mule. After Mario was nearly knocked over by the cow's behind, he angrily walked away, resentful of the crew's raucous laughter and the loss of his dignity. That was the end of my brilliant idea. We had to revert to long focal-length lenses and a real bull. I thought Mario would never forgive me but he did, and later in my London home he staged a bullfight with my children – Mario playing the bull.

Back in London to continue shooting I met Frank Sinatra, who was most friendly and happy to be with Ava. Julie and I went out with them many times; to dinner and then usually on to several night clubs in quick succession, ending up at dawn having breakfast somewhere. I soon gave up this wild nightlife – it would have killed me – but it was fun while it lasted.

Of course, at every night club we went to there was high adulation for Sinatra. They played all his songs, a vain nudge for him to sing. But he sang only once, sotto voce, for Ava, heard by our table alone. It was quite a unique experience to hear Sinatra singing without a mike, so close to us and so quietly.

When Sinatra had to return to America Ava was miserable again so I took her to see Fonteyn in *Sleeping Beauty* at Covent Garden. I was able to get a box – a rare slice of luck, indeed. Ava had never seen Fonteyn and was quite excited as the curtain rose. She was chewing gum in a contented rhythm.

Sleeping Beauty commenced with a sparkling prologue with the chewing going much faster; when I said 'There's Fonteyn', she squirmed with excitement and the jaw-speed escalated to maximum. Then I realized that the dancer who had made a whirling entrance was not Fonteyn, who later appeared to rapturous applause. I said, 'Sorry Ava – *this* is Fonteyn.' Ava stopped chewing. Her mouth dropped and she remained rigid in thrall. Only at the end of the act did she turn to me with an ecstatic sigh as though she had seen a miracle at Lourdes.

It was four years before I worked with Ava again. There had been *The African Queen* and three films with Errol Flynn. Now it was *The Barefoot Contessa* directed and written by Joe Mankiewicz; her co-star was Humphrey Bogart. In that time Ava had married Sinatra but now the marriage was over.

On *Pandora* she had not been sleeping well because of her pining for Frank and had taken sleeping pills, so I had to be careful with the lighting when her eyes showed lack of sleep. Now, after her break-up with Sinatra, she was sleeping badly again, taking more sleeping pills and I had to watch her eyes with even more attention.

There was also a new man in her life, Miguel Dominguín. I first met him when he visited Ava when we were shooting in Rome. He was attractive, easy-going, amiable. From his fresh, youthful appearance it was difficult to realize he had been close to death many times and was considered one of the great bullfighters of Spain.

At the end of the picture, I was spending some time in Madrid and he invited Julie and I to stay in his hacienda for a week. Ava had an apartment in Madrid, but was also at Dominguín's hacienda. At his swimming pool I was horrified to see a vast profusion of scars on his body. His back, chest and legs were a livid mass of dark-red weals, a grim composite of many surgeons' work. As he moved, it looked like snakes were trapped under his skin.

Life was highly enjoyable on the hacienda although there were times when Julie and I had to pretend not to hear Ava and Miguel's tempestuous battles, particularly on one occasion when Miguel threw Ava in the pool to cool her off.

One evening Miguel talked about the death of Manolete, arguably the greatest bullfighter in Spanish history. I hadn't realized that Miguel had been part of Manolete's *cuadrilla* and had been in the ring on that fateful afternoon when Manolete was killed. Miguel showed me photos in his album of the tragedy when he had rushed in to make a *quita* – getting the bull away from the fallen Manolete, but the bull had gored Manolete irreparably in the stomach. Sadly Manolete's life could have been saved if the bull-ring's medical facilities had not been so primitive.

Some days later, Ava told Julie and I that she had broken completely from Miguel, and her sister, Bebe, was already packing her many cases to go back to America. Then Miguel arrived. At first Ava refused to see him but he gently and firmly shepherded her into another room where they talked for half an hour. We wanted to leave, but Bebe begged us to stay in case there was violence.

There was no violence. Ava and Miguel emerged holding hands with tender smiles. Ava told her sister to unpack everything. She was returning to the hacienda with Miguel. As they left Bebe, who had spent all day packing Ava's extensive wardrobe, hissed, 'Ava, you're a fucking nuisance!'

Some days later we all went to a small bull-ring where young cows were put through their paces to choose those worthy to produce the best fighting bulls. Many of Miguel's friends were there and much sherry was downed before the heifers were to be introduced into the ring. Some of us were to make a few passes with the cape and pretend we were bull-fighters. Miguel asked me to have the first go and gave me his own bright magenta cape, which I have kept to this day.

With a sense of excitement I advanced to the barrier to wait for the first heifer to come out from the opposite side. With a crash the gate swung wide and a huge black shape thundered out and headed straight to where I stood behind the barrier. This was a baby COW!? It was about four feet high with wicked-looking horns, which the cow stuck viciously into the wood a few inches from my face.

I was frozen with cowardice, but I realized that I couldn't chicken out in front of dozens of people. I had to go out there, even though I was convinced I would be in hospital within half an hour – or in a cemetery.

To my immense relief Dominguín rushed to my side saying, 'No, Jack. This one is not for you – much too playful – I'll take it. You take the next one,' and he advanced to the centre of the ring with the easy confidence of a real bullfighter going to have a bit of fun. The next couple of minutes were like a surreal comedy. The young cow charged from all kinds of angles, twisting, bucking, turning in wild wrenching circles, and there was the great Miguel Dominguín frantically waving the cape all over the place like a flag-hoisting football fan.

A bullfighter with a real bull stands still as a statue while the bull charges past, but Dominguín was never allowed to stand still for a second. He was too busy dodging the wild broadside lunges and kicking legs. What kind of cape-work does a bullfighter use against backside butting? I remembered the fiasco on *Pandora* when I had suggested using a cow instead of a bull, and here was a repeat show.

Actually Dominguín's performance, in the circumstances, was magnificent and he was applauded like a Goliath as he manoeuvred the whirling beast out of the ring. Then it was time for me to have a go as

Miguel, laughing and breathless, handed me his cape again.

After Miguel had finished I waited for the gate to open with wary apprehension after what I had just witnessed, but this time a small Disneyesque heifer ambled out. I was so relieved I could have hugged it like a teddy bear. It did charge a bit, but more or less in a straight line so I was able to make several inexpert passes; to round off, I did a parody of the *mariposa*. Then Dominguín brought Ava into the ring and they held opposite ends of the cape, lifting it high to let the heifer pass underneath. Then the others joined in and the whole thing was really enjoyable after all.

There was intense rivalry between two of Spain's greatest bullfighters; Miguel Dominguín and his brother-in-law Antonio Ordonez. I had seen both in the ring. Ordonez was the perfectionist of the two, while Dominguín combined classic cape-work with incredible daring – like sitting on the narrow barrier used by panicking bullfighters to vault over. Dominguín would just sit there letting the bull charge straight at him until the last suicidal second before flashing his cape and jumping clear. Sometimes he kissed the bull between the horns. The old-guard *aficionados* considered all this as show-off stunts, but the crowd loved it and Dominguín was a hero to them.

There was great excitement when it was announced that there was to be a *mano a mano* contest between Dominguín and Ordonez to decide who was the best. The venue was Algeciras.

I couldn't resist making the trip to see this classic battle. An hour or so before the *corrida* I was at the hotel where Miguel was staying. The lobby was packed with people as Dominguín came down the circular stairs, in his matador's costume, looking magnificent, smiling and acknowledging the applause from the crowd. He caught sight of me and came straight over to shake hands, then we walked to the bar where he ordered a glass of water. Close to, I noticed he looked awful. His face was pale – even slightly green – and I asked him if he was feeling ill. Miguel smiled wanly: 'I'm always like this before the *corrida*. I am absolutely terrified.' This revelation touched me as I knew that Miguel was a man of awesome courage, but he was human after all and had the guts to say so. Suddenly, a large man with a white beard was with us and Miguel introduced me. It was Ernest Hemingway, whose classic *Death in the Afternoon* had first prompted my interest in the bullfight. Of course our conversation was entirely about the imminent *corrida*.

I would like to have talked about *The Sun Also Rises*, *For Whom the Bell Tolls* and *A Farewell to Arms*, but this wasn't the time or place with such an exciting *corrida* only minutes away. Miguel called Hemingway 'Papa', as apparently did Ordonez; in turn Hemingway loved both of them like his sons. His passion for the bullfight was based on his interest in the courage of a man who constantly faced sudden death.

The great head-to-head *corrida* began. The place was packed solid, the musicians were blaring their trumpets and the atmosphere radiated expectation. As always, there was a smell of death in the air. I felt the echoes of the days of gladiators fighting to the death. Perhaps the main fascination for the bullfight crowd is the atavistic expectation of seeing the bullfighter killed.

Ordonez had the first bull and was, as usual, magnificent, making all the classic moves with dignity and courage. When the bull was killed he was wildly applauded and given the usual tokens of honour from the judges.

Now it was Dominguín's turn. Usually, the matador doesn't enter when the bull first appears. One of his team (a *cuadrilla* of four) runs out, waves a couple of perfunctory passes with his cape, then makes a hasty exit. This is to show the matador, watching intently from behind the barrier, which way the bull hooks with his horns; some bulls hook to the right, some to the left. A bullfighter must know; his life depends on it.

On this historic occasion, however, Dominguín scorned technicalities, jumping over the barrier and walking calmly to within five yards of the *toril* – the small gate from which the bull emerges. He sank to his knees, with his cape laid down in front of him. The crowd was utterly silent at such suicidal daring.

The bull exploded from the gate and, seeing Dominguín kneeling in front of it, came at him like a cannonball. Only at the last second did Dominguín lift his cape high above him and the bull, following the cape, jumped clean over Dominguín's head to a bedlam of noise from the crowd.

Miguel had gambled on the bull following the cape above his head, but the bull could so easily not have. It could have just lowered its head and shattered Miguel's life away. Crazy or not, it was the bravest act I have ever seen. And I remembered that only an hour before he had told me he was 'absolutely terrified'.

I can hear some readers wondering how I can extol such a barbaric spectacle. They have a point. I have always had a disturbing ambivalence about it. When the reality which underlies the surface spectacle shows through, it is indeed barbaric and sometimes revolting. But underpinning the bullfight is a set of intricate technicalities and hundreds of years of tradition which, at the best *corridas*, manifest themselves in encounters of great poetry and drama.

But a game for which I do have an abiding passion is cricket. I can think of no drug more addictive, or that can lift one's senses to such heights of pleasure.

Sadly, I was never very proficient at this so very noble game. I did not have the advantage of school coaching, and though I did enjoy a spell of net practice at Alf Gover's club at Wandsworth, I doubt whether I would have been chosen for a village second eleven.

Then a magic thing happened. I joined the Lord's Taverners, a club dedicated to raising money to provide recreational facilities for youngsters. Every few Sundays I would play cricket for this worthwhile charity, whose patron is Prince Philip, and – sheer bliss – there would always be a sprinkling of famous cricketers in our team, cricketing legends like Denis Compton, Peter May, Alec Bedser, Bill Edrich – all of whom I idolized more than the heroes of Greek mythology.

The team always also included a few stage and screen celebrities, such as David Frost, Harry Secombe, Ian Carmichael, Brian Rix, and a young Richard Hearne made up as Mr Pastry, a white-haired eccentric who clowned about and delighted the spectators. I could hardly call myself a celebrity, but I just squeezed in. It didn't matter that I didn't get runs. The icons would get the runs and the wickets. It was pure Walter Mitty. Here I was, batting at one end with Peter May at the other.

On the Isle of Wight once I was fielding at cover point and Jim Laker was bowling. The batsman hit a cover drive straight into my hands like a bullet – and I let it slip through my hands. They say that when you die your life flashes before you, and such was my agony at dropping a catch off Jim Laker's bowling that this seemed to happen – but, miraculously, before the ball reached the ground, I caught it, to roars from the spectators.

When I was living in Switzerland, I had a phone call to play in a match in Scotland. I caught a plane to London, then an overnight train to Scotland, in time to play the next day. I fielded all day, then, batting at number eight, took my position at the crease. On the way out, my captain had said, 'Jack, the light's going. Hit every ball.'

So I hit my first ball hard to leg and was caught – out for a golden duck. I then took the overnight train to London and flew back to Switzerland. But what a day it had been.

One wonderful day, I had lunch with Jack Hobbs. There are three awesome names in cricket history: W. G. Grace, Don Bradman and Jack Hobbs – my childhood hero. I had watched him play at Kennington Oval when I was twelve and marvelled at his perfection; now I was sitting with him in a restaurant having been introduced by my uncle, also a cricketing man. Hobbs had retired, and told me some amusing stories. When he was just starting out, he played in a match with the legendary W. G. Grace, who was bowling leg breaks with three fielders on the leg boundary. Hobbs – always alert for a quick single – played a ball half-way down the pitch and started to run, but stopped in his tracks as Grace called out, 'Thank you youngster, just tap it back to me and save my poor old legs,' and Hobbs, in awe of the great man, dutifully tapped the ball back to him. Hobbs said that when he was asked to play in the odd village charity match, he was terrified because the local bowlers would hurl the ball down at him with very little accuracy, hoping to say that they had got Jack Hobbs out.

I visit Lord's cricket ground when I can, to see a mid-week game when there are not so many spectators. As a member of the MCC I can sit in the sacred precincts of the Long Room or in the front row outside, with the roar of London's traffic magically gone. All is silent except for the blissful sound of willow meeting leather – the soul of cricket – and the soporific gentle applause when a cover drive goes to the boundary. It is perfect Arcadian peace.

I don't play any more. I watch, and dream I could play much better now. But then I remember: 'Cricket is a game which you learn to play only when you no longer can.'

10

Huston, Bogart and Hepburn

'It will be so simple,' said John Huston. 'We'll make the whole film on a raft. We'll put a replica of the boat on it, using the raft as a stage, and we can be towed along the rivers of Africa while we shoot away to our hearts' content.' And he stretched his long frame in the depth of his armchair and took a contented sip of his brandy.

I sipped my brandy more soberly. A raft, on water. I remembered the soul-drenching horrors of that lifeboat in *Western Approaches*, and the old film axiom: animals, children and water – the most hazardous risks in movies. And water has *always* been the worst. Still . . . it sounded a novel way of making a film, drifting down rivers in Africa. It could be quite an adventure.

Director John Huston, producer Sam Spiegel and myself were in a luxury suite at Claridge's, discussing how we would make *The African Queen*. In a corner of the room, a couple of twelve-bore shotguns showed Huston's intention of doing another kind of shooting in Africa. The table – a gourmet's battlefield, strewn with the remains of good food – had had its effect, and everything looked absolutely splendid, that one enchanted evening in London, February 1950.

Looking back on it all, we must have been out of our minds. If only we could have foreseen that, a few months hence, our crew would return to England emaciated and the *Lancet* medical journal would overflow with our case histories.

The script of *The African Queen* by James Agee, Peter Viertel and Huston, was obviously a winner the moment you read it; the casting of Humphrey Bogart and Katharine Hepburn perfect. At first I had the usual reaction to an American being cast as a cockney, as well as another American being cast as an English lady, but it has been proven so often that strong personalities and good actors are more important than national authenticity in casting.

C. S. Forester's great story had been around for years – a disadvantage according to the film hierarchy, which showed yet again their extraordinary lack of instinct for a box-office winner. It had gathered dust on Sir Michael Balcon's desk for a time, but nothing came of it. Columbia bought the rights and planned to make it with Charles Laughton and Elsa Lanchester, but that didn't materialize. Then Warners bought the property from Columbia, intending to star Bette Davis and David Niven, but that also fell through. Finally, Sam Spiegel and John Huston were able to acquire the rights and set it up with Romulus Films, run by the Woolf brothers (John and Jimmy), to be made as a British-based movie.

We had a get-together party where I met the legendary Humphrey Bogart, who silently stared at me with his sombre eyes – like a gangster appraising someone before drawing his gun. Then he spoke in the gritty snarl of a tough guy in a trench-coat. 'Listen, Jack – you see my face. It's got a lot of lines and wrinkles on it. I've been cultivating them for years, and I like them. They are *me* – so don't try and light them out and make me look like a goddam fag.'

His lovely wife, Lauren Bacall, was behind him. She gave me a reassuring wink, but I had already been briefed on 'Bogey' and knew he was playing his game of mock tough guy, testing me out.

I peered at the famous face and shook my head sadly: 'Bogey, I've had many a tough job trying to light out lines on actors' faces, but this time your face has got me beat. There's too much debauchery there, I can't do anything about it, so you'll be all right.'

His eyes lit up, and that wolf grin appeared as he made a derisory gesture towards my glass of beer. 'OK, Cardiff. Put away that cissy drink, and let's have a real one.'

And that was the beginning of a friendly slanging match that lasted throughout the picture.

While we were making the usual tests – make-up, costume, hairstyle, etc. – I made my acquaintance with Katharine Hepburn, who impressed me at once. Here was no facile Hollywood glamour queen, but an intelligent woman with Toledo-steel character. I tried to convince her not to wear any lipstick on the film in her role as a priest's daughter, pre-First World War. She agreed in principle, but did not want to deglamourize herself to that extent, so we compromised: just a suggestion of lipstick and the minimum of make-up to cover her freckles – which I liked, but she emphatically did not.

There was much activity preparing for the African location. Although I knew we were taking much less equipment than usual, I requested two lamps to be sent out, to be run off a tiny generator. John Woolf was astonished.

'My dear Jack. You don't need lamps in Africa! That's where all the sun is!'

I explained that the strong overhead sun made it necessary to fill in the resulting dark shadows on faces, and reflectors would be useless on a moving boat. I also made the point that it does, sometimes, rain – even in Africa. In fact, over the opening ten days on our African location it rained nearly every day, and I was able to light the actors with my two lamps and save the company a great deal of money.

I had a wonderful camera crew. My operator was Ted Moore, who won an Oscar for *A Man For All Seasons*. Ted Scaife was photographing the second unit; he was to show much courage and skill photographing backgrounds running the rapids in a slender canoe. He also became a fine cameraman, and photographed the films I directed later. George Minassian, my assistant, had worked with me on many films; another assistant, John von Kotze, also photographed for me when I became a director.

As usual, I had the legendary Harry Arbour who had worked with me all over the world. He had started as a studio carpenter – in English studios, called a 'chippie', which in America means a whore. Then he was my camera grip and, after that, a construction manager; but really he could do anything, and was invaluable on any picture.

A long time after the completion of *The African Queen*, when John Huston was talking to Sir Alexander Korda on Korda's yacht in Antibes about his next film *Moulin Rouge*, he told Korda: 'Before we start, Alex, I want to tell you that I must have Harry Arbour.'

Korda, never having heard of Harry Arbour, said: 'I don't know this actor – who is his agent?'

When Huston explained, Korda was astonished with Huston's insistence on a mere 'chippie' before talking about the film's stars . . . but that was Harry Arbour's value.

During the pre-production, Huston went off on a 'recce' to choose the African location. The plan was to work in the British area of Lake Victoria in Uganda but, shortly after Huston had gone out, a cable arrived from him saying that the location was quite impossible. Far too pretty – like Maidenhead in England. He needed a tougher, more dangerous-looking place. After this cable, nothing further was heard of him for some weeks. Sam Spiegel and the Woolf brothers were worried. Anything could have happened.

Eventually a cable arrived, Huston ecstatically claiming he had found the perfect place. It was in a jungle territory some hundreds of miles from Stanleyville in the Belgian Congo (now Kisangani in Zaïre).

There was consternation in the London office. First of all, the company didn't have Belgian currency; it would mean a new financial set-up. Second, a lot of equipment had already gone to Uganda; this would now have to be transported over hundreds of miles through wild jungle. Then there was the health risk. The part of the Congo John had chosen was in a tsetse fly area, and our location would be two days' travelling to any form of civilization or hospital.

But John got his way, and the unit left England with about the same amount of enthusiasm as Dreyfus must have had, setting out for Devil's Island.

We flew to Stanleyville, then by train and car to a village called Ponthiaville, and after that in trucks and jeeps along bumpy roads. At one point we crossed a river by a rickety ferry of canoes lashed together. Eventually, we arrived at what was to be our home for the next few weeks. The area was called Beyondo, and 'beyondo' it certainly was – beyond anywhere.

Our camp was merely a clearing hacked out of the jungle; the buildings were made of bamboo and palm leaves. There were large huts for equipment and eating, and sleeping huts with two beds on earth floors. It had all been built in five days and was, considering where we were, very well done.

Almost immediately, there was high drama. Shouts of panic were heard as someone ran out of the bamboo lavatory having made close acquaintance with a black mamba, whose poison will kill you within ten minutes. The snake was found and hastily despatched, but the problem was that black mambas always go in pairs, so no one could use the lavatory until the mamba's mate was found, several bladder-swollen hours later.

It took a few nights to get used to the jungle sounds: the shrieks of monkeys, the howling and bellowing of so many beasts of prey – including some, we were told, gorillas – and the continuous high-pitched whine of mosquitoes.

The extreme humidity caused mould to appear on everything almost immediately. Combs, wallets, keys, etc. were soon covered in hairy green fungus.

It could hardly be called a salubrious location: the humid heat, the mildew, snakes, scorpions, crocodiles, mosquitoes, the huge black ants which ran up your legs and bit heartily, as well as the ever-present danger from tsetse flies and bilharzia. We felt it was only a question of days before we would be lying under the dank Congo earth with our names on fungoid bamboo crosses.

Our local labour came from nearby in the forest, and most of them were lepers. At first this jolted us considerably, but we were told that there is little risk of contagion unless one lives intimately with lepers over a long period. Still, this didn't make us inclined to chummy friendships.

Strangely enough, over the weeks we worked in this menacing place, there was very little serious sickness; although, before the end, Ernie Rainer (one of my three electricians) was discovered to have peritonitis and had to be driven back through the night over those horrendous roads to Stanleyville. He arrived with only a couple of hours to spare before fatal consequences would have ensued.

In spite of our resignation to all the diseases we felt were inevitable, we survived in reasonable shape. We felt at the time that, if we could get through the Congo location, our next location at Murchison Falls on Lake Albert, with its bracing high altitude and more moderate climate, would be a holiday by comparison.

Soon after we arrived at Beyondo, we discovered that a truck with important equipment on it was missing, lost on its way from Stanleyville. Harry Arbour immediately volunteered to look for it and – before anyone could stop him – he set off in a jeep. After three days of worrying for his safety, he turned up, a sweaty stubble on his face, his eyes bloodshot with fatigue – but he'd found the truck.

The river Huston had chosen was called the Ruiki, one of the small Congo tributaries, and the water was incredibly black – like squid ink – the result of millions of years of decaying trees; the effect was eerie and sinister. Along the banks, malignant-looking vines hung down, like groping tentacles, and rotting trees lay in the pitch-black water like sleeping crocodiles; the sleeping crocodiles, on the other hand, looked like rotting trees – which was confusing, as most nightmares are.

After a couple of days organizing ourselves, we were ready to go to work. The first morning, as we snaked silently down the river to the location, one of the crew suddenly yelled out in pain as he was stung by a hornet. The next morning, at exactly the same spot, another unfortunate victim was stung. This happened on five consecutive mornings. Each day, as we neared the dreaded spot, the tension was unbearable, wondering in knuckle-tight silence who would get it this time. Bogey and Kate covered themselves with blankets, as a sting on their valuable faces would prevent shooting for days. Eventually, the Africans located the nest and destroyed it – much to our relief.

The work proceeded slowly and awkwardly, as we adjusted ourselves to our cumbersome environment. John Huston's raft idea was working out well enough, but there were difficulties to overcome every day. My two lamps had to be lashed down to guard against an unexpected roll of the waters, and most of the time we had to move to one side of the raft to balance the weight of the heavy Technicolor camera, with its huge blimp, as well as the camera dolly, in order to avoid a heavy and dangerous list.

Sometimes the electric cables or the towing ropes would be caught on a sunken log, causing the raft to come to a sudden and unexpected stop with the ensuing panic as our following flotilla, having no brakes, would crash into us, with towing ropes all tangled about us like spaghetti.

When we had originally enthused about John's idea in that hotel suite in London, we had not envisaged the number of craft which had to be towed behind the raft. First, there was the two-hundred amp generator, perched on a twenty-foot launch. In front of it were two canoes lashed together to hold the cables out of the water to prevent induction troubles. Then followed a mysterious-looking windowless house made of the usual bamboo and palm leaves – also on canoes – which was Kate's dressing-room; and lastly, another launch, holding the sound equipment.

This surreal flotilla – strung out like a string of sausages – was towed by yet another launch. Of course, if our camera was pointing aft instead of forward, we had to arrange the raft in the rear of our ungainly fleet: more organized chaos.

Somehow, it all worked. The replica *African Queen* on the raft was identical to our real boat which, of course, we used from time to time. It had an identical heavy copper boiler, its furnace making bone-shaking vibrations and belching forth hot steam, but the boat on the raft was in sections and we could remove any part and work more easily, as on a stage – albeit a very crowded one.

Bogey and Kate were settling down and seemed to be enjoying it . . . almost. Bogey, in truth, hated the whole African scene. Having a yacht of his own back in California, he felt the nautical disasters very keenly, often bellowing advice to the floundering fleet like a true admiral.

Both Bogey and Kate avoided the camp food and ate mostly out of cans. We called Bogey 'old bean-belly', which made him bridle somewhat. Kate was having difficulty with her hair in the humid conditions and had to use much bottled water – a vary rare commodity – every day.

However, the scenes were looking good and John's confidence was so high that on one occasion, during a long dialogue scene, he sat on the edge of a raft with his back to the actors – fishing. This was too much for Kate, who stopped in the middle of a take and cried out furiously:

'John Huston, I refuse to act in a scene while you are fishing – and with your back to us!'

Huston half-turned his head with his bright, reassuring smile: 'Honey, I don't have to watch. I'm listening, and you sound just great. Do it again, baby.'

And she did. But after this, John was careful not to do any more fishing during a scene.

Inevitably, we had a disaster – a near-fatal one. Our weird, flotsam-like flotilla went along well enough on the straight but turning a river bend was extremely hazardous since the towed craft behind us would tend to plough straight on, laggardly sweeping alarmingly close to the banks. We were shooting an important scene lasting several minutes. This time, Huston was watching Kate and Bogey intently, oblivious of the fact that we were heading for a very sharp bend. The rest of us could see the danger, and it says much for the discipline of film crews that one never stops a scene unless the director says so. We just hung on grimly in tense silence, watching the bank looming up fast and hoping we would make it round this extra-sharp bend. We didn't. Our towing launch turned sharply, but our heavily laden raft ploughed straight into the bank with a tremendous jolt. The crash threw us all over, but worse: the monstrous heavy boiler (which was never bolted down, in order that we could move it around) began to rock violently back and forth; it looked certain to topple right over on to Kate, who had fallen beside it. Huston darted forward and flung himself protectively over her – a magnificently heroic action, but a futile one, as the weight of the huge copper boiler with its fiercely burning interior would have fatally crushed them both.

It was chaos everywhere. A lamp had fallen, but luckily no one had been underneath it. Our following craft was thudding into us as my camera crew held on to the swaying camera, but the focus of the nightmare was the boiler. Bogey and Guy Hamilton, our assistant director, darted in and somehow managed to steady it; Guy's hands were badly burned in the process.

In heavy silence, we started to sort ourselves out. There was no more shooting that day. From then on, we picked our river locations very carefully. No more sharp bends.

Our entire working day was spent on our crowded craft. At lunch time we were served by probably the most glamorous and highly paid waitress in the world – Lauren 'Betty' Bacall. One lunch time we had moored the raft against a shady bank, and had just started to eat when a four-foot green snake fell from the branches overhead right on to our makeshift table, writhing and spitting in all directions and causing much undignified panic until it was cleaved into so many pieces by Joe Vincent, our camera grip, that it looked like green salami. Not even the charms of our lovely waitress could entice us to eat any more.

The evenings back at the camp were usually of a desperately festive nature – perhaps the reaction to having come through the day without too many disasters. Party tricks were performed, usually involving Bogey and Huston. Kate did some painting in oils, and Bogey read *Lilliput* – which he pronounced 'Lillipuke'. It was rather like being in a prisoner-of-war camp without guards and, being so far from anywhere, we had to improvise when things went wrong – as when the supply of distilled water ran short for our batteries. My chief electrician, Jack Sullivan, said the only thing to do was what had been done in the war-time desert. He asked all the men to pee into the accumulators which, with some hilarity, we did – except Bogey, who declared that his urine was so full of alcohol it would certainly corrode the works. So he was excused.

Early one morning, half-way through the film, we arrived at our river location to a staggering sight. The inanimate star of our picture, our noble *African Queen*, had sunk during the night. It was just visible under the black water, half on its side. We were stunned. Guy Hamilton took over the formidable task of salvaging the vessel and we set to work with all the African labour we could find. Ropes were strung from trees on both sides of the river. With much lusty shouting, enough of the stern was hoisted out of the water to dismantle the engine and float it ashore on a raft. Finally, with all the crew perched precariously in slender canoes, we managed to get the sodden *African Queen* on to the bank, where it was discovered to have a badly bent propeller shaft. This had to be straightened in a fire, with the aid of an improvised bellows made from palm trees and bamboo. Ironically, an identical operation was performed by Bogey in the film.

It took a couple of days to get our much-abused *Queen* patched up and ready for work again, and it had been an exhausting job. Guy Hamilton had worked with unflagging energy, with all his responsibilities as assistant director on a location with so many despairing problems. Yet his energy couldn't last for ever. Soon after the *Queen* had been salvaged he said casually: 'I think I'll go and lie down for a while.' He slept for two whole days, after which the doctor said he was suffering from complete exhaustion and had to rest for some time.

Getting to sleep in my palm-tree room was not easy. The palm leaves had dried completely, and were so brittle that the sound of any small insect strolling over the walls would be magnified to a very loud crackling noise. Sometimes I would hear a more subtle sound and feel my mosquito net move with the weight of some crawling marauder. I would switch on my torch to see an enormous insect clawing its way up my net. It was not at all conducive to sleep.

One night I awoke to hoarse shouts outside: 'Invasion! Beware!' I hurriedly lit my torch and, pulling aside the mosquito net, shone it on to the wall from behind which I could hear strange panicked sounds, loud slapping and frantic oaths. Then I saw the unused spare bed in my room . . . *moving*! I thought it was a bad dream, until I realized it was the effect of thousands of safari ants which had entirely covered the bed – as well as the floor – and their energetic bustling looked like the bed itself was moving around. At that moment, I was bitten by several of these enormous creatures which had climbed up on my bed, and I started the slapping game myself. My door crashed open and an African ran in with a bucket of creosote, flinging the contents over the pulsating mass which was several ants deep. The path made by the flung creosote enabled me to run outside, still pulling ants from my body, where I joined the frantic, but unsuccessful attempts to stop this incredible invasion.

Safari ants are always on the move, as their name implies. They travel through the jungle in endless columns and our camp, with so much food about, was an obvious target. They swept through the place like a tidal wave, devouring everything edible in their path. We were up all night, sweeping buckets of creosote all over, but they kept right on – until at dawn they had gone, continuing their safari.

Shortly after this we finished shooting at Beyondo, and packed all our equipment and mouldy belongings to make the long and complicated journey over several hundred miles to Uganda, our next and final location. We travelled by truck and Jeep back to Stanleyville, then by plane to Masindi, on to Butiaba by car, finally arriving at Lake Albert where we boarded a large flat-bottomed houseboat, the *Lugard II* – which, incidentally, had been used on *King Solomon's Mines*.

Our much-battered *African Queen* chugged doggedly along obscure rivers, and some of the way by various trains, eventually joining us on Lake Albert. The journey had been more chaotic than usual. At the best of times, a film company has more moving problems than a travelling circus, but in our sort of terrain it was inevitable that much equipment was lost or delayed en route.

Sam Spiegel rolled up his sleeves and set to work, like a general sorting out the remnants of an army in full retreat. I must say, he did a magnificent job. Communications could be made by radio, but it took hours – sometimes days – and alternative contact could only be made by messages relayed via our small craft, the *Sea Bass*, going down river, then by car to the air strip which we had built ourselves, and a small plane to Entebbe – all of which could take days.

In spite of all our problems and confusion, the unit felt great relief to be in such pastoral surroundings after the dank dangers of Beyondo. Our houseboat was a romantic-looking white paddle steamer, reminiscent of the old Mississippi riverboats. The lake looked clean, not like the murky black river in the Congo, and the green countryside was crowded with just about all the animals in Africa, like a child's school book. As far as the eye could see there were elephants, baboons, monkeys, all kinds of exotic birds, hippos and crocodiles. On either bank there were so many crocodiles one couldn't count them – there must have been thousands – dozing in the sun until we approached them, when they would slide silently into the water.

The whole area was a game reserve, and hunting was strictly forbidden. It must have been painfully frustrating for John Huston, who had brought his magnificent guns to shoot elephant. Now, after a barren two months in the Congo jungle where he never got a shot at a single one, there were elephants all around him. One of us counted two hundred and forty-three of them, but was careful not to quote the number to John.

It all looked so peaceful and charming, yet I was told that Churchill had called this place 'The evil paradise'. I would soon know why.

Almost immediately, sickness descended on our unit. There was much vomiting and diarrhoea, and our holiday mood rapidly disappeared. Our doctor was soon handing out pills like a priest distributing wafers at Holy Communion.

We started work at Butiaba, where a village had been built specially for us since we had to set fire to it later, and working was quite a painful exercise. In front of the camera Kate played the church organ with convincing religious fervour, but the audience never knew that a large bucket was hidden behind the organ into which she vomited between takes. My admiration for her resolution, insisting on working in this condition, was unbounded, but I was concerned about her face looking so green in Technicolor – although, behind the camera, most of our faces matched hers perfectly.

George Frost, our make-up man, became ill one morning and I had to put Bogey's make-up on myself, enduring his wisecracks. It wasn't such a bad job, considering I felt as sick as a dog.

Malaria now hit some of the unit, and the dreaded shakes and high fever became an added burden. In spite of all this sickness, we somehow managed to carry on. Surprisingly, both John Huston and Bogey were quite free of any illness and this should have given us a clue. But sadly, it didn't, and we struggled on thinking John and Bogey were just lucky.

We shot the scenes where the Germans take over and burn the village, and had to do some impromptu casting. My camera assistant, John von Kotze, who in spite of his name was British but spoke fluent German, played a German officer; the ineffable Harry Arbour made a rugged German sergeant-major. At first, Sam Spiegel had agreed to play the officer, but he balked at having his head shaved.

Late one afternoon after we had finished work, we had an invitation to see a tree felled at a sawmill six miles away. Most of the unit felt too ill for this to be of interest, but I had always wanted to see a tree felled. A small group consisting of Bogey and Betty Bacall, George Frost, Rodney Chiltern (who lived in Kenya and was working with us on publicity) and myself decided to go.

We drove along the dusty roads in a Land Rover owned by the sawmill manager, Bob Fletcher, and then walked about half a mile through the forest until we came to the site. The tree was an enormous mahogany, eighty feet high, and twenty-six feet in diameter. The workmen had been sawing away for two days with a long saw – at least fifteen feet in length – and had cut a wedge so that the tree could fall on a chosen spot. We had to approach the tree in a wide arc to avoid the area where it might fall unexpectedly. We watched in sad fascination at this noble tree's imminent destruction.

I said musingly to Bob Fletcher: 'What happens if a sudden storm blows up? Would a high wind blow the tree off course?'

Fletcher visibly jumped, and looked around with a nervous grin.

'Don't say that. It's the only thing we don't talk about – but it does sometimes happen.'

At this moment there was a shattering clap of thunder overhead and, with Hollywood extravagance, rain fell in buckets – as though commanded by an assistant director.

Within seconds we were soaking wet, and the dusty earth a quagmire as we stood staring up at the tree, now completely unstable and swaying as the wind whirled in demonic gusts, which could blow the mahogany giant off its shorn perch in any direction at any moment.

Bob Fletcher looked as sick as we all felt as he shouted that most-used line in movies – 'Let's get out of here!' We started running back the way we had come, but the way was flooded; the only way back to the road was to run across the area chosen for the tree to fall. We ran in a panic, slithering through the mud, right beneath the swaying monster tree, with Bogey growling: 'Hey, God – who writes your fucking scripts?' until we arrived, breathless and exhausted, back on the road. We looked as if we had stood under a shower for hours. Fletcher panted that his bungalow was just down the road, and that we all could have a stiff drink and get into some dry clothes. We poured into his Land Rover like bunches of soggy seaweed.

At his bungalow, Fletcher handed round immense glasses of neat whisky as if it were lemonade, and in minutes we were all completely drunk. For some reason, Fletcher only had a spare pair of shorts and a shirt, but proffered the entire wardrobe of his wife, who was away at the time. At first Bogey said he wasn't going to dress up like a goddam transvestite, but the whisky had made us hilariously uncaring, and soon we were putting on skirts, dresses – even bras – like a Christmas charade. Betty chose a *kansu* – a long nightdress – and Bogey looked stunning in a frilly housecoat. We set off on our return to our houseboat in boisterous hilarity. I taught them the words of the song: 'Only God Can Make A Tree', which we sang in fine voice.

Meanwhile, back at the ranch – *Lugard II* – David Lewin, the well-known journalist, had just arrived from England to write an article for the *Daily Express* about the film unit, who were bravely enduring a mysterious illness.

He was sitting in a deck chair on our moored boat when he heard the unmistakable sounds of drunken singing and, round a bend in the road, appeared the incredible sight of five figures dressed in women's clothes, bawling with whisky-induced fervour 'I think that I shall never see, a poem lovely as a tree', and lurching aboard. We had certainly ruined our heroic image.

Bob Fletcher told us next day that, by some miracle, the tree had defiantly withstood the storm and had only fallen in the early hours of the morning.

The local Africans had nicknames for us, which Rodney Chiltern translated from the Swahili. Bogey was 'man with half beard'; Kate was 'the fierce one'; and Betty, who used to go around looking gorgeous in a bright two-piece, was called 'woman with no clothes'. Rodney thought it was wiser, in case David Lewin took it down for his paper, to translate it as 'woman with two pieces'.

We finished our work on land, and were now shooting the final episodes with the *African Queen* and the *Louisa* (the German war steamer), which is blown up by the noble remains of the half-sunk *Queen*. The gruelling days, handicapped by sickness, were followed by evenings on the *Lugard II*, where we desperately tried to stay cheerful in spite of the high fevers and amoebic dysentery. Bogey placed a freshly caught fish on a sleeping Kate. Needless to say, she was not amused – but it was good for a giggle.

The sickness was getting worse. Kevin McClory, one of our sound-men, was reported to be vomiting blood, and he was also suffering from malaria, shaking uncontrollably in high fever. The doctor wanted to send him back to England, but Kevin insisted on remaining.

Other doctors had been sent out by Sam Spiegel, who was desperately trying to discover what was causing this epidemic. One doctor was of the opinion that we were very undernourished (we had each lost over twenty-five pounds in weight) and needed more protein. A couple of dozen sheep were sent from Entebbe and, when they arrived, the bank looked nostalgically like an English landscape where sheep may safely graze.

The next morning, they had all gone. The crocodiles had eaten the lot.

Kate was now worse, and the doctor ordered her to bed for a couple of days. Spiegel solicitously insisted that she stay in bed for a minimum of seventy-two hours, so the company could claim the insurance.

Kate, being the iron lady she was, insisted on getting up before she was supposed to, appearing in our midst gaunt and haggard. When Huston asked her if she felt better, she snarled: 'Hell, I'm up, aren't I?'

The weight loss continued and we worked like sleepwalkers. Luckily, my camera crew were able to perform in different capacities. When my temperature reached about 104 degrees, I would lie down while my operator, Ted Moore, fulfilled my functions; in turn, I might do his job while he recuperated. It was a kind of invalid musical chairs.

There came a morning on the 'death ship', as we now called it, when the doctor reported to Spiegel that half the unit were too ill to get up, and must stay in bed for at least three days. Sam was sympathetic, but insisted that the rest of the unit must also stay in bed so that the company could claim insurance again. So, we all stayed in bed for three vomiting, dysenteric days. Someone swore they could see the vultures circling the boat, but I didn't believe it: we were too thin and scraggy to provide even a morning snack for them.

But we survived. As Ted Scaife laconically put it: 'You know the rules; if you don't like it, you shouldn't have joined.'

The doctor saw me staggering about like a zombie and said: 'What you need is Benzedrine.' He gave me a handful of tablets and I swallowed them gratefully. I was desperate enough to try anything. Amazingly, within no time, I felt like a Roman gladiator spoiling for battle. Apparently I was thoroughly objectionable to everybody, and I was told afterwards that I had tried to throw my much-loved gaffer, Jackie Sullivan, into the lake. Kate Hepburn told me: 'I didn't like you at all, Jack. Your eyes were really mean and you changed from being a nice guy into a nasty sonofabitch. Don't ever take that stuff again.' And I didn't.

Through all this misery there were lighter moments. In the middle of a tender love scene, as Kate and Bogey were gazing into each other's eyes, a hippo which had come close gave a tremendously loud snort. Bogey turned to my operator and said: 'You don't like the scene, Ted?'

Another time, when we had moored our boat against a bank, we noticed baboons cautiously approaching through the foliage. We carried on quietly, so as not to frighten them. There were dozens and dozens, slyly creeping forward, taking cover behind bushes, then moving forward again like well-trained soldiers. We worked on, none of us making a sound as we stole looks at them getting nearer in their curiosity, until they were only a dozen yards away; we held our breath as they watched us, like visitors on a set. Then one of them – perhaps the leader – sat down sedately on a log, crossed his knees and cupped his chin, uncannily like a human being in rapt study. It was too much. We broke into laughter and they fled, to our regret.

The day before we shot the final love scene, Kate insisted on going ashore for flowers to drape over the background bushes. It was another example of her resolute character. She was still far from well, but put the film before anything, and John was wise to give his blessing to her enthusiasm. She collected bunches of white flowers, which were duly draped in the background.

We did our last few days' shooting with the mighty and magnificent Murchison Falls in the background. We were now working on our real *African Queen* and the tiny boat was crammed near to sinking with us all behind the camera, photographing two lonely people supposedly miles from any other living soul. Bogey had Kate in his arms and they were gazing tenderly at each other, when the most frightening crash shattered the quiet. Our boat rose up almost out of the water, while we all collapsed on the deck in stunned bewilderment – and not a little terror. There was a horrible scraping noise as the boat rocked level again, and then we saw the reason for this unexpected diversion. An enormous hippo had risen right under our boat and very nearly capsized us. The hippo surfaced and lumbered away, giving us a filthy look.

Of course, I could not use my two lights now and, against my better judgement, I placed small silver reflectors angled to the sun to reflect light into the deep face shadows. As we were drifting on a straight course towards the Murchison Falls, there should have been no difficulty in maintaining the reflectors at the right angle – or so I thought. Without warning, we drifted right into a powerful whirlpool, and our boat spun round like a top. The reflected light went off and on the faces, like the beam of a lighthouse. Huston didn't say 'cut', and I knew why. The scene was good. In spite of the light going on and off their faces, Kate and Bogey were reacting to the whirlpool, making a dramatic effect out of it.

When we had managed to move out of the whirlpool, John cut the scene and immediately came over to me. We looked at each other. As my photography was completely ruined, I could have asked John to re-shoot the scene; but I knew I had to take a beating. John said, with his usual bright smile: 'That was a good scene, Jack.'

I smiled back: 'It sure was John. Why don't you print it?'

'I'm going to,' said John.

We grinned at each other. I knew he was going to print it anyway.

A couple of days before the end, yet another doctor arrived to try to find the reason for our baffling sickness, and this time he discovered something so glaringly obvious, it was incredible that no one had thought of it before. The water we used on the boat was pumped through special filters from the lake. It was discovered that these filters were not working, and we had been drinking unfiltered water – we had drunk every microbe in the book of tropical diseases.

It was also now clear why Huston and Bogart were the only ones to stay fit and well throughout the location. They never drank water. Only neat, germ-proof whisky.

I suppose the relief of going home from Churchill's 'evil paradise' strengthened our reserves. In fact, at Entebbe, we accepted a challenge from the local British colony to a cricket match, in spite of our exhausted physical condition. My assistant, George Minassian, was a good bowler; but the rest of our cadaverous team would hardly have caused a stir in the cricket world. However, it was a welcome break, and we enjoyed ourselves.

To the Entebbe team the star attraction, of course, was Bogey – who had never played cricket in his life. When he went in to bat, the bowlers naturally gave him the most gentle balls to hit, as no one wanted him to get out. And, after he had tried a few Babe Ruth swipes, he found it very enjoyable; he was left undefeated to the end, saying with immense pride, 'Hey, I carried my sticks, didn't I?'

The day we were waiting to board the plane, there was one last drama – a sad one. Kevin McClory had been told he must stay behind because of his malaria, but he insisted he was completely recovered and sat with us in the departure lounge at the airport, as happy and buoyant as the rest of us as we waited to board the plane. Suddenly, Kevin started to shake uncontrollably; in spite of his desperate pleas, he had to stay behind. However, it wasn't long after this that Kevin, who had been a humble 'boom boy' holding the microphone at the end of a pole, became a top executive with Mike Todd, and later was to produce the James Bond film *Thunderball*.

We shot just a few interiors in England: the scenes where Kate and Bogey had to go in the water. Using the rivers in Africa could have resulted in them contracting bilharzia – caused by a charming little parasitic flatworm carried by water snails, the larva of which eats its way through the internal organs.

Then it was all over. I don't think any of us quite realized how successful the film was going to be. Over the years it has become a classic. My youngest son, Mason, has a videotape of it, and runs it continually. Every time I see it, I wince at the recollections of our suffering, but still marvel at John Huston's magical touches and the truly perfect performances of Kate and Bogey. I know – whatever the painful difficulties – it was worth it.

Another thing I wince about: before the film started, Sam Spiegel offered me a small percentage of the film, instead of my full salary. I turned the offer down.

16 Imagine – I shot all the 'exteriors' on *Scott of the Antartic*
on this tiny stage at Ealing Studios.

17 With Hitchcock on *Under Capricorn*.
This shows the cut-up table from which actors fell backwards on to mattresses!

18 Checking Ingrid Bergman's make-up.
Her face was so perfect that it was difficult to make her look
less beautiful for dramatic stress scenes.

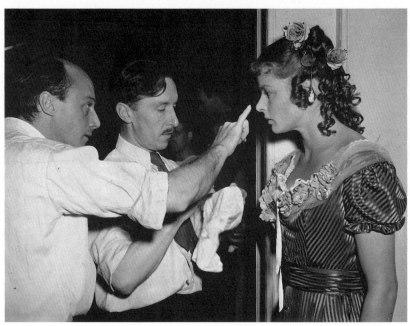

19 John Huston explains how he sees it on *The African Queen*.

20 Our weird modus operandi on *The African Queen*.
The mock-up boat on a raft of canoes, with my two lamps
and the small generator being towed behind.

21 Dancing with Sophia Loren. 'I could have danced all night.'

23 The embryonic set for the film that never was.
Errol Flynn and I look at the blueprint of our village set
against the Swiss mountains on the abortive *William Tell*.

24 Directing *William Tell* with bearded make-up to play in a later scene.

25 I took this picture of Marilyn Monroe and it has since been reprinted all over the world. It is said to be Arthur Miller's favourite of her.

26 I visited Marilyn on the set of her last unfinished film. On the left is Jerry Wald and Marilyn's coach, Paula Strasberg, is on the right.

27 Directing *Sons and Lovers*.

28 Directing Edith Evans on *Young Cassidy*.
I can still hear her famous line, 'A handbag?'

29 Denholm Elliott and Peter Lorre on *Scent of Mystery*.

30 Directing Shirley Maclaine and Robert Cummings on *My Geisha*.

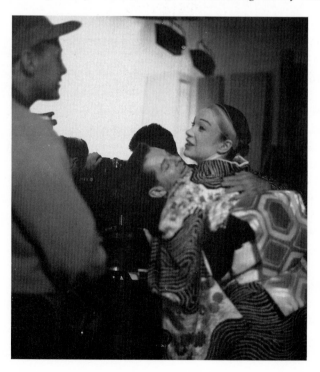

11

Flynn

In the summer of 1953 I was working on Robert Louis Stevenson's *The Master of Ballantrae* on location in Cornwall; its star was the inimitable Errol Flynn. While we were shooting, the assistant director rushed on to the set to say that Flynn had just arrived, and was drinking in the hotel bar. 'Jesus, can he drink!' He spoke with awe and some envy: 'He's just downed four whiskies, with beer chasers in between.'

The film unit broke for lunch, and I was introduced to Flynn at the bar. He was still knocking them back, but there was no sign of drunkenness, only a pleasant, slightly mocking air that typified this legendary character. Looking at him, I felt I was seeing all the pirates, adventurers, all the swashbuckling rogues of history rolled into one – and I liked him immediately. It doesn't take a psychiatrist to know why: most men envy the symbol of a wild, hell-raising reprobate like Flynn, and have a secret desire to be like that themselves.

Errol raised his glass, and winked benevolently at me. 'Hi, Jackson! – glad you're photographing me.' He tugged at his jowls with mock concern. 'Don't worry about this fat, old sport. I'll fuck this off in three days.'

In England at that time, Flynn's notoriety was confined to the popular image of larger-than-life film stars. His hell-raising exploits – no doubt trumpeted by Warner Brothers' publicity department – were those of an outrageous womanizer with a gargantuan appetite for sex, and a capacity to drink anyone under the table.

Few in England knew of a darker side. The sinister stories of smuggling, of pro-Nazi tendencies, and of spying for Germany during the Second World War were not then known. Even his rape trials and tempestuous broken marriages were all part of the image of an incorrigible playboy. The scandals on his yacht, the *Zacca*, where he would leave his harem on board while he hunted sharks with a knife clenched between his teeth, had more the aura of an Olympian satyr than an earthly scoundrel.

The location work in Cornwall went smoothly enough. Errol got on well with William Keighley, the director, with whom he had made *The Adventures of Robin Hood* and *The Prince and the Pauper* in Hollywood. The other leads, Anthony Steel and Beatrice Campbell, worked well with him, and the stuntmen respected his experience and ability. The fights are always arranged by a stunt director and it was interesting to see how Errol managed to work in his favourite fencing moves from his earlier films.

But it was back at the studios at Elstree that his skill as a sword fighter was evident. He'd certainly had enough experience, but his work with the blade was beautiful to watch. His whole being went into it. His animal grace, quick reflexes and perfect timing gave a dazzling dynamism to the duel. Each thrust and parry was a vaunting challenge, and his trick of angling one eyebrow up quizzically gave a bantering mockery to his face as he danced around his adversary. There was a balletic *frisson*, possibly unique in the whole phantasm of film swordsmanship.

Photographing him, I could see that the once Adonis-like face had suffered from the rigours of his outrageous life. His jowls were heavy, the nose slightly bulbous, and the 'debauchery lines' certainly well etched in. But he was still a fine-looking man. The perfect profile, strong chin and brown eyes still mirrored a devil's mischief, and a lurking tinder that ignited so many female hearts all over the world.

It is the assistant director's job to arrange the call for the next day's shooting. One day, when Errol was off-duty, a call was put through to him at his hotel to tell him he was required on the ballroom set the next morning. The assistant told me that Errol had been furious at being disturbed, as he was in bed with two gorgeous women. He had also requested that these two lovely ladies be put in the crowd for the ballroom sequence the following day. Next morning on the set, there was considerable interest in Errol's two bed companions. They were indeed gorgeous. One of the crew, who was well-experienced in London nightlife, said they 'were the best platers in town' (plating being cockney slang for fellating).

One of them – Lydia – turned up often in my travels; once was in Madrid, where she was doing a striptease in a sleazy nightclub. The next day she came for drinks at my house, accompanied by her Italian boyfriend with whom I had worked in Rome. Some years later, back in Rome, I was invited to the Palace of one of the most noble and important princes in Italy. In the drawing room of the sixteenth-century palace, the Prince rose from his *ottocento* damask chair as his wife, the Princess, entered. As she approached, I saw it was none other than Lydia, Errol's bedmate. As her eyes met mine, there was just a scintilla of recognition; then she smiled at me with aristocratic reserve as she proffered her hand – palm downwards.

'How do you do, Mr Cardiff?'

I bowed as I took her hand: 'How do you do, Your Highness . . .'

There were several sequences on *Master of Ballantrae* that required large crowds of extras. One day, as I was threading my way through the gaily costumed throng, directing lights from the spot-rails to be turned this way or that, a group of extras were discussing ways of making love. One of them, known as Nobby, said: 'Now, I bet Cardiff knows a thing or two – what's your favourite screwing technique, Jack?' Film extras are a mixed lot. Quite a few are drop-outs just filling in time, and some of them had, in fact, done 'time'. Some could be from high society doing crowd work for kicks, others made extra work their living. As in Hollywood, a lot of the girls were hoping to be discovered and become stars, and a lot of the men were wide-boys, who could sell you a stolen car and take you to the wildest game of strip-poker in town. What was my favourite technique? I was rather at a loss to reply, but had to say something or look foolish. 'Oh,' I said, smiling airily as I imagined Errol Flynn would smile, 'I have a very special technique.'

'What's it called?' they asked.

My mind skidded. I must call it something . . . a word leapt in front of me, a word that had no connotation to anything in my life at all, and to this day I have no idea what prompted it. 'Jasmine,' I said. 'It's called the Jasmine technique.'

They were immediately hungry for details – 'What happens? Who does what?' – but I was off the hook now. I put on a tight, secretive air. 'No way I can tell you – but it's terrific! Excuse me. I've got work to do.' And I moved on, continuing to set the lights. Within seconds, Nobby hurried over.

'What is this Jasmine? They're all crossing their legs with curiosity.'

'It's nothing,' I said lamely, 'nothing at all. Just the first word that came into my head, so you'd better relieve them of their anxiety.'

Nobby whistled. 'No. It's far too good a gag to waste – I'll see you later.'

He told me later that he had said to the curious extras: 'For Christ's sake, don't ask Cardiff to reveal the Jasmine method – he used it in Paris two years ago, and nearly went to prison. When the Jasmine technique is used, the woman has a climax that lasts twenty minutes at least. In

Paris, the girl had a heart attack and nearly died – so lay off Cardiff!'

Nobby raced over again, and whispered: 'If they ask you any more, say you don't want to talk about it.'

So, for the rest of the day, when the extras begged me to give them the details, I dutifully looked grim or pained and said that I couldn't possibly discuss it. Nobby had embellished the gag even further: 'You see,' he told the extras – who were by this time panting for information – 'there are, so far as I know, only three who know this highly dangerous technique. Ali Khan, who passed it on to Errol Flynn, and Errol who passed it on to Jack.'

The rest of the day was difficult. Every ploy was used to make me reveal the Jasmine method – including a couple of propositions as a reward; by this time the whole set was seething with erotic conjecture. But they saw that I was not forthcoming and in the end I was left alone.

The next morning, in my car on the way to the studios, I picked up a couple of camera assistants and Bunny, Beatrice Campbell's stand-in. As I was driving, she said: 'Jack, I know you don't want to talk about the Jasmine technique – '

'No,' I said curtly, 'I don't.'

'OK,' she said hastily, 'but please – one last thing. I understand you acquired it from Errol, and he got it from Ali Khan?'

'Yes,' I said, 'that's right.'

'That explains it,' said Bunny. 'That's why Ali Khan named his daughter Jasmine.'

To this day, nobody knows anything further about the Jasmine technique. I told the story to Errol and he loved it, laughing convulsively.

'But why,' he said, 'did Nobby have the climax last only twenty minutes? It could have been an hour!'

A few days before we left for our next location in Sicily, we shot a scene where bullets had to be shot against a wall, and the explosions expert had made up tiny pellets. These looked like particles of bread, which exploded with a very loud bang when thrown against a wall, or dropped on the ground. Errol was fascinated by these minute, innocent-looking particles that exploded with such a mighty noise, and he pocketed a couple of dozen.

He told me he had been invited to a reception in his honour that evening by a club consisting entirely of Indians, and asked me if I'd like to go along with him. I was a little curious that Errol had agreed to attend what appeared to be a very dull party, but I accepted. When we arrived at the club, Flynn received a great welcome from the Indians, who told him how delighted and honoured they were that he had come. Errol was smiling graciously as he accepted their homage, and was telling them how much he enjoyed working on *Kim* in India.

As Errol was holding forth to his admiring audience, telling them about his hunting experiences in Mysore, I was startled to see that he was casually – but quite openly – picking his nose. Aghast, I watched while he picked out a large 'bogey' from his nostril and rolled it between his thumb and first finger for a few moments. Then, with a nonchalant air, he flicked it away. The 'bogey' landed on the ground with a thunderous bang. I closed my eyes, and wanted to sink through the floor. Errol was at play again.

The Indians were gazing at Flynn with comic incredulity, as though Krishna had suddenly materialized before them. They couldn't believe what they had seen. Errol carried on the conversation as though nothing untoward had occurred. The Indians listened and nodded, but a little more vacantly now. Some of them were still gazing, with awe and disbelief, at the spot where the snot had landed like a mortar bomb.

In frozen fascination, I watched Errol picking his nose again, seemingly tugging another small lump from his nostril, and kneading it into a ball while the Indians gazed at him hypnotically – and with some apprehension – their eyes glued to Errol's nose. Errol went on talking easily as if it were the most natural thing in the world to disgorge a small bomb from one's nose.

He flicked this one away in the air with his thumb, and dozens of heads swung rapidly in unison – like at a tennis match – flinching as they watched it land on the floor. There was another loud explosion . . . then silence. The expressions on the Indians' faces were priceless. There were dazed mutters in their gorgeous dialect. It was too much. Errol and I broke up at the same moment, and it was such a relief to laugh away my embarrassment.

Errol then showed the Indians the contents of his pocket, and allowed them to throw a few themselves while the room rocked with excited laughter. It wasn't such a bad evening, after all.

*

In Palermo, we shot exciting sea battles using two constructed eighteenth-century galleons. The pirate stunt men were the same ones we had used in England, and by now there was a keen and boisterous relationship. The fights were much more vigorous as they fought on the rolling decks and the high fo'c'sle, or swung Tarzan-fashion from the rigging, whirling cutlasses with bloodthirsty oaths, some of them falling dramatically overboard. Flynn was in his element.

One evening after work, the film doctor told me that he was having a bit of a problem with Flynn. Apparently, Errol had just got over a slipped disc and the doctor had been giving him morphine to relieve the pain. The trouble was, he told me, he knew Errol didn't need the morphine any longer – but Errol was saying he still had pain, and kept asking for more. The doctor agreed with me that he might be hooked on it.

A film unit always has a doctor for the duration of the film. Usually, it's a young man who has just passed his medical exams and knows enough to do the right thing in an emergency. Obviously, an established doctor would never be able to give up several months of his practice for a film. Equally obviously, a well-experienced doctor would have known how to deal with a demand for a dangerous drug like morphine. I suggested to our young doctor that he made some excuse for being out of the drug until we returned to England. I didn't think any more about it, until later.

The following Sunday I played tennis with Errol. The hotel's courts were solid concrete, and murderously hot on the feet. Understandably, the courts were deserted. We played three sets, and both of us were rather battered by the end, but we enjoyed it enormously. Errol played like he duelled, with verve and quick reflexes. He won after three long, hard-fought sets. Later, when I learned that he had played with many of the tennis greats in Hollywood, I realized that Errol's tennis must have been rusty, otherwise I would certainly have been slaughtered.

After that molten game, as the sun sizzled into the sea, we had a swim to cool off. There was a high diving tower just off-shore, the top reaching thirty feet at least. In that mysterious half-light when the sun has just gone down, I watched Errol climb to the top. He stood to attention for a moment against the purple sky, and then made the most perfect swan dive I have ever seen. The effect was like a slow-motion film, he seemed to linger in mid-air like Nijinsky when leaping through the window in *Le Spectre de la Rose*.

There was no one else watching. I felt a certain sadness; in that brief twilight moment, there seemed to be an air of the finality of events. A presage of his own twilight.

Then a thought whacked into me: in those three gruelling sets of tennis he had leapt all over the court, volleyed at the net, and served with venom, at no time mentioning his slipped disc. And that swan dive: his chin arrogantly tilted up, his body curved at the right angle as he soared into the air. Not much trouble with his spine there. It had to be that he was on morphine. In my ignorance, I didn't know that he had been on and off morphine for years in Hollywood, and that the slipped disc was merely a ploy for more of the drug.

My friendship with Errol was unusual. Most of his friends were hard drinkers and womanizers. I didn't drink much, and I'm sure Julie would not have been too happy if I had accompanied Errol to his wild sex parties. Perhaps I was part of a hangover therapy: in between his bouts of drinking and sex games, it might have been that my unadventurous company was something of a breather. I suppose I was a good listener. He liked to talk of his experiences in New Guinea and we both enthused about painting – he had a Gauguin of which he was very fond – and books. I never tried to probe into his notorious past, but sometimes he would tell me of adventures with women that would double me up with laughter.

There had been a romantic conquest that he had taken weeks to achieve. The girl had been from a rich, aristocratic family in France. At first there was not the slightest possibility that she would go to bed with him, and it took all of Errol's assiduous charm and cunning before, at last, in a dream hotel on the borders of a lake, she surrendered. They made love tenderly, Errol with a heady sense of victory. In the middle of the night while his beautiful conquest lay deep in slumber, Errol was wracked by compulsive spasms of diarrhoea. Slowly, hardly breathing, he crept into the bathroom, not daring to put on the light, and accomplished his furtive mission. He was feeling for paper in the dark when he heard his beloved wake up, and sigh: 'Where are you, my darling?' In the panic of searching for paper, he felt the unmistakable contours of a lavatory seat. It was then that he realized he had used the bidet by mistake. With tortured mutterings of 'Coming, my sweet' he frantically tried to clean up the mess. Midway through his maniacal threshings, the bathroom was suddenly flooded with light. His beloved was standing there, staring in horror and revulsion at the sight of her dream prince 'completely covered in shit' – to use Errol's own words. She fainted. That was the end of a beautiful romance.

Some time after the completion of *The Master of Ballantrae*, Errol rang me in my London apartment. He was soon going to make a film in Rome and urged me to come over and work on it. 'It's great out here Jackson, you'll have the time of your life. Bring the family, you'll love Rome.'

Errol didn't have to tell me I'd love Rome. I had fond memories of my first trip in 1936 when I photographed the World Windows travelogues. So I took Errol's advice and brought my wife and three sons to the Eternal City.

The film was first entitled *Il Maestro di Don Giovanni*. The producing company, United Artists, wanted a more box-office-acceptable title, and they chose *Crossed Swords*. Errol played an ageing Don Juan who teaches aspiring novices the art of seducing women: how to swordfight, to climb balconies, and to make a fast exit through a window if a husband arrives. It was tailor-made for Flynn. The script by Milton Krims was witty and amusing, and it was also Krims's first picture as a director.

Errol's co-star was Gina Lollobrigida. In 1953 La Lolla was already established as a bright new star. Some years earlier she had represented Rome as Miss Italy of 1947. Gina was a typical *bellissima Romana*, a dark smouldering beauty with large, lively brown eyes, a pert nose, full pouting lips and a voluptuous body. At that time when proud, alluring breasts were a vital prerequisite for stardom, Gina offered all that could be desired. In France, 'la lolla' meant milk, and a cartoon in Paris showed streams of American dollars issuing forth from her bounteous bosom. She was a happy and friendly person.

I don't think Gina felt any sexual attraction for Errol. She was happily married to a handsome Austrian doctor, Miklo Skofic, and however much Errol would have liked to enjoy the attractions of his co-star, it was nothing doing.

Cesare Danova, a tall dashing Italian, played the younger Don Juan and, after some friction with Errol, they became fast friends, living out their parts with lusty enjoyment. I don't think that there was much Errol could do to further Cesare's education as a Don Juan.

Things went smoothly for the first few weeks. Errol was punctual every day, and seemed to be avoiding too much drink and drugs; but as the picture went on, I noticed he seemed to be drinking a lot of vodka – his favourite drink – even on the set. And his face was showing it. There was also a story of someone supplying him with drugs. It was, sadly, probably true.

I was living with my family in a splendid apartment in Via Lazio, just off that tourist mecca, the Via Veneto. I joined a fencing club and became an enthusiast of a real art, one which I had only photographed in fantasy. I was also, to my great surprise (and some embarrassment) awarded a Doctor's degree in Art. The Italians now called me *Dottore*, and at first

I thought they were kidding. But they were quite serious – and I was stuck with it. Aside from a grandiloquent scroll, I now possessed a small certificate in blue leather which, incredibly, proved of great value on occasions when I had been caught for speeding, or parking too long. My sons went to the Notre Dame school and in no time were speaking Italian. Johnny, my eldest, was lucky to be taught the piano by a friend of ours, Marie Vittoria, who was the wife of my camera operator, John Drake. She had been a well-known concert pianist, and soon Johnny was playing beautifully.

Sometimes Julie and I would attend the Sunday soirées at the home of the painter, Giorgio de' Chirico, overlooking the Piazza de Spagna. Apart from Modigliani, de' Chirico is the only modern Italian painter that became really important, internationally. Before meeting him, I had been intrigued by his metaphysical paintings. Those haunting landscapes of melancholy; empty squares, lit by an icy stark moonlight that cast long black shadows over deserted buildings, which seemed to be stretched in rigid terror against a dark green sky.

On my first visit to de' Chirico, I was sadly surprised that there was not one metaphysical work to be seen. Instead, the walls were covered with paintings done in his later style. They were disappointingly dull. Heavy, stiff portraits: vases of chrysanthemums, fish, bowls of fruit, and although his shining grapes were evocative of his early ovoid heads, they were all chocolate-box, and sterile.

De' Chirico himself had an alarmingly pale face and bright silver hair. His podgy features were set in a permanent pout of displeasure. His wife, Isabella, was much more vivacious and charming. She did most of the talking, while Giorgio usually sat in sullen silence. In spite of this, the Sunday gatherings were usually crowded: writers, painters, a few film people, and the usual circle of friends. From talking to them, I gathered something about de' Chirico's misanthropic outlook on life.

He had, evidently, experienced a lifetime of painful and bitter adversity. Art critics, dealers and his fellow painters – perhaps from jealousy or malice – had taken every opportunity to deride his work. The Italian press, in particular, boycotted him most of the time, and the academic authorities consistently ignored his painting, and humiliated him by giving grants and prizes to lesser artists. He hated them all with a passion bordering on paranoia.

Although it was obvious that he was not an easy person to get along with, perhaps he had a case. I don't know. Certainly most great painters had lives of crippling adversity and derision from critics and public alike, but they went on painting without exhibiting the rankling choler of de' Chirico.

On one visit, I dared to tell him that I would have liked to have seen one of his 'metafisicas'. He looked broodingly at the floor for a long moment, biting on his pipe as though he were smoking wormwood, then he abruptly rose saying that he would show me one. I followed him – not to his studio, but to a small room upstairs where, on a small easel, was a magnificent metaphysical exterior. I studied it in admiration, noting his signature and the date: 1912. I suddenly became aware that the painting smelled strongly of fresh paint. I looked closely: there was no doubt about it. It had been painted quite recently – not at all in 1912. I turned to de' Chirico: 'When did you paint this?'

He gave an irascible snort: 'I painted it – I, Giorgio de' Chirico. That's all that matters.'

I murmured the usual compliments and we returned to the crowd below. I reflected that it was all a rather sad story of a lost dream. His early work had been created from the secret recesses of his dreams, and he jealously guarded the key to them. His metaphysical canvases were deliberately obscure, and he liked to say that nobody understood them. At any rate, they were highly successful, and he had influenced many modern painters.

However, somewhere in his middle life, there had been a watershed. He didn't want to paint from his dreams any more. He abandoned his metaphysical style and started to paint in the tradition of the Old Masters. He delved deeply into the arcane techniques of priming canvases, and the secret glazes and varnishes that were used by the great painters of the past. If his honest and diligent endeavours were satisfactory to himself, they were not to his critics and public. His more realistic and romantic style was judged to be banal and superficial. It must have been galling for him to be constantly asked for more of his metaphysical paintings. Knowing they would be appreciated and fetch a high price, he painted a few from time to time and, pathetically, put early dates under his signature.

Our filming of *Crossed Swords* was becoming difficult. We mainly had exteriors left, and Roman winters can be arctic. Very shortly we all moved to the warmer region of Naples and started work in a large park where most of the trees were evergreen.

A film like this, with so much frolicking by lusty Don Juans, would obviously require plenty of lovely ladies to frolic with, and we engaged dozens of the most glamorous-looking females from all over Italy. Everybody, including this sexy assemblage, was staying in the same hotel overlooking the Bay of Naples, with the sinister Vesuvius inert in the background.

There was nothing inert about our hotel in the evenings. The lift was working overtime, as the hotel turned into a seraglio of carnal enterprise.

Errol had one official suite where he stayed with his wife, Patrice. He also had unofficial, secluded quarters on another floor. Some time later Errol collapsed, and was taken to the Neapolitan Hospital with a severe case of hepatitis. Our producer, J. Barrett (Barry) Mahon, went to the hospital and asked the doctor when Errol would be well enough to resume work. The doctor said: 'Mr Mahon, Errol Flynn is seriously ill. He has practically no liver left. He might die any moment, and I suggest you contact his relatives.'

'You don't understand,' Barry said patiently, 'we're making a movie, with Gina Lollobrigida, and it's costing a lot of money – how long will it take to get him back to work?'

I don't think that Barry realized Errol was near to dying. How could Errol Flynn die – especially in the middle of a film? The doctor repeated his advice to get Flynn's relatives over. He said that if, by some extra-ordinary chance, Errol survived, it would take at least a year before he could possibly work again. Mahon returned to the hotel in a very troubled state of mind.

It was decided that he had no alternative but to continue shooting the rest of the film without our star. Errol's stand-in was very much like him in appearance and, for the next six weeks, we shot on to Gina's face with the stand-in's back to camera. This way of shooting was difficult, and hardly allowed the usual agility with the camera. It was dull work and, when six weeks had passed, we returned to Rome.

Errol didn't die. It was a miracle. He must have had the constitution of Samson. And soon, in the Cinecittà studios, Errol walked on to the set smiling bravely, but thin and haggard – obviously weakened by his latest bed companion, the Angel of Death. I noticed that his usual strong, brown eyes had bright silver rings round the irises like those in the eyes of the ravaged Utrillo. It was sad – like looking at Errol in his dotage.

'Of course,' the doctors had said, 'it really is a miracle. But without any doubt Flynn must never touch a drop of liquor in his life again. He has no liver left.' And here he was on the set, just out of death's doorway, cracking the usual jokes with a large glass of neat vodka in his hand.

We finished *Crossed Swords*, much to the relief of everybody concerned. A few days before the end of filming, Errol invited me to lunch. He told me he was going to make his own film – something he'd thought about for some time: *William Tell*. He would produce it with his manager, Barry Mahon, and offered me my first break as a director.

'What do you say, Jackson?'

It didn't take me long to answer. It was the chance I'd been waiting so long for.

12

Great Expectations

So, I was going to be a director. Promotion in the film business is unpredictable, and can be tantalizingly short-lived. An *ignis fatuus* that has deluded many – and it was to delude me.

Somebody once said: 'Love comes by looking'. This wise maxim could certainly apply to film promotion. You have to look hard at the things you love. I looked hard at paintings, and learned about light. As an assistant, I watched cameramen work with lights, and the looking paid off. Suddenly – unexpectedly – the break comes and, if you've been looking hard enough, you'll succeed. There is a magic casualness about it. One day I had been a humble clapper boy when the director suddenly wanted six cameras on a musical number, and I found myself operating a camera on my own. A glorious moment, but next day, I was back to being a clapper boy. However, the magic opportunities occur again and sooner or later one stays promoted.

I became a successful cameraman, but had always wanted to direct. I had looked at the directors I had worked with: great ones, like René Clair, Jacques Feyder, Alfred Hitchcock, King Vidor, John Huston – and began to believe I could direct when I got the chance. But had I looked hard enough?

So many have said to me – with a kind of frankness, barely concealing their firm conviction I would never be a good director – 'You are right on top as a cameraman. Why on earth do you want to direct?' I would have thought the answer obvious. Photography is certainly a stimulating, creative art. I will always be fascinated by its power of expression; by the use of colour, light and shade, camera angles – all the tricks of the trade; with the unceasing challenge to achieve something new, daring and different. But the ultimate creative use of the medium is unquestionably in the hands of the director. In the realm of creativity, a director's scope is so boundless that there can be no comparison with a cameraman's range. A film director can evoke all the emotions in the sublimity of life, its labyrinthine roads of drama and psychology. All the world's his stage, and all the many arts his puppets to manipulate.

It is understandable that I had a passion to be a member of this godlike fraternity. It was irrelevant whether I ever became a *good* director; I was Icarus, and even if I flew too near the sun, it would be worth it. I knew that to direct an Errol Flynn film would certainly not singe my wings, but I was airborne. It was a start, and I was thrilled beyond the telling.

Barry Mahon was now Errol's co-producer. A bright young American, he had been a pilot in the Eagle Squadron in the Second World War and had actually participated in the famous 'Great Escape' from a Nazi prison camp. He had sound financial expertise, and Errol was delighted to have him manage his affairs. In Italy there were always approaches from film backers to do a film with Errol. Mahon's tactic was to ask if they could lay $60,000 in cash, on the table, before any discussion. Unsurprisingly, this got rid of the charlatans.

While Errol was setting up *William Tell*, he was approached by an Italian named Count Fossataro, a former police chief who reputedly owned a lot of property in Naples. Yes, he could lay $60,000 on the table – I believe he laid down less than this amount, but Mahon was impressed, nevertheless.

Before the deal was agreed, Mahon made enquiries at Count Fossataro's bank. Did the Count have a good standing in the bank? Oh yes, he was assured, Count Fossataro had good standing. It wasn't known then that 'good standing' in an Italian bank simply meant that he wasn't overdrawn or in debt. If he'd had only $1,000 in the bank, he would be in 'good standing'.

Anyway, a deal was made. Count Fossataro was to pay for the production shooting in Italy, and Flynn was to put up his own money for the director, the script, a co-star and the laboratory costs. All this eventually came to $500,000 out of his own pocket.

John Dighton, a fine English writer – he had worked on *Kind Hearts and Coronets* among many others – was engaged to do the script. In the weeks of preparation at Cinecittà, I assembled a film unit from the best in Italy. My assistant director was Piero Musseta; six feet five inches tall, an ex-paratrooper and diver in the war, his energy and creative help were tremendous. Nino Novarasi was doing the costumes; Arrigo Equini was art director; Ghigo Genarelli, the cameraman; Gambarelli, make-up. A superb team with whom I had worked before, including my English operator John Drake, who lived in Rome and was a trusted friend.

Errol had decided to use Cinemascope even before the first film using this process – *The Robe* – had been released; *William Tell* was to be the second film made with this process. John Dighton's finished script was excellent. I went location-hunting with my new crew, and found a perfect setting for the Swiss locations in the beautiful Val d'Aosta, with Mont Blanc dramatically close in the background. It was agreed that our Swiss village was to be built right in this luscious valley, with a breathstopping panorama of snow-peaked mountains all around. The village was built entirely of real stone. There were over fifty fourteenth-century-style houses, and a church. It was simply wonderful. I have never seen a film set so realistically executed, before or since. A small stream trickled, sparkling, through the main street; by the time I began shooting, the wild flowers, the stately conifers and all the natural flora of the countryside had settled in as if the village had been there for centuries.

The towering snow-garnished mountains were all around us, stark and celestial. Mont Blanc itself seemed so near I had the insane urge to sprint up to the summit for a lark. All this, on my first picture as a director. It was too good to be true.

I had an impressive cast. Errol's co-star was Bruce Cabot, an old buddy of Errol's – later I was to hear many stories of their escapades together. There were well-known Italian names: Massimo; Serato; Aldo Fabrizi; Antonella; Lualdi; Vera Cilenti; and Franco Interlengi.

As the days drew close to the start of filming, I felt buoyant with confidence. With so much going for me, I felt I couldn't miss. During this time Errol made occasional trips over Europe when a further distribution deal might be made, or he might get a free car on a publicity angle; on one occasion before he left, he told me that he had big plans for our future in Italy: 'If you discover a good-looking broad, do a test of her and, if she's good, I'll put her under contract . . .'

My casting director, Michael Washensky, had mentioned an attractive girl called Lazzaro, who worked as an extra but desperately wanted the security of a contract. Washensky believed she had possibilities, and I invited her to the studios for an interview.

She was eighteen, tall and lanky, and her shyness was accentuated by her scanty knowledge of English. But it was her eyes that interested me. Large, luminous and slanted slightly upwards, they were tender brown, with a subtle topaz glint. Eyes that would be difficult for any man to forget. Her nose was long and her lips large and sensuous. She had a voluptuous grace that reminded me of a Parmigianino madonna. She was definitely star material, and I decided to make a screen test. I dressed her in a black silk outfit, and she looked terrific. She had no dialogue to learn, as her English was practically non-existent, but she spoke a few words and the whole effect was charming and natural.

Errol returned from his trip to Germany and saw the test; Mike Washensky and myself were present. I noticed that Errol was a little more drunk than usual. The test was excellent; the girl had a kind of Rita Hayworth glamour, and I had shot extra-large close-ups to show those unforgettable eyes.

I naturally expected Errol to be enthusiastic but, to my astonishment, he was not impressed: 'Sorry, I can see nothing in this girl . . . nothing at all.'

Washensky said earnestly: 'Errol – please think more about it. This girl could be a big star. She would sign a seven-year contract for only sixty dollars a week.' Even in those days, that sort of money was nothing. But Errol simply would not agree. And that was that.

As you may have guessed, the eighteen-year-old girl was Sophia Loren. She changed her name soon after that test and Carlo Ponti, a much more perceptive producer than Errol, brought her to stardom in no time. A couple of years later she was just about the hottest star going, and earning over a million dollars a picture. Later, Sophia and I had a quiet giggle about that abortive test, and we agreed how lucky she was not to have signed up with Errol at a pittance for seven years.

The filming of *William Tell* started in June, 1953. I didn't use Flynn on the first day, but he sent me a telegram from Rome: 'Best Luck Pal. I know you're going to make one hell of a picture.' My crew worked with tremendous enthusiasm, and I doubt that a more exhilarating location existed anywhere else in the world: the pure bracing air, the snow-free slopes now exuberant with flowers; the diamond glints on the towering mountains against the intense blue sky. The light itself seemed holy, shining a benediction on us as we worked. For the first few weeks, it was heaven.

I was not to know then that the good Lord – who, in my experience, has a weird sense of humour – was playing one of his practical jokes. Perhaps I should not have floated quite so high in the clouds. During pre-production I had fought many battles with the Italian production office in Rome. Any attempt at good organization was maddeningly blocked by such niggardly, lire-pinching and Machiavellian intrigues that I often wondered if we would ever start the film. Actors' terms were argued up to the point of the actors walking out. Everything – sets, equipment, props, costumes – was held up by the war between Errol's side (which of course included myself) and Count Fossataro's production people, who, in the Italian way of film-making, stalled on anything to do with money.

I had sent memos daily, blasting the production office, and Errol had vehemently backed me up on the major issues. Between us, we somehow got the film started.

In spite of all this, I felt I was on to a winner. I knew I was getting good material, although – another Italian obstruction – I could not see my results on location, as the 'rushes' were kept in Rome. However, Errol had seen my material there, and loved every foot of it. It was, he said, coming together beautifully.

The story was straightforward enough. I hadn't any complexity of plot or characterization. It was simply a robust adventure, with conventional heavies and predictable story conflicts, some humour, and plenty of fast action. I shot a fight sequence in a blacksmith's where I had everything, including the smithy's anvil, made of rubber. Massive chains were swung, clouting the heavies, hammers clonked into the soldiers as they tried to arrest Flynn. The end came when the smithy himself, an Italian giant, raises the huge anvil above his head and crushes the heavies as Errol makes his escape. The rubber props were harmless, of course, but with the sounds of clanging iron and steel added later, it was quite effective.

I shrugged off the ridiculous hindrances that occurred during shooting. If an actor's costume hadn't arrived, I switched to another scene. Once, when the lunch boxes had been forgotten, I sent the crew to lunch at a nearby restaurant and, when the production office received the bill, the lunch boxes thereafter arrived on time.

My friends had warned me of the dangers of making my directorial début with the incorrigible Errol Flynn, that working with him as a cameraman was nothing like having the responsibilities of a director, that I had to keep him off the drink and on the set. I had an idea. I had brought my own trailer from England two years before, and now I had it placed right by the set. Just for Errol. Inside was a large cocktail cabinet stocked with every kind of booze. The idea was on the 'if you can't beat them, join them' principle. I had no hope of keeping Errol completely off alcohol but, if there was plenty of it right there, he wouldn't drink more than usual. It worked. From the day we started shooting, Errol was always on time – and reasonably sober.

Errol had also brought me a present. A real American Jeep. I was able to scoot along the mountain roads looking for locations. I kept it for the rest of my stay in Italy, painted it the dark red colour used by the police and it worked like a charm if I was seen speeding. Sometimes the police saluted me, thinking I was some kind of VIP.

Flynn, in fact, was behaving impeccably. No doubt because so much of his own money was invested in the film, he was a model pro. On some evenings we would have boisterous parties in the Swiss taverns and, occasionally on a Sunday, I would take my sons John, Rodney and Peter on a fishing trip with Errol, and we would cook our catch over an open fire. Errol thoroughly enjoyed himself on these 'boy scout' trips, personifying the outdoor sportsman.

On rare occasions Flynn and I would climb a mountain; breathless, but happy, we would discuss the way the film was going and, perhaps because he was so high up and near to his maker, he would occasionally brood on his life, a most intimate *mea culpa*: of his terror of violent storms; his hatred of Jack Warner and the whole Hollywood Establishment; his hero-worship of John Barrymore, who had drunk himself to death ('What a way to go, Jackson.'). There was no doubt that was the way he wanted to go, too.

Once, when we were talking about women, he stared pensively down at the tiny villages so far below us, and confided that he didn't really take sex that seriously; what was important was the chase – the conquest. He got a kick out of shocking people, and enjoyed the outraged reactions of the scandalmongers. I asked him how his wife, Pat, bore all this. He gave a short laugh, then spoke with cool finality: 'There's no question about Pat minding what I do. She knows the way I live, and we have a complete understanding. That's the way it is, and it couldn't be any other way.' He flashed that sardonic grin: 'Jack, my attitude to women is that there's always another man for the woman you've left and, for yourself, there's always another woman.'

I just can't believe that Flynn could have been a cold-blooded spy for the Nazis. He just wasn't the secret agent type. Perhaps in his buccaneer life-style he might have taken some document to Mexico in his yacht just for the hell of it. But I'm sure he was no Philby. A touch of the James Bond, perhaps, so far as glamorous women were concerned, but that was all.

With a casualness that completely deceived me, engrossed as I was in my exuberant work, a tiny smudge appeared on the spotless horizon. At first there were just rumblings and rumours: some of my crew had not received their money that week; props, wardrobe and other things had not been paid for. The *élan* subsided a little. Italian film crews and shady production accountants were old bedfellows.

What had happened was that, when Barry Mahon had gone to Rome to collect the money for salaries and production expenses, he discovered there was no more money in Count Fossataro's account. What money had been there had been transferred to Naples. Horrified, Mahon flew to Naples; there, the banks told him there was no money in Naples, either. The story of the Count's valuable property in Naples was not quite true; it was his wife who owned the property, and Count Fossataro possessed nothing. Mahon flew back to Rome, dazed. He tracked down Fossataro, who apologized and gave him a cheque. It bounced. There was no more money from the Italian side, as contracted. We continued working. My crew were marvellous; Flynn and Mahon talked reassuringly to them. United Artists has agreed to guarantee distribution, and might also put up the money to finish the film. The Italian government was also being approached for financial support. There were other parties interested in financing the rest of the film – everything would be all right.

But the crew were uneasy. They were used to this sort of thing in Italy. A lot of films were started with hardly enough production money to last a week. Then the producers would make the rounds of the banks, saying that they had just started a 'wonderful' film starring so-and-so and, piecemeal, gathering the necessary money as they went along. On most occasions the crew would only get a portion of their agreed salary. The rest would be in *cambiale* – a sort of IOU – and the balance of their salaries would be paid when the film was making money at the box office.

But, towards the end of the filming, the producer would give the crew a confidential tip-off. The film wasn't working out that well. It wouldn't make much money when released, and they would be well-advised to settle for half – or less – their *cambiale* figure, which would be paid to them at once. It always worked, and the producers had thus paid far less in salaries.

The shady dealings were quite something, even for the film business. A production manager would take under-the-table percentages from the extras, a cut from the car hire, and many other rake-offs. If only eighty horses turned up, instead of a hundred, he would say nothing and pocket the difference. A production manager would start on a film with obvious evidence of poverty. As the picture progressed, he would look more and more affluent and, before the end of the film, had bought a new car. From rags to *la dolce vita*.

Even in our grim situation it should have been simple enough to follow the Italian practice of making the bank-rounds saying 'We are shooting a picture with Errol Flynn' and pick up enough for completion.

But, by this time in Errol's career, he was no longer a gilt-edged security. His reputation had ruined his chances in that field – even in Italy.

Inexorably, the pace and rhythm of work slowed. Barry Mahon was in Rome trying to raise money. Errol was, understandably, worried. He had invested half a million dollars of his own in the picture. Once or twice he went off to Rome while I carried on without him. I received cables: 'Stick with it, Pal. We are doing our best down here. Love to you all, Errol.'

The aura of disaster seeped pathetically through the unit. But there was still a touching loyalty from everybody. They carried on working for weeks without money but, with accelerating set-backs, the work was grinding to a crawl. One day I arrived on location to be told the lights had been taken away. I told the cameraman we must somehow manage with reflectors – but the next day, the reflectors had gone also. We made a few reflectors with the silver paper from cigarette packets, and carried on for a while. But every day brought a new stranglehold.

Errol was now making excuses not to come to the set: 'Jack, the doctor has ordered me to stay in bed. Sorry, couldn't let you know last night. Please shoot all you can, chum. I'll try to get there this p.m.'

Bruce Cabot, who had behaved so well on the film, now gave up in disgust and returned to Rome. The costumes were suddenly taken away; with no costumes, the actors went away, too. I continued shooting; long-shots of the glorious Courmayeur valley, its very beauty mocking me. I always hoped, up to the last, that somehow the money would arrive and we would all be saved.

Then the *coup de grâce* was delivered, more lethal than a thrust from Errol Flynn's sword. The Cinemascope cameras, on hire from New York, were seized by the hotel and locked up until the bills were paid. What was left of my loyal unit wandered aimlessly about the village. Wives were phoning from Rome wanting money to live on; the situation was desperate. Most of the crew hadn't enough money even to return home. I had rented an apartment in the village for which the Italian company had paid three months' advance rent, deducting it from my weekly allowance. Suddenly, I had a visit from the landlord. He had never received any money from the company. They had certainly deducted it from my allowance, but had used it for something else. Now the landlord wanted his rent. I had hardly any money left, and had to sell my 16 mm camera to pay this bill.

Then the unions acted. They sent money for the crew to travel by train back to Rome. I had just enough money to get back by car and, before I left, I paid a last visit to the stone village we had built in the valley. My art director, Arrigo, was with me and he broke down, crying like a child.

I took a last look at this beautiful place, now deserted and silent. I murmured 'Fuck Count Fossataro', and, with this bitter but useless epigram, I left. I am told that the stone village still stands today, perfectly preserved, an object of curiosity for passing tourists.

Back in Rome, I somehow managed to live on very little money. It's strange, but one feels more vulnerable being broke away from home; but I no longer had a home in England, and my family and all my possessions were with me. I sold things from time to time: some furniture, a painting and, finally, my car, retaining the little Jeep that Flynn had given me.

Ironically, I was owed nine million lire for my work, tragically unfinished, but I didn't expect to see that for some time – if ever. I still stubbornly hoped for a miracle. There was just the possibility that the film could get off the ground again. Errol and Barry Mahon were working feverishly to get a new financing deal but, although Columbia and Herbert Wilcox came to Rome to look at the situation, they all backed away when they encountered the complex demands of the Italians. For some time, law suits were flying back and forth, vindictively. Everyone was suing somebody or other. Bruce Cabot fell out with Flynn, and was suing him for his salary; he also seized both Errol's and Barry Mahon's cars in Rome, which made Flynn hopping mad in view of their long friendship. Count Fossataro was, of course, right in the cross-fire but, being on home ground, was able to wriggle out of trouble.

It was a bitter and hopeless time. I saw a good deal of Errol and his wife, Pat; but any hopes of starting the film again faded as the weeks went by. There were too many debts and labyrinthine law suits and, comically enough, Guido Martufi, the little boy who was to have had the apple shot off his head, was growing up fast, and was nearly as tall as Errol.

Rome was as good a city as any to be broke in. It's the only place I know where one can eat well on very little money. My friend John Drake, and his pianist wife Marie Vittoria, were constant companions. There were so many interesting people one could spend a stimulating evening in some off-the-tourist-beat trattoria. On a special occasion like a birthday – or a rumour that money was forthcoming to re-start *William Tell* – we would eat at Alfredo's in Tresteveri where Alfredo himself, a spectacular showman with a huge walrus moustache, would twirl the fettuccine with the solid gold knife and fork given to him by

Douglas Fairbanks and Mary Pickford. Perhaps mesmerized by his panache, we would eat the most superb fettuccine ever.

Sometimes I would have a drink at the bar of the Excelsior Hotel, a most extraordinary bacchanalian beehive where groups of highly dubious 'film producers' clustered. Deals were bartered like make-believe Monopoly. One would proffer a sensational new Italian star, if the other could raise money to make a film. A scriptwriter is conned into writing a screenplay for nothing but the promise of a lucrative share of the profits when the film is released. They huff and they bluff, setting up dream projects which will never see the light of day. They talk in millions of dollars and most likely couldn't raise a hundred between them.

One evening at the Excelsior Errol Flynn called me over. 'Jack, I want you to meet his majesty, King Farouk.' I shook hands with a plump, balding, rather repellent-looking man with gold-rimmed glasses framing weak grey eyes. His Majesty nodded affably, and said: 'How do you do, Mr Cardiff. Tell me how do you kiss a duck's arse without disturbing the feathers?'

I must have stammered a little as I answered: 'I'm really not quite sure, your Majesty.'

He then demonstrated with a short, sharp blowing noise, immediately followed by a rapid squeak of a kiss – 'But you've *got* to be quick!'

I laughed dutifully, a bit put-out by that profound introduction to the man who ruled over 40 million Egyptians.

I studied him over our drinks, and perceived an ordinary, undistinguished man with not the slightest aura of sovereignty. He could have been any middle-aged playboy; I felt that if I had brought up the fascinating mystery of his ancestor, Akhenaton, he most likely would have giggled a smutty limerick about him, or just stared at me vacantly before ordering another drink. Although I met him several times afterwards, my first impression remained: he was a royal drop-out – or rather, a royal thrown-out.

I was at a party when Farouk was present. He had been eyeing an attractive girl with barely-concealed lechery and, when she left the room for a few moments, he slid out after her. In a very short time he returned with a noticeably bright red patch on the side of his podgy face. The girl had repelled his advances with such a hefty wallop that the face which had been embossed on so many millions of Egyptian stamps looked like a casualty of the printing dye.

*

William Tell was taking an unconscionable time a-dying but, by the autumn of 1953 as the leaves withered and fell, it symbolized for me the final fading of all hopes of a miraculous resurrection of my film. I had to face the fact that my first picture as a director was stillborn. The Lord giveth, and the Lord taketh away; he also took away the prime cause of the disaster – Count Fossataro died, bankrupt, soon after.

By October, I was just about broke. I sold my *Encyclopaedia Britannica* for peanuts. Something had to happen. And it did. Joe Mankiewicz came up to my table in a restaurant. I knew of him as a brilliant writer, now turned director, who had enjoyed great success with *All About Eve*. He was now going to direct *The Barefoot Contessa* with Ava Gardner and Humphrey Bogart. He wasted no time: 'Jack – don't be a sucker. Forget *William Tell* – it's finished. Come and photograph my picture. It will do you the world of good.'

13

On the Payroll Again

I had slipped a few rungs down the ladder, but I could always shin up again with a bit of luck. Joe Mankiewicz was very professional and considerate, often talking to me about the scenes from a director's point of view. He gave me a valuable tip about scriptwriting: 'After anything you have just written – even a paragraph or a sentence – just say one word to yourself, "Why?", and if you can't explain the purpose or necessity of what you have written, you must throw it out.'

Ava Gardner and Bogart were old buddies and the shooting went smoothly, ending up with a pleasant location at Positano.

At that time in Rome I had an Italian domestic help called Tina who was also a truly marvellous cook. I invited Mankiewicz to dinner and he drooled ecstatically at Tina's cooking. Just as I was reflecting how lucky I was to have such a gastronomic paragon, Tina stunned me by giving her notice, saying she wanted to join her boyfriend in Sicily.

Some weeks later, Mankiewicz invited me to dinner. The food was wonderful. There are no prizes for guessing who the cook was. Never trust a director who loves good food.

During the picture Frank Sinatra flew into Rome. Ava's relationship with him was still stormy. I had seen her trying to reassemble the pieces of a letter from him which she had torn up in a tearful frenzy and which she had been trying to put together again because, she told me, 'I still love him'. A lavish party was held at the Grand Hotel with Frank and Ava present. During the evening I found myself alone with him. He was very depressed about Ava. Innocently – but stupidly – I told Frank about Ava trying to piece his letter together, saying she had torn it up because she still loved him.

Frank's blue eyes flared and for a moment I thought he would take his anger out on me. But then he relaxed with a rueful smile and went looking for her, leaving me wondering if he was going to kiss Ava or sock her.

I was at a bullfight in Mexico finishing *The Brave One* when Dino de

Laurentiis cabled me from Rome asking me to photograph *War and Peace*. I stalled him. I can't remember why, but I didn't want to do it. I think I was reluctant to labour on a project so huge it would take at least a year to make. I told my producer Frank King how I felt. He thought for a moment, then said simply 'Just ask for double your salary. That will let you off the hook.'

Doubling my salary to avoid *War and Peace* didn't work; my terms were agreed and I spent the next year in Rome working on this mammoth project with King Vidor, the director of such classics as *The Big Parade*, *The Crowd* and *Duel in the Sun*. Of course, I had to imbibe the book thoroughly; obviously, it helps to absorb the general atmosphere for lighting purposes and *War and Peace* was crammed with visual drama.

There were many candlelight scenes – it's always been a challenge to obtain realistic effects in those situations. Of course, even with modern fast film one can't use candles to light a scene, so it has to be simulated. I usually mix ochre and grey paint and spray a thin coating from the bottom of the candle up to an inch from the top. This gives the effect of the flame glowing through the top of the candle. Then I hang a lamp from above, exactly over the candle. This gives a realistic effect of the candle glowing as if from its source. The lamp has a dimmer on it so that the light fluctuates – as it usually does owing to air currents – and I use an amber filter to accentuate the mellow light. The tricky part is placing lamps on the actors that have to appear as emanating from the candles. It's easy enough if an actor is seated at a table and his shadow is thrown on the wall exactly in line with the candle source, but when several actors are in the scene and are moving about, it becomes complicated; then you must be careful to place the candle or candles in positions where a single light could cover the actors. Sometimes I have to use several lamps which fade out on dimmers as other lamps fade up so that the light always appears to be from one source. It's a headache, but well worth the effort to obtain realistic candle effects.

Our leading lady, Audrey Hepburn, had a fascinating face to photograph. At that time Audrey embodied the feminine spirit of her age, with her cropped hairstyle, the fringe, and eyebrows made up so thick and bold. She was imitated by thousands of women for a long time afterwards. The public loved the perky urchin look, with that melodious drawl – sometimes a purr – and above all, those huge, beautifully expressive eyes.

Her ballet training had given her an elegant poise. She also had an innate dress sense. Anything she wore looked straight out of the pages of *Vogue*, her slender body was just like a fashion model's.

A problem on *War and Peace* was the duel sequence. Pierre (Henry Fonda) and Dolohov (Helmut Dantine) face each other at forty paces on an 'exterior' snow landscape which had to be created in the studio. The large set at Cinecittà had a cycloramic backing with trees and heavy snow everywhere. The scene called for an extreme long-shot using a wide-angle lens so the duellists with their seconds were two tiny figures low in the frame. Unfortunately this meant that the overhead spot-rails, which were lower than usual, would be in the picture. The alternative was to use a lens that brought the actors much too close for a dramatic long-shot. I told King Vidor I had an idea that might work and he gave me the time to try it.

I put the wide-angle lens on the camera anyway which showed the duellists as two tiny figures with, of course, all the spot-rails – and even the studio roof – in the picture. Now I rigged a sheet of glass a couple of feet from my camera lens and, using the same paint that had been used on the cyclorama backing, I sprayed the top part of the glass until it merged into the distant backing and completely masked the spot-rails. Now I had to obtain a sunrise effect. I used a lamp concentrated to full spot to make a bright circle of light on the backing horizon with pink and lemon filters to effect a dawn colour. Then I placed a small lamp close beside my camera which was brightly reflected in the sheet of glass. This also had the pink and orange filters on it. I manoeuvred the lamp reflection until it was exactly centred on the aureole of light on the backing. Although a tiny lamp, its reflection in the glass looked exactly like a dawn sun on the horizon. Finally, I used a fog filter to soften the scene like a misty dawn.

Dino de Laurentiis came on to the set just as I was spraying paint on the glass and called out in his spaghetti accent, 'Cardiff, what-a the hell you do?', and when I told him he made a typical Italian gesture of scepticism and walked off – probably to look up a cameraman to take my place when I was fired. But when he saw the rushes he was delighted, and kept showing it to all and sundry.

Quite often when setting lights on a scene a cameraman has an idea that isn't in the script. Audrey Hepburn – Natasha – is in a coach that is leaving the ruins of Moscow before Napoleon arrives. She hears that the man she loves – Prince Andrei – is badly wounded and is in the same mass exodus. She leans forward with painful intensity and wants to see him, but is told that it is impossible and so she slowly sinks back, her eyes brimming with tears.

I was lighting Audrey's stand-in, leaning forward in the coach, when I had an idea: when she sinks back in the coach she could lose the light from the window and be hardly visible in the darkness of the coach; only her eyes would be dimly seen with her tears flowing like the weeping Niobe turning to stone. I suggested this to Vidor, but he wasn't enthusiastic; 'Jack, I have to see her face, to see the sadness . . .' Well, I thought, the tears would have done that. King Vidor was a great director, but cautious. I lit the scene with most of her face visible. Oddly, Audrey's eyes didn't brim with tears, so if I had sold my idea and let her face go into the darkness, I might have been considerably embarrassed.

Working with Henry Fonda again reminded me of his crazy antics on *Wings of the Morning*, eighteen years before, but now he was much more subdued. I don't think he was too happy working with Vidor. Every morning there were interminable script discussions round a table on the set where the scenes to be shot that day were discussed by Vidor at great length; it was all rather heavy going. Sometimes there were sharp disagreements. Vidor wanted Fonda to carry a dog on the long trek in the snow out of Moscow. Fonda was vehemently against this idea but in the end agreed to do it, obviously against his will.

This sequence was also shot in the studio – snow being hard to come by in August in Rome – and I had over two hundred arc lamps, each one covered with architects' paper to soften the shadows and obtain an overall dull light.

We shot Fonda walking the length of the studio in the snow carrying the dog in his arms; then we repeated the shot several times – when cut together, he would appear to have been walking for miles.

Fonda would walk the distance, the dog in his arms, stumbling slowly against the wind and the snow with the camera tracking him; then, when Vidor called 'cut', Fonda would abruptly lift up his arms and drop the dog. He did this on every take, with his face expressionless. We all caught the humour, except King Vidor.

I had an uncomfortable feeling, after some months, that the cast were not in a fever of enthusiasm. On such a monumental epic, with such a long shooting schedule, it must have been difficult to maintain a continuous dedication to their roles. Another jarring situation for the actors was the mixture of nationalities, with its consequent farrago of accents. There was Henry Fonda, an American; Audrey Hepburn, very British; Helmut Dantine, Austrian; Oscar Homolka, German; Anita

Ekberg, Swedish; Vittorio Gassman, Italian. John Mills played a Russian farmer with a thick Somerset brogue. All this in the highly Italianate ambience of Cinecittà in Rome.

I was nominated for an Oscar on this film, but that year *Around the World in Eighty Days* won the cinematography award – I should say 'awards' since sixty cameramen shot it. My sour grapes are excusable – how an artistic endeavour by one person can be equated with travelogue photography by sixty different cameramen, I'll never know.

14

Sophia

I went from Tolstoy to Ben Hecht, who was writing a script for my next job, *Legend of the Lost*, to be shot mostly in the Sahara desert. The story was of a man looking for his father presumed lost in Timbuktu some years before. He hires a dubious character – a Foreign Legion drunk – to guide him on the hazardous desert journey. An Arab prostitute hooks on to the party and they eventually reach their objective.

I cannot remember how I, a cameraman, got to be present at an early script discussion but here I was with my friend, the director Henry Hathaway, in a Hollywood office of the distinguished writer Ben Hecht who had scripted *The Front Page*. Hecht was amiable to work with and completely professional. His office had – without exaggeration – dozens of glass jars crammed with pencils sharpened for instant use. I have since worked with many scriptwriters who usually make notes from the discussions then write the scenes and dialogue later in private, but Ben would take a sheet of blank paper, whisk out a pencil and write a complete scene in a matter of a minute or two. If Hathaway said he didn't like it, Ben would calmly crumple it up, throw it in his waste paper basket and immediately write a new version. I had never seen anything like that before. It was so effortless – and sadly lacking in depth, as it turned out.

Rossano Brazzi played a man searching for his father, John Wayne played the crapulent Foreign Legionnaire, and Sophia Loren played the Arab prostitute. Unusual casting you will agree. I can't imagine anyone less like an Arab prostitute than Sophia Loren. She wore a nicely laundered dark green dress down to her ankles which was buttoned modestly up to her throat. She was in her early twenties and with her fresh un-Arabic complexion and her wonderfully lucent eyes, she radiated purity.

John Wayne in real life was just like John Wayne in movies: calm, genial, with that easy-going drawl. It would appear that nothing bothered him – although once a month he locked his door and got completely plastered. It seemed to work perfectly.

On the first day's shooting, the Duke came on to the set. I was astonished to see him wearing his large stetson hat, cowboy boots and trousers and his guns at the ready in twin holsters. No hint of a Foreign Legionnaire here. I whispered to Hathaway: 'Why is he wearing the cowboy outfit?' Hathaway stared at me as though I was mad. 'He always wears the cowboy outfit.'

The work was pure hell. The Sahara desert during the day was a shimmering, ferocious furnace, but at night so numbingly cold that it was like being in cryogenic suspension. We slept in every garment we possessed, a couple of pullovers, as many socks as we could manage, overcoats – everything. We were already dressed when we got up at 4 a.m. every day, but our feet were still frozen and special Norwegian ski boots were sent out just for the dawn hours.

Our trucks' engines were always frozen and had to be started by putting flaming torches under the engines. Every morning we set out on a two-hour journey to our location. Our road was a dusty track on which at least one truck always sunk axle-deep in the sand and had to be dug out. By nine in the morning the temperature had risen from arctic cold to blazing heat. The extreme changes of temperature caused desert pebbles to crack open like fretful fireworks. And that sand: the ever-present gusts of desert wind wafted it into our eyes and throats; it got into everything – including our lunch.

Hathaway was at his worst, screaming maniacally at those who left footprints in the sand, until we were all afraid to move. I remembered one of Hathaway's cynical dictums to me earlier: 'If you want to be a sonofabitch, be a good one.'

In those diabolical conditions we worked with mechanical stoicism, accepting the daily torments like doomed prisoners in a chain-gang. And in this preposterously unromantic atmosphere, I fell in love with Sophia. Nothing apocalyptic in that; everybody falls in love with Sophia. She must be the archetypal *femme fatale*, but, strangely, she had little awareness of her great powers of attraction. People just fell in love with her – usually to her embarrassment. Certainly most of her leading men, Cary Grant and Peter Sellers to name but two, were hopelessly in thrall to her, although it came to nothing.

On our grim location, Sophia was hugely popular with her cheerful demeanour and sense of fun – her laughter was pure delight. I told her she walked like a giraffe. She said her mother was the only other person to make the same observation. She had a slender, pliant grace that reminded me of the elongated figures of Parmigianino. The crew adored her – and of course so did I.

But, extraordinarily, my feelings were not entirely one-sided. One weary day on our desert shoot, I was standing next to Sophia on a sandy ridge. There had been a delay and the unit was standing idle, resigned to the heat and the gusts of sand. Sophia was standing close to me and we both stared ahead without talking. Then she murmured something that froze my senses. I won't repeat what she said here; suffice it to say it was simply a young woman who, like a schoolgirl, was expressing a crush for a much older man.

Funny, although those words of hers are etched in my memory like the Lord's prayer, I can't remember my reply. I probably mumbled something gauche and inarticulate as I was, frankly, stunned. That night, after dinner at our 'hotel' (a half dozen small grotty rooms which housed the actors, director, and myself), Sophia and I sat outside on the steps of the entrance talking for hours. It was the beginning of a chaste but fervent love that was kept secret throughout the film.

Two of my trusted friends knew, including Ken Danvers the stills photographer, who took some pictures of us; otherwise no one had any idea. We had secret code words and phrases which passed between us on the set. During our working day, with the crew clustered all around us, Sophia and I were as prominent as goldfish in a bowl, so we simply had to hide our feelings. Letters were passed by hand to each other; all fire and rapture. It was kids' stuff; a juvenile passion on her part that had shown in my case (I was twenty years older) the frailty of my mind. It seemed I had lost my grip on reality. I was devoted to my wife and children, but now I was in a sort of hypnosis, as though my family didn't exist.

Many have said Sophia was the most beautiful woman on earth, and a photographer's vision and work is all about beauty. Michelangelo, who disliked making portraits unless his model was very beautiful, is quoted as saying: 'All my life I have only to see beauty, to fall in love with it.' Of course this goes for all those who paint or sculpt – or even photograph. Beauty is pure rapture to them. But in my case, I most certainly overdid it.

Another thing that I overdid on this location was to air my French with the wrong accent. It was in a helicopter and my camera was angled down on to a train of camels and mules on which Sophia, Wayne and Brazzi were swaying and plodding across the Sahara desert.

It was a great shot, but my camera was too close. So, '*au-dessus, s'il vous plaît*' I shouted to the pilot who spoke no English. Now as most schoolboys know, *au-dessus* is French for 'higher' but the French for 'lower' is *au-dessous*. The fractional difference is in the pronunciation. For 'higher' one must purse the lips like kissing a pea.

I forgot to kiss the pea and the helicopter sank noisily down. The mules and camels panicked, unseating some riders, and galloped in all directions over the Sahara. I was in the doghouse with Hathaway for the rest of the day.

Towards the end of our location shooting, Sophia told me that Rossano Brazzi was boasting to people on the unit that she was making a play for him and was knocking on his wall at night, but that he wasn't interested. Sophia was fuming at this wild untruth and swore that she would get her revenge at the right moment.

The moment came when we returned to Rome for studio work. She had a struggle with Rossano in a tent and during the scene Rossano suddenly yelled in pain and ran off the set holding his bruised manhood. Sophia had got her revenge.

When we all returned to Rome my wife Julie and my two sons came over from London. I think it was a shock for Sophia to see them. Over the following days I saw less and less of her. We both knew it was the end of love's young, but truncated, dream. In the middle of a scene Sophia burst into tears and ran off the set. Everyone was mystified except me.

Years later, when I was directing a film in Nice, I realized Sophia was staying at the same hotel as me, the Negresco. I resolutely made no attempt to get in touch with her, but after some days Sophia rang me and said, teasingly, 'What are you, some kind of nut?' I muttered excuses and she invited me to have lunch with her at the nearby studios. I noticed as I approached the studio gates that Sophia's devoted maids were spaced at intervals to guide me to her dressing-room and there we faced each other in silence for a moment. Then we embraced like brother and sister. She had prepared a scrumptious steak with a very good wine, and it wasn't until coffee time that our unconsummated attachment of so long ago came up – casually enough. Sophia smiled and said, with a mixture of simple dignity and a certain tenderness, 'It was my young love. It was very beautiful.'

15

Marilyn

For the first time in my life I had to have a security pass to meet a film star. Marilyn Monroe's arrival in England had generated more than the usual press hysteria. Such was the frenzied lusting to get near her – the all-American dream girl, the celluloid embodiment of erotic fantasy – that she had to be wrapped in a cocoon of protection like a Head of State, and her rented house at Egham was more like a military fortress as I presented my security card.

Some weeks before, Laurence Olivier had asked me into his office at Piccadilly and told me that he was going to make Terence Rattigan's *The Sleeping Prince* (retitled *The Prince and the Showgirl*), and 'Miss Monroe' had requested that I should photograph her. He spoke with a certain reserve, and I felt embarrassed. Larry had always been one of my heroes. I could see that he didn't like being forced to accede to a request that was obviously a demand. I knew the rules of the game: a director has the right to choose his own cameraman.

For years in Hollywood, stars have insisted on having their favourite photographers who, because they know every wrinkle and curve of the stars' faces, can devise the most flattering angles and lighting – as well as avoiding the unflattering ones – and have retained these guardians of their beauty on picture after picture. But this was England, and this was Laurence Olivier.

'How do *you* feel about it, Larry? Did you have someone else in mind?'

Larry smiled. I felt his feelings about film protocol were allayed.

'Don't be ridiculous. I'd be happy if you'd do it.'

So there I was, passing the last guard on the porch of an imposing Edwardian house in part of the Windsor Great Park, about to meet the fabulous Marilyn.

I was asked to go upstairs, where I met Arthur Miller on the first landing. His face gave me rather a shock. It reminded me of Christie, the murderer – the same diamond-bright glint from deep-set brown eyes behind thick, horn-rimmed glasses, the same deeply incised creases in the cheeks. His hairline was also similar, but he was much more youthful-looking than Christie, and I felt ashamed about making such a sinister comparison. No murderer he, yet my involuntary connotation with Christie was ironic. After Marilyn's death, he would be accused of brutally murdering her image in *After the Fall*.

Marilyn had just woken up, he said, and she would be out in a minute; we chatted about the forthcoming film while I observed his easy, forthright manner. He was refreshingly un-Hollywood, and without the charisma I would have expected of a world-famous playwright.

Then she appeared. A door opened behind me; there was a blur of soft material as Marilyn sped swiftly into Miller's arms, not looking at me until she was hugged in his bear-like embrace. Then she slanted a shy, sleepy smile at me. I had never seen this Marilyn before, in any film or photo. This was no hot sex symbol; this was a little girl, with her face pressed into Daddy's chest, shyly curious of a visitor.

Her face was still rosy, flushed from sleep, and her buttercup-gold hair tangled like a Botticelli cherub. Her eyes had the unreal clarity of the porcelain eyes in a doll; large, wondering, wide apart and slightly turned down at the outsides; and the mouth, timorously half-parted lips; the saucy turned-up nose – here indeed was a delightful evocation of Renoir.

She didn't say anything to me at all – not even 'hello'. She just looked at me with a kind of possessiveness, like a child showing Daddy her prize handiwork from school, and Daddy cuddled his baby with proud tenderness. Still no word to me. Only a soft murmur to Miller, as she gazed at me in cosy triumph.

'Isn't it wonderful, darling? He's the greatest, and I've got him!'

I gave them a silly smile, feeling uncomfortably gift-wrapped. That was my first impression of Marilyn Monroe: a wide-eyed innocent child, as pure as springtime. Could I have been so naïve? But everyone had the same reaction when they first met her; her beguiling innocence was not deliberately put on, despite some cynics' opinions. She seemed to have the vulnerability of a child and you instinctively wanted to protect her. Larry told me long afterwards that he, too, had had the same reaction when he first saw her: 'But she's only a child! My God, I'm going to fall in love with her!'

'The child' and I had breakfast that morning, and we talked about the film. As I listened to that breathy voice, shy, tremulous, with sudden soft laughter, the sort that causes poets to invoke celestial metaphors, I was completely under her spell and left the house quite convinced that I had just met an angel.

Then my mind pulled up with a seismic jolt as I recalled the tawdry tales of Marilyn's climb to fame that were more than just public gossip, in my case. I had been told some pretty lurid stories by friends who had worked with her: to put it mildly, Marilyn's love-life had not been exactly unblemished. The spell of Marilyn as a cherub from heaven was broken – at least, for that moment. Marilyn was hauntingly lovely, but she was not exactly a Vestal Virgin.

I was now busy on pre-production with Larry. I had worked with Olivier the actor before, but now he had the formidable task of both acting and directing – and with Marilyn Monroe as co-star.

Certainly he was wed for ever to the theatre but, after his great filmic success with *Henry V*, *Hamlet* and *Richard III*, he was now very aware of the use of the camera for dramatic expression and the hypnotic persuasion of editing; this, combined with his vast experience of stage technique, gave the crew plenty to think about. A few of us called him 'Larry' but to most he was 'Sir'. Even the 'Larry' invoked a certain deference – like Mr Quelch, referred to as 'Quelchie' at Greyfriars. In fact, working on this picture was very much like public school. The atmosphere was definitely sixth form.

There was Anthony Bushel, ex-star British actor, now associate director and personal assistant to Larry, the quintessential School Captain: 'Come on, you chaps – don't let the side down.' Tall, still with a matinée-idol charisma, his golden curls thinning inexorably, but always with that public-school confidence. He was passionately loyal to Larry. There was Hugh Percival, our associate producer, an urbane Dean, sucking on his huge quirky pipe with a scholarly air as he discussed production procedures. He and I soon discovered our mutual love of books and, to my delight, he presented me with a first edition of Sir Thomas Moore's *The Hidden Hand of Shakespeare*.

Teddy Joseph, our production manager, could have been a junior house-master. A brilliantine-stiff lock of hair stuck permanently on his domed forehead, his glasses were so low down on his nose that the grimace from keeping them from falling off gave him the air of having wandered on to a film set and finding it quite revolting.

There was Colin Clark, son of Sir Kenneth, who was a trainee assistant, but could have been a prefect, and another 'good man' from Greyfriars.

And, occasionally, Terence Rattigan (who at his first meeting with Marilyn called her a 'shy exhibitionist') would come to see us. Definitely a distinguished 'Old Boy'.

There was, through my eyes, an atmosphere of noisy schooldays at

Pinewood, a chatter which would instantly cease as Larry and the chaps went to work.

Larry's magisterial aura was a natural echo from his life-long performances as all kinds of kings. Even during pre-production, dressed casually in tweeds and grey flannels, there was the unmistakable authority of one whose complete mastery of the craft of theatre was beyond dispute.

Listening to him talking quietly about the work ahead, I superimposed over his modest image the colossus I had seen in his spellbinding performances, and heard his soft liquid tones change into that glorious bellowing battle-cry at Agincourt: 'Cry God for Harry, England, and St George!' The critics said his performance as Titus Andronicus was his masterpiece, and Kenneth Tynan called Larry 'the greatest actor alive'.

How lucky I have been to see such acting magic in my lifetime.

Larry prepared everything with his usual meticulous attention to detail. For our coronation sequences, we ran old newsreels; we checked all our London exteriors for camera angles and sun positions; materials and colours were tested for the brilliant sets of Carmen Dillon – a trusted stalwart from *Henry V*; there were talks with Technicolor, make-up tests, and, lastly, two weeks of rehearsal – without Marilyn – at Pinewood Studios when the sets were just chalk-marks on the floor, and Larry went through the camera movements for all the scenes. Larry's infinite capacity for painstaking details was beyond the usual pre-production commitment; it was exhilarating.

During discussions at his office in Piccadilly one morning, Larry looked at his watch and suggested that we pop outside to see the Queen pass by. I suppose he had inside information, for there were no crowds outside – just a couple of policemen hovering near the gate at Hyde Park Corner. No sign of HM. Then a policeman strolled over to the gates to stop the traffic, and we could see the carriage approach through the park. It was all so casual. It was as quiet and peaceful as a Sunday morning. And there she was ... Elizabeth, Queen of England, sitting upright in an open carriage, dressed in the scarlet and gold uniform of the Coldstream Guards with a close-fitting tricorn, her brown curls just showing. She looked serene and quite beautiful. If I'd had a cloak, and if there had been a puddle, I would have thrown it on the ground.

I saw her glance for a moment at No. 146 next to our office. She must have often looked at this house when she passed, for that was where she was born.

I talked to Marilyn again. I was going to do some photographic tests on her. Her dressing-room at Pinewood had been personally checked weeks before by Milton Green, her producer and manager. It was painted white and gold, with beige curtains, and there were to be security men posted there to see that her privacy was not invaded.

Marilyn told me she had used a new kind of make-up on *Bus Stop*. It was very, very pale – almost white. The role of Cherie was that of a tawdry night club hostess who rarely saw daylight, and the pale make-up was obviously to enhance this effect. Much to my concern, Marilyn wanted to use it on *The Prince and the Showgirl*. I told her that too pale a make-up was likely to make her teeth look grey – had she seen the final print of *Bus Stop*? No, said Marilyn, but she was going to run the film privately, and we would see it together.

There were just four of us at the private screening at 20th Century Fox in Soho Square: Marilyn, myself, my wife Julie, and another woman, the wife of one of the Fox hierarchy. Before the film started the ladies went to the powder-room where, Julie told me afterwards, the Fox woman was saying that she had just come back from a trip to Rome – and how devastatingly handsome the Italians were. 'Dark men are so much more sexy than fair men, don't you agree, Miss Monroe?' Marilyn had replied: 'I don't think it matters really, as long as they *think* darkly.'

I greatly enjoyed *Bus Stop*. Marilyn gave a most moving performance as the pathetic night club girl, but her chalky white make-up, although very effective for that role, was definitely unglamorous; when her teeth showed, they looked like a row of lead bullets. Marilyn was shocked and angry, and that was the end of the white make-up.

After that, I did my test of Marilyn and this time she had a good make-up. I pulled out all the tricks of lighting I knew and, when we saw the test on screen, she looked beautiful. I knew Marilyn was happy in my hands and wouldn't worry about how she looked in the picture.

The great day arrived: we started shooting. Larry, the Grand Duke of Carpathia, goes back-stage at a London theatre and the cast is presented to him. Marilyn, who is one of the dancers, is requested to have supper with his Grand Ducal Highness by Larry's equerry (played by Richard Wattis).

The day went well. Some said afterwards that Marilyn had been very nervous. Larry would have well understood; he had once said to me 'If any actor doesn't have butterflies in his stomach at the beginning of each performance, he is no actor.'

It was a closed set. No one but the crew was allowed to be present. This upset the press, of course. There was an enormous trailer on the set for Marilyn. Arthur Miller was apt to linger inside with his new wife – somewhat energetically sometimes – and the waiting game gave us all tender reflections on honeymoon bliss (although I don't think Larry was quite so benign about it). There were times when, just as we were about to shoot a scene, Marilyn would drop everything and dash over to embrace her husband who had just come on set. It was irritating for Larry, but he endured it with stoic dignity.

From the beginning, Larry was taking the advice of Josh Logan, who had directed Marilyn on *Bus Stop* and who had written to Larry about the way he had handled her. He urged Larry to have infinite patience and never – but never – lose his temper and shout at her. That would be fatal, he said. Logan extolled Marilyn's natural talent and reiterated that she must always be treated with extreme delicacy when she was late, or forgot her lines, you must grit your teeth and bear it. And that's what Larry was doing. He treated her with soap-bubble delicacy, but eventually the bubble had to burst.

In the beginning, however, we were happy enough at work, with Larry coming on the set proudly wearing his new MCC tie, having waited for a membership of this famous cricket club to be 'given out' and, for a rare moment on this film, his face looked boyishly happy.

In those fairly calm days – not exactly halcyon, but before the stormier weather – I had decided to take some private pictures of Marilyn dressed as a Renoir girl. I already had a collection of Renoir period clothes which I used for models for my paintings. The time agreed was 9.30 on a Sunday morning – a bit optimistic, since Marilyn rarely appeared on the set before 11 a.m., but I duly turned up at Miller's house at Egham with my still camera and a couple of lights; Marilyn's ever-faithful make-up man, Whitey, was also there.

Marilyn was sound asleep, Miller told us, so we had breakfast and read the Sunday papers. The morning drifted on in lazy Sunday fashion. Miller suggested tennis, which I could never refuse, and we played until lunch time. Marilyn was still fast asleep, so we had lunch and talked the afternoon away. She finally made an appearance at 7.30 in the evening, looking like a radiantly beautiful child, smiling shyly – and not a word about being nine hours late. I dressed her in the Renoir clothes. The black silk blouse was a problem. The Victorian maiden who had originally worn it didn't have Marilyn's prodigious 'pair of lungs', but a large safety-pin at the back did the trick. I took several pictures in colour and also some normal black and white pictures – well, hardly 'normal', as I used a wind machine to blow her hair across her face, and spread

Vaseline over a piece of glass in front of the lens. It was one of these black and white pictures which became Arthur Miller's favourite, out of so many thousands of pictures of her, and it hung in his study until it was abandoned, much later when Marilyn and Arthur parted. She signed one of the windswept pictures to me: 'Dearest Jack, if only I could be the way you created me. I love you. Marilyn.'

There was a day at the studios when Marilyn told me excitedly that she had a new disguise for going unnoticed in crowds, and would I like to see it? Marilyn in public was, of course, a big problem. She could so easily be injured by the frenzied curiosity of the mob. I went to her dressing-room and she presented her 'disguise' to my astonished eyes with a jubilant flourish. It was a large wig, coloured the most glaring bright orange I had ever seen. If anyone had worn it – let alone Marilyn – they would have exposed themselves more than did Lady Godiva. I gently pointed this out to Marilyn and suggested a mouse-coloured wig, a head-scarf and, perhaps, an old raincoat. Later this disguise worked very well, and we went to a Bruton Street art gallery together where Marilyn saw some Impressionist drawings.

Marilyn didn't chat much with the crew. Most actors, after the first couple of days, get to know the camera operator, props man, sound crew, etc., and by so doing obviously feel more relaxed. But Marilyn just didn't fraternize. Not that she was stand-offish, but she had such an aura of blank remoteness, of being in another world, that it made her inaccessible to friendly small-talk. Anyway, she had her entourage always close by, an assiduous shroud of protection: Paula Strasberg, her dialogue coach; protective hubby, Arthur Miller; her producer-manager, Milton Green; and her make-up man, Whitey, whose real name was Alan Sneider.

Considering all the weird people that were tangled in Marilyn's life, Whitey stood out as a monolith of common sense and reliability. His patience and loyalty to Marilyn had an aspect of parental devotion and, mindful of her fragile mind, her strange waywardness, he had to have extraordinary tact and patience. His work transcended that of a normal make-up man. Whitey would be on call at any hour of the day or night to make Marilyn look her best – whether it was at the studio or afterwards, at a party or theatre, or sometimes, he told me, when she was still lying in bed, comatose from sleeping pills and very late for work. He had been her make-up man for some years and was one of the few people in her life she really trusted.

Once or twice I would be talking to Whitey in Marilyn's dressing-room when she arrived. I would move to leave, but Marilyn would ask me to stay and chat while Whitey made her up. She never talked about the film upon which we were working: no peevish grievances, or comments about Larry. It was the other side of the schizoid coin: Marilyn, talking about normal things, quite relaxed and happy. She liked poetry, and I gave her Dylan Thomas's poems, which she read avidly. One could see her determination to read as much as possible, not only with a view to playing a role, but generally to improve her knowledge. I guess we were both in the same league. She adored Charles Adams's black gallows humour; but, on reflection, it all fitted in with her horrific girlhood, and her own brand of survival humour.

However relaxed I thought she was as we chatted, I would observe a subtle change in her manner as the make-up approached completion. A withdrawal into quiet. She knew she would soon be going on the set, and an inward panic seemed to be taking possession of her. She would make some excuse to delay things, to stay longer in that dressing-room. On one occasion when she was at last ready, she suddenly decided to phone someone in New York. 'Honey,' said Whitey, 'that might take you an hour, and they're waiting on set.' But Marilyn, with a trance-like false brightness, insisted on making the call.

It was obvious she didn't want to face people. Whitey had told me that this was the biggest problem in Marilyn's tortured life. She had an escalating hidden terror of being stared at by countless eyes.

Once, on a Jack Benny show, Marilyn had been waiting in the wings for her entrance and, when her cue came, she had frozen; Whitey 'had to kick her in the butt' to make her go on stage. He said that often when he was making her up she would be on the verge of hysteria. There were many reasons, he said; but without a doubt, one on this picture was that she was scared of the day's work ahead with such a brilliantly talented man as Olivier.

There was a vast gulf between Marilyn and Larry. How could she help being overwhelmed by the great Olivier, legendary giant of the theatre, a man who had articulated nearly all the great roles in Shakespeare, possessed of so many accolades and friends with fine cultured minds? What a jolting contrast to childlike, frightened Marilyn. Ironically, she was a bigger star to world film audiences than Larry; she came from a different galaxy (tinsel-glittering Hollywood, which had evolved from tawdry nickelodeon to a tasteless dream factory), quite alien to the noble lineage of the theatre. Surely Marilyn and Olivier was the casting misalliance of all time: *The Prince and the Showgirl*, indeed!

If Marilyn was overawed by Larry's god-like image, she was compensated – but I think more confused – by the weird idolatry showered upon her by her acting coach, Paula Strasberg, of the Method school of acting. I overheard Paula telling Marilyn startling things: how important she was to the whole movie business; that she was quite unique; the whole world adored her; yes, she was the greatest woman living, etc., etc. Fond as I was of Marilyn, I thought this was unnecessary. Perhaps it was a psychological ploy to bolster Marilyn's fragile ego; perhaps she really did require inordinate doses of praise like that. Anyway, Marilyn seemed to accept Paula's worship without demur. It is hard to see how Marilyn survived both Larry and Paula, and kept her balance. Certainly Paula's method must have divided her mind.

Then there was Vivien Leigh: Lady Olivier. At the beginning, Vivien was a daily visitor on the set, always looking attractive and elegant with her wide, brilliant smile and beautifully articulated English voice, so different from Marilyn's. I don't think there was any doubt that Marilyn was crushed by 'her Ladyship', and felt awkward and inferior in her presence. But Vivien, who was pregnant at that time, was soon sadly to have a miscarriage, and the visits virtually ceased. Marilyn knew that Vivien regretted that she wasn't playing the part she had originated with such success in the theatre, and also that Larry wanted Marilyn to play the role the way that Vivien had played it. This collided head-on with Marilyn's own interpretation, and her reliance on spontaneity. If Marilyn was put out by Larry's theatrical approach, Larry was certainly frustrated by Marilyn's Method style – which he hated. And there was the continuing problem of her conduct and lateness.

As the work continued it became obvious that the pace was slackening considerably. Larry and his producers talked to Milton Green and Arthur Miller about the problem of Marilyn, and how the shooting schedule would have to be revised. I know Marilyn resented Miller's involvement, and the pressures that were put on him to keep the production from collapsing, so Miller's mantle of go-between was not a sweeping success. He could only phone the studios to say that Marilyn would be – unavoidably – two, three, four hours late, or that she was ill and couldn't work that day at all.

Eventually, Marilyn would come to the studios as if nothing had happened and, if anyone solicitously asked her how she was, she would smile a happy 'Fine'. Of course, we on the unit could only guess what dramas were happening off the set. When we were rehearsing or shooting a scene, Larry and Marilyn would appear reasonably amiable as they worked together with the rest of the cast – but we all knew, and felt, the tension.

Sybil Thorndike – a very lovely lady – was always kind to Marilyn, and marvelled at her aura of wholesome innocence which Larry had, wryly, to acknowledge. Larry said to Sybil one day in front of me: 'Look at that face. It could be ten years old!'

All the stars I photographed had some kind of facial flaw which a badly placed light would disclose, or emphasize, and Marilyn was no exception – although she was as near-perfect as any cameraman could wish for. She had a classically sound bone structure; her cornflower-blue eyes were the right distance apart, and her full mouth was perfectly formed. But I had to be careful about her nose, so delightfully retroussé, for, if the key light was too low, a blob would show up on the tip. She actually mentions this in the film, saying to Larry's paean: 'You skipped my nose, because you noticed the bump on the end.' Marilyn's face was, in fact, so flawless that, were it a painting, it would be criticized as too perfect. Bacon said: 'There is no beauty which has not some strangeness in its proportions.' Luckily, the almost too-perfect proportions of Marilyn's face came magically alive the moment she breathed, and her face became a bemusing paradox: that of an innocent sex siren.

Her whole body had a touch of over-ripeness – how Renoir would have adored her! She was indeed a little overweight and was worried very much about her tummy protruding in her tight white dress, which she wore throughout the picture. She would try to pull her stomach in during a take, and begged me to watch very carefully and let her know if it was showing. I couldn't very well call out, 'Push your tummy in, Marilyn!' so I invented a code word which I could call out as a technical last-minute injunction before the camera turned over. The code word was 'Tom', which was the name of one of my electricians, so I could safely call out 'OK, Tom!' and no one else would take any notice. There must have been times when Tom was rather bewildered by my constant calling out of his name just before shooting, only to be waved away with '. . . it doesn't matter'.

This secret code worked very well, until one day when Marilyn had to say, 'Here's to more love in everybody's life' – instead of which she said, 'Here's to more Tom in everybody's life'!

Colin Clark, the trainee assistant, invited me down for the weekend to Saltwood Castle, the home of his parents Sir Kenneth and Lady Clark. I was delighted. I had always wanted to meet this very distinguished man whose books on painting and all aspects of art were so enthrallingly instructive. It was a wonderful weekend. Sir Kenneth and his wife, Jane, were warm and genial hosts, and Sir Kenneth spoke illuminatingly. Years later, when his brilliant *Civilisation* captivated so many millions, I reflected how lucky I had been to have had a personal seminar on so many beautiful things.

He showed me his superb Renoir, which he kept in a bedroom; I was astonished when he told me that it was too expensive to insure. Later I was to own a Renoir, from Somerset Maugham's collection, and had the same problem.

That evening over dinner we were discussing the first night of the forthcoming Bolshoi Ballet at Covent Garden. It was the first time this great ballet was coming to London, and I had desperately tried to get a seat – but it had been hopeless. Imagine my joy when the Clarks invited me to share their box on that evening. It turned out to be even more exciting than I could have imagined. The Russian *corps de ballet* was breathtaking; I had never seen anything like it before. What elevation! They seemed to soar ten feet into the air. Some ballet purists condemned their athletic virility as circus acrobatics, but to me it was a great gust of fresh air, sweeping away the dust of choreographic dogma.

Soon after this weekend at Saltwood Castle, another evening materialized: the première of Arthur Miller's play, *A View from the Bridge*. Arthur had been experiencing much difficulty with the casting. He wanted tough-looking and tough-sounding workman types, but most of the actors he interviewed were handsome and elegant, with refined British accents inevitably showing through the false patina of cockney – or worse, American slang. He had searched long and desperately for the sort of dock labourer types so easily found on the American stage.

Marilyn had invited my wife and I to go with her and Arthur, joining Larry and Vivien at their London house from where we would all go on to the theatre. I was awestruck – the Oliviers, the Millers and the Cardiffs. Just the six of us, going to a first night. I must say, I find it hard to believe myself that it really happened. But it did.

It was a black-tie affair. My heart always soars at first nights, and this was a very special one indeed. Julie and I arrived at the Oliviers' Belgravia house. Marilyn was changing her dress somewhere upstairs, and we had drinks while we were waiting.

I had not visited the Oliviers' house before, and I saw at the end of their large drawing room a small landscape painting. 'Isn't that a Daubigny?' I asked Larry.

He gave me a puzzled look. 'But you haven't been here before, how sharp of you to know at that distance, and at first glance.'

It wasn't sharp of me, but second nature. I have spent so much time studying art that nearly always when I see a 'good' painting, even at a distance, a mental computer displays its identity to me.

There was a loud whoop from Arthur, followed by an exuberant 'Attagirl' as Marilyn came down the stairs. She was wearing a tight-fitting bright red velvet dress. Somehow, her tumescent breasts were not falling out – but they should have done, according to Isaac Newton, as they nodded rhythmically on each step of the stairs. I saw Vivien flick a look at Larry, but his face only showed the amused tolerance of watching someone's child in Mummy's clothes at her birthday party. He'd made up his mind to relax that evening. Arthur encouraged her: 'Why shouldn't she show off her God-given attributes; why should she have to dress like her maiden aunt?'

We decamped in the most enormous Daimler. When we drew up, like royalty, at the flaring lights of the theatre, our car was instantly engulfed by a surging mass of screaming people, and that was very scary – at least to me. As the car door opened, police heroically held back the crowd like a rugby scrum, with frenzied screams of 'There's Marilyn!', 'Vivien Leigh!', 'Laurence Olivier!'. The Oliviers and the Millers somehow pushed through the throng to reach safety inside the foyer – but the Cardiffs didn't make it. The gap closed, and Julie and I were cut off. It seemed ages before the police made a path for us. This time the comments from the fans were rather different: 'Who's that?' 'Nobody important.'

Getting to our seats wasn't easy, either, however distinguished the audience was – and there were many famous faces to be seen. Marilyn's flamboyant luminosity was enough to make even the polite stalls assembly press close to her, as if they'd forgotten where their seats were.

A View from the Bridge was powerful theatre, and there was much applause as the curtain came down for the interval. It was considered far too risky for Marilyn to go to the crowded bar, and so a small room was provided for us where the attendants usually made teas and coffee for the interval. This small room was immediately crammed with friends and well-wishers, as we drank champagne to toast Arthur, with Marilyn beaming with pride for her husband.

Then the bell rang for the second act. I saw Marilyn stiffen in that strange withdrawal, exactly as she did when she was in the make-up room at the studios, and she quietly asked for another glass of champagne. The conversation noise sagged to a tactful diminuendo as everybody waited for Marilyn to make the first move back to our seats, but she stayed there, in that tiny crowded room; I knew she was going through the private hell of not being able to face that audience . . . of 'going on the set'. The bell rang a second time, and in a kind of awkward politeness people began to retreat, but Marilyn still stood there with that blank look I knew was self-torture, until Arthur Miller gently but firmly hustled her out of the room. As we watched the rest of the play I thought soberly about Marilyn's problem, and I knew there'd be many more to come.

Over the following days we lumbered on, knowing how difficult it was for Larry. Marilyn's upsets were more frequent and she was absent more often. It was evident by now that Marilyn was questioning Larry's direction. We couldn't fail to hear what went on; there is little privacy on a film set. During rehearsals and shooting there is always a piercing quiet so that any soft murmur is heard by the entire crew: it's as intimate as a cottage parlour. Larry would rehearse, and tell Marilyn about a dramatic point, but her remote look made it doubtful that anything had penetrated. Then Marilyn would walk over to Paula Strasberg, and there would be a whispered discussion while Paula gave her views on how the scene should be played. This sometimes lasted several minutes, while Larry waited nearby, his incredible patience hardly hiding his humiliation and rage. Sometimes Marilyn would walk away while Larry was in mid-sentence, and have her hair done while she pondered on her own – or Paula's – views on the scene. On one occasion, when Larry was explaining the underlying motivation for a line of dialogue, Marilyn turned to Paula and said petulantly: 'What's he mean?' Larry just walked away, while Paula talked about the subtleties of Method acting.

There was something unreal about it all. The great Olivier, magnificently costumed in heavy military felt, cumbersome medals, epaulettes, belts, riding boots and thick make-up, with his hair plastered down and a monocle wedged in his eye, would be all ready to shoot a scene. Having wearily rehearsed Marilyn for ages, he would be about to say 'Roll the camera' when Marilyn would go over to Paula in the shadows and talk again, while Larry waited – in sweat and silent fury. The remark that Paula made to Marilyn which has been quoted so much is true: I can vouch for it. Tom Heathcote, my electrician, was moving a cable near Paula's feet when he heard her tell Marilyn: 'Now remember, darling, think of Frank Sinatra and Coca-Cola.' At last Marilyn entered into the scene – and forgot her lines.

Larry's major problem was being unable to watch Marilyn's

performance from a distance when they were acting together. On one occasion he used a weird ploy to act in the first part of the scene, and watch the last part from behind the camera. In the scene he had to walk to the back of the set where a writing desk was in the left-hand corner. When the camera momentarily panned off him to hold Marilyn close in foreground, Larry ran out of picture and a double took his place. Being out of focus at the back of the set, nobody saw it was a double, and Larry could stand by the camera and watch Marilyn.

There was no doubt that Paula's Method technique greatly confused Marilyn and slowed her down. It also made her much more unsure about the way she should play a scene. Sometimes we would shoot more than twenty takes – over thirty, sometimes – before Marilyn would remember all her lines. Well, hardly ever *all* the lines; in the end, Larry would print several takes, hoping that what line she had forgotten in one take would be remembered in another, and the whole could be cut together in the editing.

The extraordinary thing was that when we watched the rushes the next day in the viewing theatre, it worked; Marilyn was simply wonderful. She had a luminous quality which was pure magic.

Sybil Thorndike said: 'You watch her act in a scene, and it seems nothing – too vague and underplayed; but when you see her on the screen, it is just wonderful.' And that was what kept Larry, and all of us, from total despair. We knew that the ultimate result would be something special.

None the less, I marvelled at Larry's stamina against such adversity. The continued presence of Paula Strasberg on the set and her effect on Marilyn was almost unbearable. Larry complained to Milton Green and Arthur Miller, saying Paula was driving him out of his mind; but Marilyn relied on her so much that nothing could be done.

The English crew were, of course, solidly on Larry's side, and Marilyn must surely have felt this, although the crew were always polite to her. For me, there was a painful conflict of loyalties. Much as I had always hero-worshipped Larry, I just couldn't help loving little-girl-lost. She was so endearing sometimes; like once when she was near me, she made a funny kind of cough, and clutching my arm, whispered: 'It's taken me years to disguise a burp into a cough!'

There was another occasion when I noticed her hands looked unusually rough and red. I said: 'Your hands are red, Marilyn – you need make-up.'

She looked at them with that far-away gaze of hers and said: 'That's all that scrubbing floors at the orphanage.' I wondered . . . all those years ago, and still signs like that? Was she fantasizing? Was it all a part of a self-destructive caricature of her past?

The 'problem child' image was emphasized when Bumble Dawson, our costume designer, had trouble with Marilyn's white dress. Marilyn was constantly spilling food down the front. Usually there are always at least a couple of spare identical dresses in case of an accident, but the spilling over-ran the supply – until Bumble had the bright idea of making the dress in two parts, the front like a quick-change napkin, and that made things easier.

There had been childish tantrums, too. Marilyn had never forgiven Larry when he had – rather misguidedly – instructed her, 'Be sexy, Marilyn,' and she had retired to her trailer in trembling fury.

Was Larry deliberately ignoring her talent? Did he believe only her body could act? She had to be cajoled back on the set, but it always rankled; from then on, Marilyn sarcastically called Larry 'Mister Sir'.

The strain was beginning to tell on Larry. His abundant energy was running down at last, and his nerves were visibly frayed. One day, when Marilyn arrived very late, Larry finally exploded: 'Why can't you get here on time – for fuck's sake?' and Marilyn, wide-eyed and smiling angelically, said: 'Oh – do they have that word in England too?'

There had been more arguments about the way scenes should be played, with Marilyn, under Paula's influence, ending up in a haze of indecision. How Larry hated Paula. She had told him to his face that she thought his performance was 'artificial'. Somehow the studio roof didn't fall in, but afterwards, he referred to her as 'that beast'.

Then a break came from out of the blue. I didn't know the details at the time, but the story leaked out via the grapevine of the crew that Marilyn was heart-broken about something she had read in Miller's notebook. We didn't know what it was; all we knew was that Marilyn was in an overwrought state and taking more pills. She was being hysterical with increasing tempo, and a woman psychiatrist who had been attending Marilyn in New York was flying to England immediately. The psychiatrist's presence undoubtedly seemed to help Marilyn and she arrived on the set a little more punctually. What happened next has always been shrouded in secrecy, but it appeared that Larry seized the opportunity of Marilyn's improved state to request that Paula's services be dispensed with. There were theories among the crew. Some believe Paula didn't want to leave, but had been persuaded to withdraw to allow Marilyn to re-establish some rapport with Larry. It was officially said that Paula had to return to New York on family business. Anyway, she went – temporarily or not – to New York, and Larry was free of her.

There is no doubt that Larry and Marilyn worked better together and everything was going much more smoothly, until – again in a cloud of rumour and secrecy behind the scenes – it was said that the heads of our company were pulling every string to prevent Paula returning to England. Marilyn found out, and there was an enormous row. Somehow Marilyn was persuaded to finish the picture without Paula. The collective pressure from Arthur Miller, Milton Green and the psychiatrist made Marilyn see that she must finish the picture, as there was so little shooting to be done. Larry, like a gladiator recovered from near-annihilation in the arena, was refreshed with new energy for the end of the fight. His phenomenal patience and fortitude deserved a special Oscar.

One day towards the end, Marilyn touchingly apologized to the unit: 'I hope you will all forgive me. I've been very, very sick all through this movie. Please don't hold it against me.'

There was a wondrous evening for her before shooting finished. She was invited by the Queen to a command performance at the Empire Theatre, Leicester Square. I told her what a treat it would be (I had been there on the first command show, with *A Matter of Life and Death*), and begged her most earnestly to dress with some care, something in good taste, without showing too much cleavage that could embarrass the Queen – and herself, too.

Marilyn thanked me and declared she would certainly take my advice, and wear a modest dress. Of course, she didn't. On the great night she wore a dazzling gown of gold lamé, revealing just about everything – and again her exuberant breasts defied Newton's law of gravity. Arthur Miller's point had been taken again: why should she not show off her God-given glory – even to the Queen?

It was quite a while before I saw the Millers again. I had a letter from them while I was in Rome, just before the opening of *The Prince and the Showgirl* at New York's Radio City, saying that they felt the picture would be very successful – although Arthur thought it was odd that many of the takes to which Marilyn had objected were in the final print: 'It's probably going to bore some people who are not swept away by your marvellous photography'; and Marilyn wrote: 'We keep missing you.'

At the première, views were mixed, but most praised Marilyn's performance – 'One of great talent . . .', 'It comes as a pleasant surprise, for Marilyn Monroe who has been half-actress, half-sensation so far . . .'.

Marilyn received several awards outside America, including Best Foreign Actress in Italy, but she was still denied even an Oscar nomination.

I was at the Beverly Hills Hotel in Hollywood when I had a phone call from Marilyn in New York. I told her I was setting up *Sons and Lovers*, and when I mentioned that I was flying home in a couple of days through New York, she invited me to lunch.

I arrived at the Millers' apartment at Sutton Place in New York at eleven in the morning. Marilyn was asleep. With memories of my photographic sessions with her, I feared I wouldn't see her before my plane left that evening. Arthur and I talked a lot and had lunch as Marilyn was still sleeping. After lunch, Arthur reported she was awake and getting up; he also brought in a black eye-mask which Marilyn thought I might need if I was tired. I was touched. The mask was smudged with her make-up and I thought of the times she must have used it to shut out the world.

She appeared at last, smiling apologies, and we spent a few hours together before I had to leave. Marilyn insisted I take the eye-mask for the plane trip. She also gave me a book to read – a proposed film for her: 'Perhaps we'll make it together, Jack.' It was called *A Lost Lady*.

A year later, I received another call from her. I was staying at the Beverly Hills Hotel again, but was out when she called. The message was from an El Dorado number. I called back, but she had gone. Why had she wanted to talk to me? I had heard that her life had been even more chaotic. *The Misfits* had just been completed and, evidently, had been a soul-scarring experience. And, far worse, her marriage was over.

As it happened, I saw her very soon afterwards. I discovered that she had just arrived at my hotel and had taken a bungalow there. I phoned her and she asked me to come over – 'right now'. It was nine at night. The interior of the bungalow was lit only by a table lamp; Marilyn was wearing dark sunglasses and surely couldn't have seen much.

She was so pleased to see me; her smile was wan as we embraced, yet somehow it was more sincere than her broad smile on camera. Her face was pale and strained. This was nothing like the Marilyn I had known. There was a bitterness and deep hurt; I could see that an avalanche of troubles had crushed her spirit. We sat down on a settee and had a drink, but it was decidedly not a happy occasion.

She told me *The Misfits* had been a most harrowing picture. There had been all kinds of despairing problems. Now Clark Gable had just died, and this had upset her terribly: 'I cried all night,' she said. In a way, she felt herself to be the cause of his heart failure. I tried to put that idea

out of her mind, but she shook her head: 'Kay [Gable's wife] thinks so.'
I didn't know then that, because of this, Marilyn had attempted suicide.
And it had been a close thing.

She said flatly: 'Arthur and I are finished.' I said how very sorry I was,
but I don't think she heard much of what I was saying. She sat looking
at the floor through those black sunglasses, talking in a toneless reverie:
'Arthur saw the demon in me . . . a lot of people like to think of me as
innocent, so that's the way I behave to them . . . if they saw the demon
in me they would hate me . . . I'm more than one person, and I act
differently each time . . . most of the time I'm not the person I'd like to
be – certainly not a dumb blonde like they say I am; a sex freak with big
boobs . . .'

In a weird irony, a lot of what she said I'd heard before – quoted in
press interviews. This is not uncommon, especially with film stars. They
say things which sound good and go down well, and they repeat them
from time to time.

Then she started to tell me the bizarre story of the Payne-Whitney
Clinic. Her voice was low at first, a self-explanatory analysis. It was
natural, wasn't it, to expect a normal clinic for someone run down? How
could she have known what kind of place it really was? Then, with
passionate incredulity: 'Jack, it was a nuthouse!'

At this she jumped up and wandered round the gloomy room. There
was much pain and bitterness in her voice as she told me the full story.
She had taken the advice of her doctor and gone to what she thought was
a simple nursing home in New York. Nobody had told her that the
section to which she was taken was for the mentally ill. At first, she didn't
notice the iron doors that clanged shut behind her, and the barred windows.
Then she saw that there were no handles on the doors of her room. The
door to the passage had a window pane so that patrolling nurses could
check up on her all the time. Her lavatory had no door at all.

As she realized the sort of place she was in – 'locked up with all those
nutty people' – she naturally enough went into panic. 'What are you
doing to me? I'm not crazy. I want to get out of here!' She was told this
was legally impossible. Only a relative could be authorized to take her
out. But Marilyn had no relatives – apart from her mother, who was
herself incarcerated in an asylum. No husband now – Arthur Miller was
out of her life. There was nobody to get her out of this nightmare. She
frantically wrote to the Strasbergs, pleading for help, but her letter was
ignored. Years later, however, this letter was sold for thousands of
dollars at Sotheby's.

Her voice took on the edge of hysteria as she went on: 'Jack, I was *afraid* – I still am . . . There's my mother – paranoid schizophrenia . . . and *her* family – all destroyed by the same thing – insanity. Was I a nut, after all? There I was, in a cell like I was mad . . . I was hysterical – who wouldn't be? And they were going to put me in a straitjacket. I knew that if I stayed there for long, I really would be mad.'

I sat on the settee, frozen. It was painful to listen to, but I knew it was a release for her to talk. She told me that she was finally allowed to make one phone call; she phoned her ex-husband, Joe Dimaggio, surely the most reliable and faithful man in her life, and it was by his influence that she was able to get out from that terrifying place – to which she should never have been sent anyway. 'Thank God for Joe,' she murmured.

She was still racked in outrage. The mechanical pacing continued, to and fro. Her voice had become a moaning catharsis: a querulous outpouring, sometimes so incoherent I couldn't understand. And some of the things I heard, I would never repeat to anyone.

She was most bitter about those who had let her down. They showed so much interest in her but, 'They were always on the make . . . I've been used by so many people, in so many ways . . . I was abandoned right at the beginning and, where it really matters, I'm still being abandoned.'

And then the tears came silently, in a flood. She turned to me as I went to her, and the tears were running in surging release as she ran into my arms. I sat her down and took off the sunglasses. She sobbed and shuddered, and I cradled her in my arms like a child.

After that night, I never saw her again.

I was in a Roman inner courtyard of high apartment buildings when I heard a high-pitched cry, then more cries echoing back and forth. I opened a window. It was like a scene in an Italian opera. Windows were opening as neighbours looked out and voiced the news just heard on the radio. '*Marilyn è morta! Incredibile . . . poverina . . . Oh, poverina!*'

A year before her appalling end, Marilyn had asked her make-up man, the ever-faithful Whitey, to promise her that: 'If I get killed or die, or something, you'll make me up; make me look good – before anyone else sees me?' And Whitey had promised he would do that.

On the Monday following the tragic August Sunday in 1962, he got a call from Marilyn's lawyer, Milton Rudin, who had been told long before that none but Whitey was to touch her body in the event of her death. Whitey, still very shaken, went to the morgue with his wife-to-be, Margie.

Marilyn was lying in a chilled steel box and Whitey had to 'make her look good'. After fifteen years of making her up on so many occasions, through so many stormy pictures, he was to end it in this eerie and macabre fashion. He was understandably nervous and needed a stiff drink to help him in this ghoulish task. He made-up Marilyn for the last time: foundation, undershading, eye make-up, a little powder, and finally he traced her stilled mouth with red lipstick. And Margie touched up her hair.

Marilyn's death was shocking – indecent and utterly tragic. Soon afterwards, Larry made a telling statement: 'She was a complete victim of ballyhoo and sensation, exploited beyond anyone's means.'

But the ballyhoo continued beyond anyone's imagination. The world – even now – will not let her go. Her death, still shrouded in mystery, only intensified the obsession of people to know more about her. The books still pour out, with new angles and 'revelations' about new alleged lovers – even newly discovered husbands.

She was cruelly manipulated in life, and cynically exploited after her death; she who was one of Hollywood's most pitiful victims is now with the immortals of film mythology.

Anyway, I loved her – not as a myth, or because of any of the fables that shrouded the real Marilyn, but simply as a warm, lovely person, all woman yet, somehow, all child, who was at heart a pure soul. Pure? In the teeth of all the smears . . . yes, pure in heart. I believe she was untarnishable.

> Like the sweet blushing apple
> On the highest branch,
> High of the topmost, which the gatherers forgot,
> Forgot? No, but they couldn't reach it . . .
> *Sappho*

16

Strange Interludes

Richard Fleischer, the director, and I were on a recce in Norway to choose locations for the forthcoming production of *The Vikings*. We had hired a seaplane to see the awesome eerie beauty of the Norwegian fjords which were bounded on both sides with immense towering cliffs that seemed to shut out the rest of the world.

The seaplane was tiny with cramped seating room and both take-off and landing were more than a little nerve-racking as the plane ploughed through the icy black water to get airborne and then soared crazily towards the top of the cliffs – and barely cleared them. To make matters more perturbing, the pilot had told us that morning – with questionable sensitivity – 'You're lucky to have this seaplane, the other one crashed yesterday.'

The Vikings was Kirk Douglas's baby. He had been trying to get it off the ground for some time, but the money boys wanted two stars for box-office security, and Kirk just couldn't get a co-star interested. Eventually Tony Curtis said he would do it, but only if he could have the leading role – Kirk's role.

With considerable fortitude – and perhaps desperation – Kirk agreed and the production was set to start a few months later. During this preparation time, while the script was being polished and finalized, Kirk's secondary role somehow became the leading role again. Tony didn't realize this until well into the middle of the picture, and must have been rather bemused.

It wasn't an easy picture to work on. We lived on a large ship anchored near our Viking village; we had built it, as well as some magnificent authentic-looking Viking longships.

True to Norwegian conditions it rained steadily for days on end. Kirk was naturally worried as the rain threatened to wreck the budget. I suggested we shot in the rain. It would surely be accepted that the lusty Vikings would have ignored bad weather conditions; it would enhance their legendary toughness. Kirk and Dick were delighted with my suggestion and we accordingly shot regardless of the weather. It certainly gave mood to the film, but on some occasions we had problems with the wind direction for our Viking ships. When the wind was too weak to fill their huge sails, the ships were fitted with auxiliary motors so they would appear to be sailing. But sometimes the wind would be in the wrong direction when the ships were approaching camera; so, although the motors drove the ships towards us, the wind-filled sails billowed the wrong way – concave instead of convex. It looked hilarious, and you can witness this weird nautical miracle in the released film.

We shot our interiors at studios in Munich. On one set, a 'stone' wolf pit which Ernest Borgnine is forced to jump into to be devoured by a horde of savage wolves, an unforeseen problem arose. When we set the camera to look down on them from Borgnine's point of view, instead of them reacting with blood-curdling growls in anticipation of a Viking meal, the dogs were totally placid and peaceful. Some of them appeared to be sleeping. The dog trainer yelled at them. We all yelled at them. We pelted things down at them, but the ferocious-looking beasts just looked up with bored disdain.

Someone had an idea. Pieces of cloth soaked in turpentine were put on the end of long poles and our prop man leaned over the parapet trying to jab the turpentined end under the dogs' tails. It didn't work: trying to position a ten-foot pole on a moving dog's anus was impossible.

Another idea was tried. Our brave props man walked right into the wolf pit carrying rags soaked in turpentine, lifted up the wolves' tails and swabbed the turps in the correct places. The dogs simply licked the turpentine off and then relaxed into boredom again.

Then a strange thing happened. Tony Curtis, who wasn't in the scene but had come to watch, went near the camera to peer down at the ridiculous sleepy dogs. When the dogs caught sight of Tony they all went mad with fury, leaping up and howling with rage. Tony backed away from their ferocious frenzy, disappearing from their view, and the dogs instantly relaxed again. Tony had found some old peasants' clothing, including a big floppy hat which belonged to one of the dog trainers, and had worn them for a joke. For some reason, this was responsible for the dogs going wild. We started the camera and got Tony to appear before the dogs who, the moment they caught sight of him, went berserk again. Thus, we got the scene.

At the end of the film, Kirk is killed in battle and is given a majestic Viking funeral at sea. The setting was magnificent: the Viking longships against a deep sunset and Kirk's body (a dummy) on a pyre awaiting the torch for burning. Although it had to look as if in flames, we obviously couldn't burn our valuable vessel, so butane gas was rigged at key places which would give the effect of the ship being on fire. When we had got enough footage the special effects crew would then emerge from hiding and turn the butane off.

We shot the scene from an adjacent modern vessel. The sun wouldn't set until 10.30 p.m., so the light would last for hours.

A fire vessel was standing by in the event of something going wrong, which of course it did. We gave the signal to light the butane, turned on the camera, and obtained a most poignant scene. Dick said 'cut' and we all felt very pleased with ourselves, as the order was given by walkie-talkie to turn off the butane.

The special effects crew turned off the gas, but to our alarm we saw that the flames had taken hold and our Viking ship was burning for real. Instantly, the order was given to send our emergency vessel to put the fire out. But the fire vessel's motor wouldn't start.

As we listened to the ship's engine turning over without success, we saw the special effects crew on the Viking ship frantically trying to douse the flames and realized we were approaching disaster. When the Viking sail burst into flames, the special effects crew dove into the sea.

It would be an understatement to say there was much confusion. Although it only lasted a few minutes, it seemed like a nightmare in slow motion. Finally, the fire-launch's engine came to life and it sped to the blazing ship with all its hoses going, eventually putting out the fire.

Kirk usually insisted on doing all his stunts himself no matter how difficult or dangerous, but this was one occasion when Kirk hadn't protested at the use of a dummy. I think he was very wise.

I joined Richard Fleischer once more, in 1977 when he was doing *The Prince and the Pauper* in Budapest. One incident remains firmly embedded in my memory. Our unit was crowded into the lobby of the Gellert Hotel, all packed up and ready to move on to a new location sixty miles away. Over the swell of talk a sudden cry of horror was heard from the producer Pierre Spengler. 'Oh my God! Stop the unit from leaving.' It transpired that one of the young assistants on the film had been examined by a Hungarian doctor who had pronounced him infected with syphilis. The assistant had been bringing us tea and soft drinks every day from the first day of shooting, so it was decided that the whole unit must be tested for syphilis. We were taken to a rather primitive hospital, and the method for blood testing was equally primitive. A needle was pricked into a vein in the arm which was then squeezed to let the blood drip into a metal pot.

We moved on to the new location where the atmosphere was like an Agatha Christie murder case. Who was the syphilis carrier? And who had it now? Everyone viewed each other with brooding suspicion; there was an undercurrent of mild hysteria amongst some of the younger women. The bar was very busy. News had come in that the results were on the way and would be posted on a notice board in the hotel lobby. As we waited, the suspense was suffocating.

Richard Fleischer's wife had just returned to Los Angeles and Richard phoned her that evening: 'Mickey, darling, I think you'd better be tested for syphilis.' Mickey must have tottered back in horror wondering what her husband had been up to until Richard explained.

The results of the test arrived. Quite a few people were found to be positive, including my son Mason who was then six years old. One of the girls who was positive fainted: she had just got engaged. Another victim had hysterics and locked herself in her bedroom. Others who were positive were stunned as if they had received a death sentence. During this nightmare both Richard and I had the same idea. Richard phoned his doctor in Los Angeles and told him the macabre story. His doctor appeared to be gasping on the other end of the phone – not from horror but from paroxysms of laughter. He told Richard that if anyone had caught syphilis from a used cup, a touch, or a lavatory seat, it would make medical history. Syphilis could only be passed on by sexual intercourse. I had also phoned my doctor in Switzerland who said the same thing: that it was quite impossible for anyone to catch syphilis in this way. The whole thing was sheer nonsense.

The unit was told and the relief was like the gates of heaven opening, but no one would ever forget the day the unit caught syphilis.

17

Expectations Fulfilled

My career as a director had not, so far, been an awesome success: two low-budget B-pictures. The press had not been kind. Their verdict on my new career was 'Why should Cardiff (flatteringly labelled "Britain's best cameraman") leave his safe pinnacle for the hazards of direction?' Leonard Moseley of the *Daily Express* had written a caustic review of my first effort, *Intent to Kill*, advising me that I should return to photography as soon as possible.

Then, in 1960, I struck lucky. The head of the London branch of Fox was Robert Goldstein, a typical American executive: middle-aged, somewhat epicene in manner, a moonlike face, with large horn-rimmed glasses which were always perched on top of his head, making him look rather like a snail. He wore expensive silk suits and his Rolls-Royce had a BG 1 number plate. But I mustn't be unkind, for it was he who gave me my big break as a director. He also gave me problems, though, as will be seen later.

He told me, in his walnut-panelled office, that he had me in mind to direct D. H. Lawrence's *Sons and Lovers*. I lied – show biz style – and told him I adored the book when, in fact, I hadn't even read it. The moment I left Goldstein's office, I dashed into Hatchard's and bought a copy. As I read it, I felt a fecund possessiveness. Perhaps I could be a creative part of this powerful human story. Perhaps this was the chance I'd been waiting for.

Goldstein had told me that the big boys in Hollywood had to be convinced that I could do it, so he had already sent my two earlier films for their verdict. Some days later, I learned I had passed the test, although my two modest films could hardly have had them frothing with excitement. Perhaps they had seen a smidgen of promise, enough to allow me to direct what was to them, after all, an ordinary low-budget picture in England.

Off to Hollywood and much more opulent walnut-panelled offices where I met Buddy Adler, head of production at 20th Century Fox and

Jerry Wald, who was to be the producer, a large genial man said to be the model for Bud Schulberg's *What Makes Sammy Run*. I was given three disparate scripts of *Sons and Lovers* to read. They were terrible, as little like Lawrence's book as Jackie Collins is to Tolstoy. With shaky resolution, I told Adler and Wald my reaction. There was a loud silence. I knew I could have been sent packing there and then. Buddy stared at me, then murmured, 'Did you have another writer in mind?' I said I wanted an English writer, one who knew Lawrence and Lawrence's country, someone who would keep close to the book, which, after all, was an acknowledged masterpiece. To my relief, Buddy agreed and Jerry Wald, having seen Buddy's approval, also nodded enthusiasm, so it was back to England to find an English writer and prepare the picture.

Before I left, there was a touch of fantasy. I was ordered to try and get Vivien Leigh for the part of Morel's mother and Jack Hawkins for the father. I was aghast. The beautiful, elegant Vivien Leigh playing a miner's wife? And the cultured Shakespearian voice of Jack Hawkins as an ignorant, drunken coal miner? But I said nothing, already having other ideas as I flew back to England.

First I approached John Osborne to write the script. We talked in his London apartment. He mused about an approach to a screen version, looking up at the ceiling, his hands shaping ideas in the air as he spoke of gritty Nottingham and the brave show of summer in the grimy surroundings; the wild flowers holding their own against the soot and sulphur of the pits; Paul's relationship with his mother, Miriam, and Clara Dawes. (Neither of us knew then that I would cast his wife, Mary Ure, to play Clara.)

But gently, he declined. I think with regret. He had other things to do, and that was that. However, I was lucky finally to get T. E. B. (Tibby) Clarke, a truly talented writer with stunning successes behind him: *The Blue Lamp*, *Passport to Pimlico*, *The Lavender Hill Mob* – all his own original screenplays. Though hardly Lawrence material, he greatly admired Lawrence and, after some discussions, he went to work while I went on to cast the picture.

The key casting, of course, was the son, Paul Morel – Lawrence himself as a young man. This was a period when Bob Goldstein played a producer's role, asking me to test the most preposterously unsuitable actors. I had little or no help from my real producer. Jerry Wald was thousands of miles away in Hollywood; in fact, he never once came to England, neither during pre-production, nor during the shooting of the picture.

I treated Goldstein's weird casting suggestions politely enough and duly made tests of actors who were quite unsuited, including Richard Harris, whom I respected for his zany Irish ebullience; although the test I made was hilariously enjoyable, Harris himself knew it would never work. Goldstein even wanted me to test Sean Connery, but I talked to Sean and we agreed that it just wasn't on. Nobody then knew that Sean would become the world famous James Bond, but even so I could never see him as an adolescent Lawrence.

While this vital key role was in limbo, I went to see Vivien Leigh in a play at the New Theatre and, in her dressing-room, told her about the role of Mrs Morel, the coal miner's wife. I laid on the coal grit in a miner's cottage with gusto, as of course I didn't want her to accept the role. She looked most doubtful at my description of the sooty ambience: 'I don't want to look crummy, Jack.' I tried to sound honest and practical: 'Well, Viv, darling, you live in grimy poverty and perpetual coal dust. You have to scrub the dirt off your husband in a zinc bath every night, and one of your sons is twenty-six years old. I'm afraid you'll look crummy most of the time – but it's a wonderful part!'

She turned it down. Hiding my relief, I told Goldstein and said I would like to try for Wendy Hiller, who was so effective in *Major Barbara* and *Pygmalion*. Goldstein shook his head so violently his glasses nearly fell off. 'You can't have Wendy Hiller. She's in a play in New York.' Then came a big slice of luck for me. By chance I read that her play had just folded and I was able to phone her in New York. Yes, she would be delighted to play Morel's wife, and Goldstein had no alternative but to sign her up.

I then told Goldstein I wanted Trevor Howard, who was most interested, to play the father. Goldstein was curiously hostile to this request, but I didn't know why until later. Two days afterwards, he phoned me to say he had signed Harry Andrews for an extremely low figure – I believe it was £10,000. Trevor Howard's money was £26,000. So Goldstein had gone for a bargain.

This was war. Trevor came to see me, bemused and angry. Nobody had spoken to his agent about making a deal for less money. I was embarrassed but asked him how much less he would have considered. Trevor said he wanted to play the role so much he would have done it for half of his regular money. At this time I discovered why Goldstein wanted nothing to do with Trevor's agent, Al Parker. Apparently Parker had tried to organize a list of signatures to send to Fox in America to get Goldstein replaced, as he was considered incompetent and impossible to deal with!

Fate came in right on cue. Buddy Adler had just flown in to London and was in Goldstein's office and so, barging through secretaries, I dashed in to confront the two of them. I said, tersely, 'I can get Trevor Howard for twelve thousand.' Goldstein glared. 'I've already signed Andrews for ten.' Buddy held up his hands, 'Now wait a minute.' He paced around a bit, then said curtly to Goldstein. 'Pay off Andrews, sign Howard.' That was victory number two.

After that, without further hindrance, I was able to cast Heather Sears as Miriam and Mary Ure as Clara – who provided Paul Morel's initiation into sex. I was on cloud nine.

Then the storm broke. The gods in Hollywood thundered their wrath over the long-distance phone: 'What the hell are you doing? This film is being made and financed by an American company, to be shown all over America, and there's not one goddamned actor who is known in the States . . . Who's Wendy Hiller? Who's Mary Ure? Who's Heather Sears?' And Trevor Howard, he's hardly a big name in America. Now listen, Cardiff . . .'

That was it. I was instructed to have a big American name to play the son, Paul. Dean Stockwell, who had been a hit in *Compulsion*, was required. This was an order – 'If I still wanted to direct the picture', and I surely did.

Apart from having no choice, I honestly couldn't come up with an alternative. There were plenty of talented young English actors who would have probably given fine performances, but then, much more than now, the leading role had to be a star name in the box office. When *Sons and Lovers* was released, some English critics chided me for casting an American to play the leading role, knowing nothing of the compulsory order by my bosses in America.

During pre-production, I had to make yet another trip to the Hollywood mandarins to discuss the final shooting script and cast. There were further talks with Buddy Adler – more friendly now since Dean Stockwell was playing the lead. And lastly, Jerry Wald told me that the Sherlock office – the American censors – wanted a meeting to tell me about the censor cuts. Alarm bells clanged in my head. Censor cuts?

The meeting was duly convened. A few gentlemen in sober suits sat in Jerry Wald's office and told me of the scenes and dialogue that they could not allow and which had to be changed. There was a scene in the barn where Miriam cannot bring herself to respond to Paul's ardent embrace and recoils trembling. Paul sadly tells her he can't always be so spiritual: 'I'm flesh and blood . . . Being afraid, that's not pure, it's a kind of dirtiness.' He moves to the barn door to go. On an impulse she rushes to him; as he holds her, she says fiercely, 'You *shall* have me.' All this was Lawrence's dialogue in the book. 'No she can't say that,' said the Sherlock gentlemen, and Jerry Wald told me cheerfully that he had already had the corrected line typed and showed it to me. Instead of Miriam saying 'You *shall* have me,' she was now to say 'I *do* love you.' This was the new punchline, as banal as a quotation in a Christmas cracker. I looked at them. They were serious. And there was more. I listened, hiding my feelings with difficulty. Each censored line had been corrected and retyped by the affable Jerry Wald, all the force diluted to the level of a child's primer.

In the night scene at the farm mill, Paul and Miriam had made love, but it had been a disaster because of Miriam's frigidity. Paul says bitterly, 'You hated it . . . you shut your eyes and clenched your hands. To you it was a sacrifice, and I feel like a criminal.' A general shaking of heads at this one. I read the new bowdlerized version and this time I didn't know whether to double up or throw up. It portrayed Miriam, stretched awkwardly on a couch, looking bewildered, saying: 'What's the matter, Paul?' Paul is standing by the window looking out. He says, without turning, 'You *would* have hated it and I *would* have felt like a criminal.'

At the end of this incredible session, I knew it was hopeless to argue, especially as Jerry, my producer, had condoned every correction; it was all a bathetic *fait accompli*. I knew what I had to do. I went back to England resolved not to alter a single word of the script.

The starting date was getting close. I had checked the locations and the casting of minor parts. The main location was to be at Eastwood, Lawrence's own country, in the industrial Midlands of Nottingham. In fact, I used the actual house where Lawrence was born and spent his youth. And luckily I was to be able to reopen the old Brinsley coal mine, the original pit where Lawrence's father had toiled.

The shooting schedule was squirmingly tight. For all the Nottingham locations, including the dramatic pit disaster, I was given only one week. Goldstein was determined to show Hollywood that the picture could be made on a really low budget. The original schedule had been for the summer months, but we were shooting in December when the winter light was gone by three in the afternoon.

Lawrence's book glows with the flora of summer. I squeezed in some snowdrops for one scene by the canal, but it was a bleak compromise. Mainly because of this absence of the colours of summer I made the film in black and white. There was no objection from Fox. It was cheaper.

Certainly black and white gave it a more realistic power. The press was to think so too. One critic wrote 'The coal mining background is near perfection. It is redolent with coal dust.' But, really, I would have preferred flowers.

The evening before our first day's shooting, our wardrobe truck was stolen. All our period costumes lost. Disaster time. We got the Nottingham police on to it, and the truck was discovered early next morning, weirdly enough in a local army barracks. No time to find out why. I was 'on' – with butterflies in my stomach, like my father on first nights. But this was dawn, at the old coal mine, and the giant wheel, unused for years, was starting to turn with a rusty screech, causing the pigeons to scatter against the morning sky.

The winter weather was horrible, but excellent for the atmosphere I wanted. My cameraman, Freddie Francis, did wonders in the daunting light; and for this and his sensitive studio photography, Freddie deservedly won an Oscar. My assistant director, Peter Yates, was soon to make his name as a director with *Bullitt*.

The local film extras were, I suppose, unique. Not only were they the actual people of the Eastwood community, but many came from families close to Lawrence's real life. Imagine my reaction when a woman came up to me between set-ups and told me with a certain shyness, 'My mother was Clara.' I looked at her, a woman in her forties, dressed in Edwardian costume – she could have been a ghost standing before me – but she was real. This was Phyllis, the daughter of Alice Dax, from whom Lawrence had drawn the character of Clara in the novel. She told me her parents had kept a chemist's shop at Eastwood. Her mother had been a keen social reformer and had the same suffragette sympathies as the book's Clara. 'Mother had a very strong character indeed and had clashed with Lawrence at times. Of course, Lawrence changed quite a few things for his book, but it was mother all right.'

It was so stimulating to talk to someone so closely connected to the real story I was portraying on film. There were more surprises. When I returned to my hotel that evening, a man was waiting to see me in the lobby. Well dressed, perhaps in his sixties, with a confident intelligence, the first thing he said was: 'What are you doing to my sister Miriam?' I could only stare for a moment, hardly believing my ears. Could this really be Miriam's brother? The real sister's name was Bessie Chambers, so this had to be Professor David Chambers who had been a child at the time that Lawrence made so many visits to the Chambers' home – Haggs Farm, two miles out of Eastwood.

He spoke of his sister with love, but also with the candour of a brother. 'She was a shy, sensitive thing. She didn't have a great sense of humour, but Lawrence certainly had. I played with him often . . . he was fun . . . in the winter evenings when he came over, I, of course, was put to bed, but he used to read to the family – books and sometimes poetry. My family said he was domineering at times; he put on airs, but we all loved him.'

I asked him about the religious dominance of his mother over Miriam – Jessie in the novel – and he confirmed it. They both absorbed religion passionately and, no, sex was never mentioned.

'Jessie was, in fact, considered to be a bit odd by our family. She was unable to be just an ordinary woman. She was too intense. Of course she and Lawrence were close; they both had a love of learning and discovery, but there were some things in her behaviour which grated on him. I was only a child then, but my family spoke of these things long afterwards.'

When David left, I jotted down all I could remember, wishing I could have met him earlier, but it helped me to understand better the character of Miriam.

The first week's shooting ended bang on schedule. I had worked quickly and had a fast crew. The actors were behaving well in the dismal weather conditions, and I had a good relationship with them – essential for any director. Actors must have confidence and believe the director is concerned with their performance. It was a successful, if exhausting week. Back at Pinewood, the real work started. The performances, relationships, the tempo had to be right. On my tight schedule I had no time for the luxury of safety margins. I had to 'cut in the camera' and know where I would use each shot. It was more or less a television technique, shooting longer stretches of a scene with the minimum of closer shots from different viewpoints. I had learned a lot about the advantages – and disadvantages – of this technique when I worked with Hitchcock on ten-minute takes.

I had no producer 'in the field'. Bob Goldstein stayed in his London office and made not one trip to the studios. Jerry Wald stayed in his Hollywood office, sending useless advisory letters from time to time. So I was on my own as far as supervision was concerned. I was happy enough about this. My production manager, Teddy Joseph, could handle any problems that arose. And arise they did.

The first problem concerned shooting with snow. Near the studios was a lake and a mill house, a perfect setting for the scenes where Paul and Miriam agonized over their relationship. There were rumours of snow coming, and I told the production department to be ready to take out all the equipment at a moment's notice if any should fall. There was strong opposition to all this. I was told that organizing a full day's shooting at short notice on the chance of snow could be a disaster. Bob Goldstein told me on the phone to forget it. Too risky.

I awoke at dawn the next morning and saw snowflakes falling. I raced to the studios and told everybody to switch the schedule to the lake scenes. Amid much protest and advice not to expose myself to wasting a day's shooting, I insisted on the move and completed the whole sequence in one day. The lake was frozen over, and I made Paul throw a stone to skid on the surface. It was perfect. I was winning.

Back in the studio I was shooting a tricky sequence where Paul takes Clara home after an evening at a vaudeville. He misses his train, and Clara says he can sleep there – she will sleep in her mother's bed. It's late at night, and they are surprised to see that Clara's mother is still up. Paul and Clara hope the mother will retire – they are burning for each other – but the mother takes an interminable time tidying up, and in their frustration they play cards, watching the mother as she potters about, carrying things to and fro. In the end the mother brings a candle for Paul; there is nothing for him to do but go upstairs to bed.

I deliberately played this sequence in a slow tempo of frustrated waiting. The lateness of the night, trains shunting tiredly in the background. The two young people ache for each other as they play cards, but the mother swishes back and forth increasing their frustration.

Next day Goldstein phoned me from his office. He had seen the dailies and was very concerned. 'It's so slow, Jack. You've lost your snappy tempo.' I told him not to worry, it would be adjusted in the editing. It was like talking to a child.

In spite of the stifling obstructions of Goldstein, I began to sense the film taking shape. But there was also a nervous feeling, near to panic sometimes. Was I making something worthy of such a literary master-piece, having to work on such a low budget and short schedule?

Obviously, a book must suffer from being adapted for a film. So much of the structure and depth is lopped away, reducing hundreds of book pages into a stunted digest. My writer, Tibby Clarke, had met this challenge and made the best compromise possible, but we had to take liberties with the novel as every film writer has to do. Lawrence himself made many adjustments to all his works: the first version of *Sons and Lovers* was written *before* his mother died, and there were three versions of *Lady Chatterley's Lover*, each quite different in story and content.

Astonishingly, the second version is still waiting to be published in English!

Inevitably during the shooting of a film, there comes a question about dialogue. An actor finds a line awkward to say, although it looks fine on the page. When this happened on *Sons and Lovers*, I would immediately refer to Lawrence's book – which I always carried by my side like a devout Christian clutches his Bible and, *voilà*, there in the book would be the perfect line of dialogue. It never failed. Later *Time* magazine was to comment: 'Much of the dialogue is Lawrence's, and it's a reminder of what a remarkable dialogue writer he was.'

However onerous the responsibilities of a director, there are compensations: happy moments creating new ways of film expression; getting away from clichés; doing something different.

Who hasn't experienced that flash of inspiration when a sudden idea produces a 'Eureka' of satisfaction? So, too, a film director has that tingling pleasure when an idea lights up in his head to make a scene more interesting, something new that will articulate the story in a novel and persuasive way.

For instance, Paul and Miriam are sitting by a lake in the peaceful countryside. They hear the muffled explosion of the mine disaster. Easy enough to show them reacting to the distant explosion and realizing what it is, but what could be done to make it more interesting?

I had a gadget placed just under the surface of the placid lake which vibrated after the explosion, causing shuddering ripples on the water. They both stare at it for a moment, then Paul shouts, 'It's the mine!' and they race away.

Many ideas came during post-production. Sound effects, for instance. Paul's mother has a row with her husband about Paul's going away for a weekend with Clara. The mother, weeping, sinks to the ground holding the bedrail as the father shouts to her, and her whimpering cries echo over the following scene, merging with the shrill, slightly derisive cries of seagulls as Paul and Clara scamper happily over the sands.

Bob Goldstein nearly ruined that sequence, saying it would be too expensive for the first unit to go to a seaside location, so a very small second unit was sent, with doubles for Paul and Clara. The dialogue scenes were to be done in the studios.

I saw the two doubles on the screen and it didn't work. They didn't look like Dean Stockwell and Mary Ure, and they didn't run with the same visual personality as the real stars.

I phoned Goldstein telling him I wanted a retake with the real actors on the following Sunday. 'You must be crazy,' Goldstein said. 'Paying Dean Stockwell and Mary Ure for Sunday work would cost a fortune.' 'It's all right, Bob,' I said sweetly. 'I've talked to Dean and Mary. They'll do it for nothing.'

But there was another hurdle, just before the camera equipment was due to leave for our seaside location. Goldstein was on the phone again. 'What's this tracking dolly on the list? You can't take it – it would cost an extra sixty dollars freight.' 'Oh, Bob,' I exclaimed, 'why didn't you tell me earlier? The truck has already left.' The moment I put down the receiver, I raced to the transport department and told them to hit the road!

I used the dolly to track sideways with the running couple seen in the distance, to take them under an iron pier for a smooth transition to the scene underneath.

It was this constant battling with Goldstein that brought out in me a cunning I never knew I possessed. The big crisis came when Goldstein phoned to say I was two days behind schedule. Although I protested the schedule had been unrealistic, Goldstein was adamant on showing Hollywood how much cheaper films could be made in England.

He told me he had torn several pages out of what was left of the script so we could get back on schedule. Which pages? When he gave me the scene numbers he had torn out, I couldn't believe it. They were some of the most important scenes in the picture.

If I had then resigned from the picture, I knew Goldstein could replace me without much trouble. I had no alternative but to employ a stratagem I didn't like, ethically: pitting the actors against the company. I was on the best of terms with my cast, and I called them all into my office and told them the position. They were dumbfounded. What could they do? The only way, I told them, was for *all* of them to protest to Fox in Hollywood. If I walked out I could easily be replaced, but Fox couldn't afford to reshoot everything if they all walked out.

The cast agreed wholeheartedly and each of them sent cables to Buddy Adler saying that their best scenes had been cut and they wanted them put back. Buddy Adler phoned me. What the hell was going on? Why were the actors so insistent on replacing the scenes? I told Buddy that the excised scenes were vitally important; and if they were cut out, he wouldn't have a movie. It was as simple as that. The scenes were replaced at once.

Sons and Lovers was completed soon after this silly drama, and everybody was happy – except perhaps Robert Goldstein. He told me that I had half a day for inserts, which are close-ups of things like letters, watches, etc., which one never has time to shoot on the set. This had to be shot in the afternoon of the following day. I reminded Goldstein I had to get a long shot of the city of Nottingham, which had always been put off. 'No time or money for that now,' said Goldstein. 'Forget it.'

How could I forget such an important shot of the city which figures so importantly in the film?

The next morning I got up at dawn and caught a very early train to Nottingham. With my still camera, I climbed a high building overlooking the city, clicked the long shot I needed, and returned to Pinewood by lunch time, with one still picture of Nottingham which was developed and printed in a few hours. During my afternoon insert time, I photographed it with the movie camera, with cigarette smoke drifting in front, and my camera slowly tracking and panning to disguise the stillness of the photograph. It was quite successful. Goldstein squinted with suspicion; he thought I had gone with my crew to Nottingham on the sly.

We were nearly finished. My film was already rough cut. After each day's shooting, I had worked with my editor and the film was already in good structural shape, although without music and sound effects. Now came the big obstacle. I took the rough cut to Hollywood. Buddy genuinely liked it and so did Jerry Wald. But now I had to show it to the Sherlock censor department – the gentlemen who had made all those ridiculous but mandatory cuts in the dialogue, all of which I had brazenly ignored. The theatre looked, to me, like the Old Bailey Central Criminal Court. There were rows of film censors, all in smart suits and ties, with the stern looks one has for a felon on trial. Buddy Adler sat next to me as the lights dimmed. We ran the film and I sat tensed in the flickering darkness. The lights came on at the end, and I held my breath like a prisoner waiting for the jury's verdict.

The foreman turned to me. 'Well, Mr Cardiff, I see you've ignored our censor cuts.' I thought by his grim expression he was going to produce a black hat and pronounce sentence. He pursed his lips: 'All of them, in fact.' I nodded mutely, having nothing to say before sentence was passed on me. 'But,' he said, 'I have to tell you that everything you've done is in such good taste that it works without offending and we're not going to cut a frame of it.'

Buddy and I had a drink afterwards. I was elated, but Buddy looked gloomy. 'Well,' I said, 'that was a triumph, wasn't it?'

Buddy shook his head morosely. 'Jack, it's a disaster. We haven't got a picture.'

I was dumbfounded. 'What on earth do you mean?'

'They didn't fight us on anything,' he said. 'It often takes weeks before some kind of compromise is reached; a cut here or there, maybe a whole scene cut, if we can keep other scenes in. But these guys haven't cut a single word. So it must be too tame. We've nothing to fight about.'

I forgot to be amused at Buddy, ignoring the persuasion of good taste. I had an idea.

'Well, Buddy, why don't we give them something to fight about? Why don't you let me shoot that scene you said was taboo, which you cut out of the script?' This was, in fact, a key scene. It focused on Paul's Oedipal relationship with his mother. From the beginning Buddy Adler had veered right away from it, but I had managed to make it fairly apparent in the overall story.

The scene that Buddy had cut showed Clara in bed, watching Paul washing himself, and she taunts him: 'About me, you know very little. About *me*.'

'What do you mean?'

'I never seem to have all of you. It's as though you were taking someone else . . . Is it me you want, or just *it*?'

'Have you ever been loved more than I love you?'

'It isn't the act of loving. You're just incapable of giving *yourself*. As though something – or somebody – was holding you back.'

'Shut up,' Paul shouts. He grabs her on the bed, and they embrace fiercely.

It was good Lawrence, and I wanted very much to get this scene in my picture.

Buddy considered my suggestion thoughtfully, then snapped his fingers. 'Let's do it. It's a big gamble – they'll fight this like crazy – but let's do it.'

I shot this extra scene at Fox Movietone Studios in New York. Mary Ure was lying in bed naked, covered only by a single sheet; Paul, stripped to the waist, is washing at a basin. The scene played very well. I finished it in one day. When I returned to my hotel, there was a long cable waiting for me. Buddy had got cold feet: 'Dear Jack, here are your instructions for the extra scene. Mary Ure must not, repeat not, be naked in bed. There must be a minimum of four sheets on the bed and, lastly, Mary must not, repeat not, say "Is it me you want or *it*?" Regards, Buddy.'

I replied at once: 'Dear Buddy, your cable arrived too late. I have already shot the scene. You wanted a fight with the censors. Now you've got a good one. Good luck. Regards, Jack.'

A week later I was delighted to hear that Buddy, after quite a battle with the Sherlock censors, had won the day. Not one frame was touched, and the new scene was in the picture.

It's hard to believe the enormous change in censorship over the last few years. When Rhett Butler said to Scarlett, 'Frankly, my dear, I don't give a damn,' it was considered very bold indeed; and when Eliza Doolittle said 'Not bloody likely', there were gasps from the audience. When *Sons and Lovers* was released in England, the British censors wouldn't allow Mary Ure to say 'Is it me you want or *it?*' without giving my film an X certificate! The ineffable Goldstein cut the whole sequence out because of this one tiny word. I was out of the country at the time, and there was no one to fight like Buddy Adler had fought. Anyway, the sequence was put back later.

Back in London, Goldstein told me the British Film Producers had seen my rough cut and had chosen it as the British film of that year to go to the Cannes Film Festival, which was in two weeks' time. Of course I was delighted but had to explain patiently to Goldstein that there was simply no chance of getting all the post-production work done in two weeks.

We had no music yet. I had wanted Mario Nascimbene, who had composed the score for *The Vikings*, and whom I knew in Rome, but Goldstein had never agreed to his terms and nothing further had been done. Most musicians can take weeks – months, sometimes – to compose a musical score, and then there's the final cut, sound effects, dubbing, negative cutting, etc. Cannes was only fourteen days away!

Goldstein simply said, 'Jack, do you want it to go to Cannes or don't you?' Dear, dear man.

So, my art director, Tom Morahan, was upgraded to associate producer so he could supervise some of the post-production work while I flew to Rome to work with Nascimbene on the music.

Incredibly, the music was written in three days and nights. Nascimbene would play a theme on the piano and we would work out all the music passages far into the night. Despite the amazing speed at which he worked, Nascimbene wrote a wonderful score. Back in London I recorded the music and did the final dubbing in record time, and somehow it all came together just in time for Cannes.

And so I came to be at the Cannes Festival. The soaring music ended the film and the applause surged into me like a great flood of joy, making up for all the battles I'd had on the film. Buddy Adler gave his cynical advice: 'Jack, you must enjoy every second of this; who knows, it may never happen again.'

The press reviews were the best any director could ever hope for in one lifetime. Leonard Moseley of the London *Daily Express*, who had been so hostile to my first film as a director and had suggested that I return to photography as soon as possible, now wrote of *Sons and Lovers*: 'One of the most moving, compassionate and genuine films I have ever experienced.'

The American reviews were also good. The *New York Mirror* said: '*Sons and Lovers* is a brilliant film . . . brought to the screen with such rare fervor and consummate artistry that it is even more rewarding to watch than read. I urge you to see it. I personally consider it one of the finest films ever made.' The *Chicago American* said: 'It stirs new faith in movies. This is a wonderful film, wonderful in every department. Although its subject deals predominantly with sex, it is never guilty of poor taste or deliberate sensationalism.' And the *New York Post*: 'The opening sequences of *Sons and Lovers* are so marvellously right that they astound you, as does all great art when it expresses a whole world without a flaw. Director Jack Cardiff . . . steps up among the great ones. There is no letdown from his unbelievably high level. *Sons and Lovers* can safely be placed among the literary masterpieces which have been acted worthily for the screen.'

Am I showing off? Of course I am, but why not? You don't get reviews like that very often – perhaps once in a lifetime.

18

The Aftermath

The dizzy success of *Sons and Lovers* led to several directorial offers – mostly from Hollywood – and, dreamlike indeed, the great David O. Selznick invited me to Venice to discuss a future production.

There I was, in bathing shorts, plodding back and forth on the beach of the Lido Hotel with the great man who had produced so many cinematic triumphs, including of course, *Gone with the Wind*, offering story after story to tempt my appetite.

David O. Selznick, the apotheosis of the Hollywood mogul, was also large of physical stature and his overweight form was not flattered by knee-length shorts, but his enthusiasm for story ideas was as bracing as the adjacent Mediterranean. We continued our discussions over dinner at the hotel, when his wife, Jennifer Jones, joined us. Apart from her outward beauty, I had the impression that her pleasant politeness only just veiled her true inner feelings, which were just waiting to erupt. Selznick had told me from the beginning that whichever story was chosen would have to include Jennifer in the lead. There was another stipulation: that his name was not to be used in connection with any film. I supposed it was to do with contracts, but it was rather off-putting.

I told him that my favourite of the stories he'd told me was that of the real-life heroine of World War Two, Christianne Granville, who bravely smuggled many Allied soldiers out of enemy terrain and was never honoured or even thanked by the British government, dying unrecognized as a chambermaid in a London hotel. Selznick agreed it was a strong and poignant story and we parted in an atmosphere of warm enthusiasm.

Over the following weeks I was relieved that nothing further came from our Venetian sand-plodding. I had heard about Selznick's mania for working to the limit – usually aided by Benzedrine – on everything connected with his films. His countless memos. His obsessive interference with anything he felt he could improve on. King Vidor had told me on *War and Peace* that he had walked out of *Duel in the Sun* in protest at Selznick's meddling. So I suppose I was lucky to escape all this.

Incredible as it may seem, in the midst of several other tempting directorial offers, I went back to photography.

Joshua Logan phoned me from New York. 'Jack, I'm going to make *Fanny* in France. You simply must come and photograph it.'

I was a bit taken aback – 'Josh, I'm a director now.'

'I know you are,' said Josh, 'but, Jack, you should do both when something like this comes up. People will respect you for it.'

What a sly persuader Josh was. I flew to Paris and had the time of my life. After the grim battles of directing, it was a holiday – and it was French hours too! French hours means arriving for work at midday – having had lunch – and working straight until 7.30 p.m. We didn't have to get up at dawn or work late into the night.

We had many wonderful parties and it was blissful to have the whole morning free. My eldest son, John, who was working on the camera, had time to take flying lessons just outside Paris. His teacher was a World War Two pilot who had a startling method to impart resourcefulness while in the air. He would suddenly switch off the engine and John would have to land in the nearest field. He soon learned to land his engineless plane in any field with confident aplomb.

All the actors were congenial company to be with: Leslie Caron, Maurice Chevalier, Charles Boyer, Horst Buchholz and my old friend Lionel Jeffries, who has always had an outrageous sense of humour.

Josh Logan had a sumptuous apartment near the Etoile where splendid parties were frequent. One evening Dinah Shore came and after dinner she sang so many old favourites for us with Harold Rome on the piano; often when we begged her to sing a song again, she would do so with a serene smile. What a lovely person she was.

Maurice Chevalier had an enviable collection of Impressionist paintings; a superb Cézanne, three joyous Renoirs and several flamboyant raw-coloured Fauves, including one by my favourite Fauve, Derain. Leslie Caron had been a ballet dancer and she very kindly posed for me in a period ballet costume while I made drawings and pastels in the Degas style.

After Paris we had another enjoyable location at Marseilles, at the famous waterfront where Marcel Pagnol had made the original *Fanny* trilogy in 1932. And here we were thirty years later, but this time with colour and a new set of stars. When our film came out some film buffs loftily preferred the old classic immortalized in France by the great Raimu, but I maintained Logan's *Fanny* had more heart and Leslie Caron was infinitely more appealing.

*

After photographing *Fanny* it was back to directing again. I loved the idea of directing: to feel a project inside you, like a foetus in a womb, to be confident that you are telling the story, with all the skills – artistic and technical – at your command, to have a perfect script and actors who will brilliantly articulate it so that audiences all over the world will be intensely moved by your work.

Unfortunately such idylls are often a mockery of reality. Directors become engulfed, as I have often been, in all kinds of adversity: conflicts with stars and with some producers who are directors manqués, heads of studios, budget politics; and in avoiding one problem, you often come up against a worse one.

A successful director, to stay on top, requires beguiling charm, the cunning of Odysseus, strident persuasion and ruthless resilience – none of which, I'm afraid, I possess in great quantity.

As a cameraman, I have gaped at the bombastic ranting of some directors and envied them, in a way, because I just couldn't scream and rave like that. But what I lacked in bellicose ruthlessness, I made up for in psychological manipulation. On *The Magic Box,* which I photographed, Robert Donat was suffering the horrors of forgetting his lines. In a scene with Michael Redgrave he kept 'drying', take after take; Redgrave, on the other hand, was always word perfect. Each time Donat dried, he would apologize wretchedly to Redgrave; the poor man was a complete nervous wreck. I suggested to the director, John Boulting, that he whisper to Redgrave to 'dry' himself on the next take. Michael received the suggestion with aloof condescension. During the next shot Redgrave fluffed his lines and apologized profusely to Donat. On the next take Donat was word-perfect and we got the scene.

Ironically, years later, I was directing Michael Redgrave in *Young Cassidy.* Redgrave played W. B. Yeats and had to make a long speech outside the Abbey Theatre in Dublin. While we were setting up the shot Redgrave came to my trailer and said, 'Jack, my speech is half a page of dialogue; I shall never get through it in one take. I hope you can break it up.' Funny; over the years Redgrave had lost his perfect memory for dialogue and was now a bit like Donat had been. 'Don't worry, Michael,' I assured him. 'I shall break it up with close-ups.' But I was lying. The drama of the scene would suffer if it were broken up. There was also rain in the scene and to intercut 'pick-ups' would have spoilt the spontaneity.

'Anyway, Michael,' I said, 'I have to rehearse the scene all the way through for the rain. Don't worry if you "dry", just pick it up and carry on till the end of the scene – it's only a rehearsal.'

We turned on the rain and I called 'action'. Redgrave's performance was magnificent, he was word-perfect right through the scene. When I called 'cut' he rushed over to me: 'Oh, Jack, if only it had been a take! I'll never get through it again like that.'

'Don't worry, Michael,' I said. 'That *was* a take. You were marvellous.'

Young Cassidy was originally to have been directed by John Ford, but after a few days' shooting he had become ill and was flown back to Hollywood. I was urgently summoned to Ireland to take over the film – a daunting task, not having even read the script, nor met the glittering cast, which included Rod Taylor, Julie Christie, Edith Evans, Michael Redgrave, Maggie Smith and Flora Robson. It turned out to be a most creatively satisfactory experience. It was a joy to work with such a fine cast and a great script. I was proud of a sequence I directed of a rioting crowd in the Dublin streets. It took three days to shoot with several cameras and I cut the scenes in very short sections – sometimes just a few frames – to underline the panic and horror.

When the film was released the reviews were very good, but many critics praised John Ford's direction for scenes I had done myself. One critic commented: 'It is easy to see the difference between John Ford's direction and Cardiff's.' Another declared 'The riot sequence is superb – obviously the work of the master, John Ford.'

I suppose I should have been flattered that my work should be considered to be the work of the master, but in fact I was indignant. I measured John Ford's work on the film. It totalled four and a half minutes out of two hours' screen time. I wrote blistering letters to the critics, but it never does any good.

I had long felt that films could benefit from the pervasive influence of smell. Aldous Huxley's *Brave New World* had the 'feelies' whereby the audience turned metal knobs on their seats to relish kissing and other erogenous sensations. So when Michael Todd junior offered me a film which would be 'the first smellie', I was delighted. It was called *Scent of Mystery* and the cast included Denholm Elliott, Peter Lorre, Paul Lukas and Diana Dors. The story took us through the glorious vistas of Spain.

One evening in Cordoba, when I was having dinner in a local restaurant, my assistant director dashed in, breathless with panic: 'Jack, Peter Lorre is dying.' There he was, unconscious, lying on a table in his hotel room, his face a pale grey and his belly weirdly enormous. His breathing was shallow, but every few seconds his body shuddered from huge spasms like colossal hiccups.

Extraordinarily, there happened to be a convention of doctors in Cordoba that day, and a group of these learned men were gathered round the body of Peter and shaking their heads. 'He has about one hour to live,' said one doctor, and the others nodded wisely. I was stunned. Peter was a lively and intelligent man to work with, and now he was dying in front of us. The doctors were talking in rapid Spanish, arguing with some kind of animation. It was explained to me that Peter's terminal condition was the result of a blockage in the arteries and one doctor had the crazy idea of using the centuries-old technique of blood letting. I was requested to return in an hour, as the cluster of doctors gathered round the impromptu operating table.

Amazingly, the 'crazy idea' worked. When I returned Peter was out of danger and a few hours later he was sitting up talking in French. Of course, he could no longer run in the chase scenes. We advertised in the Spanish press for a double and luckily found a most realistic Peter Lorre II to do the running for him.

One day soon afterwards I asked Michael Todd what news he had about the smells. I knew there was a man in Switzerland, Professor Hans Laube, who was working on the various smells outlined in the script and I asked Michael if he had received any samples yet. I was shocked when Michael answered that he hadn't seen anything yet. I suggested that Laube should send some samples to us – of the sea, tobacco, apricots, etc. – as soon as possible. Two weeks later a box arrived with half a dozen samples. I took out a bottle labelled 'apricots' and inhaled excitedly. It smelled of cheap eau-de-Cologne. I tried 'sea ozone'. That too smelled of eau-de-Cologne. Every sample smelled the same: a third rate perfume, nothing at all like they were supposed to smell.

Michael and I were horrified. Michael telephoned Professor Laube who assured him that everything would be perfectly alright on the night of our big test in Chicago in two months' time. All we could do was trust the professor and pray.

Our big night duly took place in Chicago. The cinema had a thousand seats and most of the audience were trade people. On the back of each seat a tiny pipe with fitted with a spray to project smells to the viewer seated behind. The pipes ran under the floor where an enormous dispensing machine had been installed acting as a 'smell brain', having stored every aroma to be projected during the film. In addition to the eight tracks on our 70 mm film, there was an extra track carrying the smell signal. As the film travelled through the projector an electric signal triggered a mechanism which projected a small quantity of aroma-laden air on cue to every seat in the audience.

Well, the magnificent machinery worked wonderfully. The only trouble was, the smells that were projected towards the eager nostrils were exactly like cheap eau-de-Cologne ...

The film was released in New York where the critics all had wrinkled noses and acerbic tongues.

Then came a bathetic *coup de grâce*. In a nearby cinema, a few days before the New York opening, an enterprising gent showed an awful 'B' film and installed incense in the air conditioning, triumphantly advertising his film as 'the first smellie'.

More directorial projects followed, including *My Geisha*, *The Lion*, *The Long Ships*, *The Mercenaries* and *Girl on a Motorcycle*. Today, few people know much about *My Geisha*, starring Shirley Maclaine. It ran in London for a few weeks, but it has to be classified as a flop. The funny thing was, at the usual sneak preview in Hollywood it had an 85 per cent rating, which meant it would be a huge success. But it wasn't.

Norman Krasner, one of the best writers in Hollywood, wrote an excellent script. However, the story had one cardinal element which challenged belief; that an actress could disguise herself as a Japanese geisha girl in a film audition and not only get the leading role, but her husband, who was directing the film, never realized it was his wife throughout the filming. This bothered me, but no one else shared my concern and we went ahead. The entire film was shot in Japan, and working there was an enjoyable experience.

I managed to pay a masochistic visit to the horror city, Hiroshima, which left me numbingly depressed for long afterwards. Although the city is now rebuilt, the area at the epicentre of where the first atomic bomb in warfare exploded is left untouched as a kind of shrine, grim and ghastly, too terrible to describe.

Back in Hollywood I worked on the editing and cut it from three hours to two. This was very near the bone, but it worked beautifully. However, shortly after I returned to England I received a phone call from my editor. The film had been shown in New York to Barney Balahan, who was the big boss of Paramount, and he had cut half an hour out of it. I was devastated. I knew now the film was ruined. When it was released in London the chattering critics echoed each other with one voice: it was completely unfeasible. A man would surely recognize his own wife. Several echoed another objection, 'How dare they cover up our Shirley'. And that was it.

The book, *The Lion*, by Joseph Kessel was a sensitive and moving story about a little girl in Africa who had raised a lion from birth and, when the lion was fully grown, was the only one who could handle it.

From thousands of miles away in Hollywood a fully-grown, ferocious-looking lion arrived in Africa with the trainer Ralph Helfer and his assistant, Stewart. It was, of course, a tame lion specially trained for films. His name was Zamba ('King' in the film) and he really was quite tame, at least with men. A photograph was taken of me using the lion as a pillow while reading a book entitled *How to Make Friends and Influence People* which made a fun Christmas card. However, you can never be sure with wild animals. Zamba was housed in a compound a hundred yards away from our hotel and every day at dusk Stewart had to take Zamba his dinner in two meat-laden buckets. One evening as he approached he saw to his astonishment that Zamba was sitting down *outside* the compound. He walked up saying, 'Zamba, you rascal, how the hell did you get out.' Then he heard a hungry growl behind him. He whirled round and saw that Zamba was *inside* his compound and, horror of horrors, the lion outside was a wild one who had scented Zamba's presence and was paying a visit. The huge wild lion was staring at Stewart with that low growl that precedes a spring. Stewart 'stood not on the order of his going' and, throwing the meat on the ground, went.

In the case of our young actress, Pamela Franklin, I couldn't take the slightest chance. First a piece of her clothing was given to the lion to smell, then she was introduced to Zamba from a distance of fifty feet and then in gradually decreasing distances until it was clear that Zamba had no objection to her company.

One evening Ralph Helfer, the trainer, came to see me and said it was necessary to find out if Pamela had reached the age of puberty. He told me that a couple of months earlier, when he was using the lion in a film, a woman who was menstruating had walked on to the set and the lion, scenting her condition, had sprung and killed her. I talked to Pamela's mother and yes, Pamela had just reached puberty. So that was an added problem and we knew we would have to adjust the schedule accordingly.

A few days later Pamela was allowed to touch Zamba and in no time at all was cuddling the lion like a pet doll. But those who saw the film didn't realize that just outside the picture frame were two professional hunters on either side of the camera with rifles always aimed at the lion in case of a sudden attack on Pamela. My nervousness can be imagined. On every scene with Pamela my heart was in my mouth – no, in the lion's mouth – but Zamba was a real sweetie and gave no trouble.

We somehow finished the film without anyone getting torn to pieces. The *Daily Express* was close to the truth: '*The Lion* is a marvellous film. I marvel at its happenings and speculate hardly at all how these happenings are made without any drop of real blood having been spilled.' Well, it was a close thing.

When I worked with Joe Mankiewicz on *The Barefoot Contessa*, he called me his 'partner in purgatory'. He was primarily a writer – one of the Hollywood greats – but he turned to direction because his scripts were always being altered – and ruined – by directors and producers.

On my own path to purgatory, he wrote in a letter: 'You poor bastard. There seems little doubt that God intends you to be a director. What he's doing to you he only does to directors. Keep your chin up and keep swinging.'

Well, it was extremely difficult to keep my chin up on *The Long Ships*. When Columbia sent me the script I immediately sent it back without reading it. I had worked on *The Vikings* and had no desire whatsoever to direct a similar project. Anyway, I was talked into it. Richard Widmark was the star and the first thing he did was demand that the script be rewritten. He wanted it done by a friend who arrived in a large white stetson. My misgivings were well-founded when I read his rewrite. It was pure Abbott and Costello, and that was the first time I walked off the picture. I was enticed back with the promise of another writer, Beverly Cross, whose script was accepted and we started work in Yugoslavia.

A sizeable village had been built in the country outside Belgrade with a Norwegian-type fjord running through it. When I inspected this fjord I asked how deep it was. Six inches I was told. I couldn't believe it. Viking long ships had to navigate this fjord and it was only six inches deep?! I was told that the previous director had not bothered to get out of his car during the recce, and had simply ordered the village to be built 'over there'. Canals had to be blasted to allow the ships to enter and leave – and I felt like leaving myself.

At eight o'clock in the morning of the first day's shooting the producer, Irving Allen, sat in his producer's chair watching the work. Richard Widmark went up to him and said, 'Mr Allen, I don't want you on the set when I'm working.'

'Read your contract,' was Allen's reply. Widmark walked off the set back to his hotel. That day, the telephone wires were humming. Columbia sent messages to Widmark that if he wasn't on the set the next day Columbia would sue him for 4 million dollars. Apparently Widmark was also told by his agent that he had no legal right to keep the producer off the set and the next morning Widmark came to work with a face like thunder. For the rest of the picture the atmosphere was extremely tense.

Irving Allen was not a popular producer. I had been warned about some of his ploys. He would sometimes use a second unit to shoot scenes he wanted in the film which the director never knew about and after the 'director's cut' – when the director can do nothing more but go home – Allen had been known to order up fresh prints of everything and re-cut the film to his liking. I had insisted on using my friend John Drake as the operator on the second unit. Allen had wanted an operator of his own choice and I knew he was prejudiced against John. Some weeks later the second unit had a shot slightly out of focus. This was the fault of the focus puller and had nothing to do with John. Allen was in London at the time and sent an order firing John. I sent him a cable: 'Your intentions revealed like a loathesome sore unbandaged. Why don't you fire me too? Cardiff.' He sent a cable back: 'I'll get around to it. Allen.' But he never did.

It was a soul-destroying film to work on. No doubt it required a tough director like Henry Hathaway to scream and rave. Widmark was grimly carrying out his contract. He rewrote his own scenes and when Sidney Poitier arrived the contagion of discord affected him also and he rewrote his scenes as well. Sidney, apart from being a very good actor, was an extremely good writer and improved his scenes, although it was hardly a harmonious situation.

One doesn't have to be a psychiatrist to see that my work was affected by all this. I was constantly involved in arguments with Widmark. Occasionally, he would send me a note in the evening apologizing for his behaviour. I still have them. In a strange way I felt sorry for him. He was undoubtedly a fine actor and his letters to me before we started the film showed his conscientious involvement. Perhaps, with all the prestigious films behind him, he felt he was trapped in a film he didn't believe in.

Towards the end, however, I couldn't stand any more of the friction and one day I walked off the set and, I hoped, off the picture. That evening Mike Frankovich, the head of Columbia in Europe, came over from London and we had a meeting. Widmark was present and I aired all my feelings with passion. Frankovich, of course, made peace, saying it was nearly the end . . . it would be a big success, etc., and I was back for the last days of shooting.

Oddly enough, it went down well with audiences as a fun adventure yarn. But it had certainly been no fun for me.

Rod Taylor and I became good friends on *Young Cassidy* and I directed two more films with him: *The Liquidator* and *The Mercenaries*. *The Liquidator* was the first to make fun of the James Bond ethos but, because of a weird litigation situation between the producer and MGM, it was locked away in a vault for two years. By the time it was released it was sadly out of date.

The Mercenaries was set in the Belgian Congo but shot in Jamaica, because in Africa we couldn't find a suitable steam train – a vital part of the plot. Although it was a very violent story, the actual violence happening in the Congo at that time was much more than I could show in my film; in my research I encountered evidence so revolting I was nauseated. The critics complained of the violent content, but today it would hardly raise an eyebrow.

During shooting, Noël Coward, who lived in an away-from-it-all property in Jamaica called Blue Harbour, invited my wife and I to see his exotic hideout, and on a rare Sunday off work we paid him a visit, marvelling at his new home with its superb views in all directions. We were taken high up a small mountain on his property which he called 'Look Out', and there, in an old stone house, we found Coward and his companion, Coley, painting at easels. Noël was a wonderful host and we spent a most pleasant day in lively conversation, being entertained by his amusing stories.

Nothing could have been more of a contrast to the savage mercenaries than *Girl on a Motorcycle*. The book by André de Mandiargues had won a Prix de Goncourt and showed a girl obsessed with her ex-lover while married to another.

Originally, I cast a German girl to play the lead. She was perfect for the role. A few days after engaging her she was rushed to hospital with a drug overdose and I never saw her again.

Marianne Faithfull was suggested to me and, after meeting her, I agreed to her playing the lead.

To show a girl on a motorbike for almost the entire film was a stimulating challenge. I used many techniques, one of which was solarization – half-negative, half-positive; it had been used before in small doses, but

I was able to use it thanks to a computer system devised by a brilliant backroom boy from Technicolor, Laurie Atkin. I shot the scenes straight, then they were taken to the BBC's telecine department late at night when BBC work had finished. There I had Atkin's magic box with dials on it and I could adjust the solarization to any part of the scene I desired on a tape which would then be transferred to film at Technicolor. It was thrillingly successful and allowed me to solarize sex scenes, for instance, that no British censor would ordinarily allow.

I was making this film in two versions, French and English. My French version came out first and the French reviews were wonderful. *Le Figaro* said, 'Jack Cardiff has reconstructed the book with remarkable intelligence. He switches from past to present so subtly one doesn't notice the difference in time ... Cardiff reveals other talents. He creates strong links between the poetry, fleeting but unforgettable, of the scenery and the motorbike. In the erotic sequences their bodies dissolve into a psychedelic whirl. All this adds up to a great film. Don't miss it.'

Although the reviews outside London were excellent the London critics were awful. One critic sneered at a line of Alain Delon's: 'Your body is like a violin in a velvet case', and I was astonished that they had been so mentally lazy and had missed the point entirely. *Alain Delon did not say this line.* When the girl is approaching the town where her lover lives she *imagines* him using this erotic metaphor when he unzips her leather riding outfit, which has a lining of felt, she being naked inside. Of course, he could not have said this line since she was killed on the way to him.

Ironically, this film was the second highest grosser that year and was very lucrative for me.

The British film industry is infuriatingly illness prone. We have superb technicians, directors and writers, but they are frequently out of work, mostly because of financial sickness – lack of funds and faith from the money men.

We have kindred ties to centuries of British theatre: proud dynasties of great actors and writers, including Shakespeare. What a glorious heritage for British films. So why is our industry periodically infirm?

I believe the main reason is that we no longer have great producers like Alexander Korda, Sam Spiegel, Michael Balcon and the Powell–Pressburger team. The flour magnate, J. Arthur Rank, had a brave try and Pinewood Studios produced many quality films but it died and, you may have noticed, they are all dead now. The new ones have much promise; David Puttnam, Ridley and Tony Scott, but we need more like them.

During yet another industrial film crisis, I was living in Switzerland – *ipso facto* presumed retired. I had been out of work for some time and had gone through the sad break-up of my marriage, when I was offered a photographic assignment in Australia which I grabbed. Thereafter, I photographed clusters of epics, working with Arnold Schwarzenegger on *Conan the Destroyer* in Mexico; in Egypt on Agatha Christie's *Death on the Nile* which had a galaxy of stars: Bette Davis, David Niven, Peter Ustinov, Maggie Smith, Mia Farrow, Angela Lansbury, Jack Warden and Jane Birkin; then again in Mexico with the ineffable Sylvester Stallone on *Rambo: First Blood Part II*; in New York and Belize on *Dogs of War* with Christopher Walken and Tom Berenger; in Vermont on *Ghost Story* with Fred Astaire, Melvyn Douglas, John Houseman and Douglas Fairbanks Jr.

After that I had a painfully abortive six months' stint in China on *Tai-Pan*, on which I did some of my best work, but the film was shown for only two weeks in LA and, to my knowledge, nowhere else since.

If all these jolting vicissitudes sound like whingeing, well it's certainly not so. My life has been – and still is – wonderfully stimulating in all kinds of weather. When fickle-fingered fate has bloodied my nose, I do what Noël Coward used to advise, 'Rise above it', and I think of the good times. There has been such an abundance of good times that when I spread them out in my mind, I experience that wonderful feeling of flight – and that really is something.

I get the occasional fan letter, not in shoals like film stars, but the odd few a month. To receive genuine appreciation from people of all ages from all over the world, who are not professional critics, is quite refreshing. One of them told me recently that I am the only one in the film business to have won the Golden Globe award for both direction and photography – so hurrah for statistics.

I've had my share of the slings and arrows and sometimes outrageous fortune, but when I felt I had succeeded in what I had set out to do, even if some critics excoriated me, I was amply rewarded in spirit.

Success – Huxley's 'Bitch Goddess' – has flirted with me often enough, though not quite leading to wedlock. I am still very much involved in work and my painting, and the urge to create still runs hot in my veins.

I never worry about the end of my story. Sophocles put it so beautifully:

> One must wait until evening,
> to see how splendid the day was.

Index